# BORN IN THE WRONG CHAIR

## The 3 Stages of Awareness: A Neurodivergent Journey to Truth, Healing, and Action

*A Memoir of Discovery, Resilience, and Reclaiming Identity*

by
Fabien William Auger

**Born in the Wrong Chair**

The 3 Stages of Awareness: A Neurodivergent Journey to Truth, Healing, and Action

Published by FWA Publishing
fwa@frenchwithattitude.com
www.frenchwithattitude.com

ISBN 979-8-9932989-0-0 (paperback)

Cover and interior design: FWA Publishing

First edition 2025

# Dedication

To my parents, for their strength and discipline.

To my aunt, who always believed in me.

To the children still misunderstood, unheard, or unseen.

To every ND (neurodivergent) out there trying to make sense of this world.

To myself, for never fully giving up, even when I wanted to.

To the friends who held me through the storms, the partners who carried burdens that weren't theirs, and everyone who loved me back to myself when I forgot the way home.

You are the invisible architecture of this story. Your love taught me that I was never as alone as I felt.

# Epigraph

*"Tchimbé Raid Pa Moli"*

# TABLE OF CONTENTS

# Author's Note

This book chronicles my journey from confusion to clarity, from shame to self-acceptance. It's the story of discovering, decades later, that I'm neurodivergent, and that everything finally makes sense.

I share my truth not for pity or praise, but for recognition. For every person who has felt like a square peg in a round world, who has been told they're "too much" or "not enough," who has wondered if they're fundamentally broken.

You're not broken, you're just born in the wrong chair.

This is about building a better one

# PART I: KNOWING

## Chapter One: The Smile That Betrayed Me

I was always smiling.

It wasn't a performance. It wasn't a strategy. It was simply my face, this light, this involuntary beacon I carried into classrooms, family dinners, the streets and spaces of my childhood. I didn't know it would one day feel like a liability, a flaw, a reason for people to question me, reject me, or worse, dismiss me entirely. I didn't know it would become evidence against me.

When I was eight, my teacher stopped mid-lesson and called me out in front of the class.

*"Why are you always smiling? What's so funny?"*

Her voice sliced the air. Everyone turned. I froze.

My smile faded. My insides dropped. I wasn't laughing at anyone. I wasn't mocking anyone. I just had that look, a look that said, "I want to be here, even if I don't understand everything."

In French, we have a phrase: *être à côté de la plaque*, which translates to be off-base, out of sync. I didn't realize until much later how this dissonance, this subtle mismatch between what I felt and what the world perceived, was shaping every corner of my childhood.

# The Paradox of Hypervigilance

I always knew there was something slightly "off" in how I spoke, but I didn't have a name for it, not even a real awareness, until someone weaponized it.

In 9th grade, there was a classmate whose last name was full of slippery syllables, the kind that caught against the curve of my palate. My mouth simply didn't want to cooperate. My palate isn't flat like most, it's subtly arched, which makes specific letter combinations scratch or bend when I try to pronounce them. I've worked hard over the years to train my tongue, but back then, it was raw and unrefined.

His name wasn't particularly long, but it had those sounds. *Agnostic. Adlayer.* Words that scraped. I tried my best. I wasn't mocking him. But he acted like I was.

He turned it into a game, one I never agreed to play. Mimicking my voice behind my back. Correcting me with an exaggerated tone in front of others. "It's not that hard," he'd say, smirking. I smiled the first few times, trying to play along. That's what I was good at, masking discomfort. But inside, I felt exposed.

Then he went further. One day he accused me of stealing a ring, a cheap one, from one of his acquaintances, someone from the housing projects. He knew I hadn't done it. I knew he knew. But that wasn't the point. He wanted to embarrass me. Frame me as the "suspicious one." The "different one."

And something in me cracked.

I didn't fully understand it at the time, but I was having a bipolar episode. Almost on demand. As soon as two things clicked in my mind, that he was mocking me, and that I was being falsely accused, I flipped. The shame, the betrayal, the rage, all mixed into a fire I couldn't contain.

I stood up and cursed him out in front of everyone. Loud. Raw. Threatening to fight him if he pushed me again. I didn't really mean it, but I also knew he wouldn't call my bluff. He backed down. Chickened out. And for once, my intensity, this thing I always tried to keep hidden, got me out of trouble.

Later that year, he tried to steal my jacket. Again, I confronted him. Again, the fire in me made him shrink. He handed it back without a word.

Looking back, I can see the bigger picture. That I wasn't just "moody" or "difficult"–I was neurodivergent. Undiagnosed. Masking every day until my nervous system snapped. My speech pattern wasn't laziness. My reactions weren't disproportionate. They were early signs of bipolar episodes, of sensory stress, of unrecognized trauma.

And yet, no one asked if I was okay.

Not the teacher who watched me shout across the room. Not the students who laughed. Not even me.

Instead, I learned how to hide even deeper.

I began practicing my pronunciation in private. Whispering difficult words. Breaking them down phonetically. I'd go over syllables again and again until they smoothed out, just enough to not draw attention. I didn't want to stand out. I wanted to blend in, to speak like the others. To avoid becoming a target again.

This is how masking begins.

**Not as a decision, but as a defense.**

I was the curious kid with a thousand questions inside and no instruction manual. I saw everything. I felt everything. I scanned every room for signals, faces, tones, energies. I could pick up on the tension between two adults whispering in the hallway, or the way a classmate's voice changed ever so slightly when they were lying. I noticed everything, except the instructions right in front of me.

Because when it came time to act, to respond, to perform as expected, I was already exhausted. Already overwhelmed. Either I was scanning everything all at once, or I was staring at **nothing**, numb, frozen, fogged.

My mind was like flying a plane that refused to land, constantly circling, constantly checking, constantly trying to make sense of a world that operated on unspoken rules. And when I did speak? It was often "too much" or "too late."

Research from the **Yale Child Study Center** and Dr. Stephen Porges' **Polyvagal Theory** reveals that children on the autism spectrum often exhibit what seem like "inappropriate" emotional responses, like smiling during discipline or laughing during conflict, not because they don't care, but because their nervous systems are in overdrive.

The smile wasn't fake. It was a life jacket. It was regulation. For many neurodivergent people, smiling is a self-soothing response, a way to signal "I'm okay" even when drowning inside.

## The Cultural Context: Growing Up French Caribbean

My family was traditional French, with strict Caribbean roots on my mother's side and wartime discipline from my father's. The cultural expectations were clear: children should be seen and not heard, emotional displays were weakness, and conformity was survival.

In our household, dinner wasn't just a meal, it was a performance review. We stayed at the table long after the food was finished. It wasn't optional. You sat. You listened. You absorbed. No interruptions. No excuses. No fidgeting.

The conversations flowed over my head in rapid French, switching between topics I couldn't follow: politics, family drama, financial concerns. The adults spoke in code, their words layered with meaning I couldn't decode. I'd try to read the room, to understand when to nod, when to look serious, when to laugh.

As a child, I'd try to laugh when the adults laughed. Not because I understood the jokes (they were often about politics, death, money, or something subtle and cruel) but because I wanted to belong. I wanted to be part of the rhythm, the timing, the *knowingness* that filled the room.

But my timing was always off. My reactions were always a beat behind or ahead.

## The Immigration Story: Context for Conformity

My mother had arrived in France in the 1970s as part of the wave of Caribbean migration seeking better opportunities. My mother came from Martinique with dreams of education and respectability. My father, from France, carried the military discipline of his own father, a man who had fought in both World Wars and believed that structure was the key to survival in a hostile world.

They worked multiple jobs to establish themselves. My mother was studying during the day and was an aupair evenings and nights. My father, after the War enrolled in the army. After the army he went on to work on airplanes engines. My mother spoke French at home, but Creole with her friends on the phone, insisted on perfect French in public. She also speak English, German, Spanish and Mandarin. My dad always insisted heavily on her teaching me English at a young age. They navigated a culture that was simultaneously familiar and foreign, French in language but metropolitan in ways that felt exclusionary to people from the islands.

For them, having a child who stood out for the wrong reasons wasn't just embarrassing, it was dangerous. In their experience, being different meant being vulnerable. Being noticed meant being judged. And being judged, for immigrants who already faced suspicion and discrimination, could mean losing everything they'd worked for.

When I acted out, when I couldn't sit still, when I asked too many questions or laughed at the wrong times, it wasn't just childhood behavior, it was a threat to their carefully constructed respectability.

## Shame, Served at the Table

My mother came from Martinique in the early '70s, chasing survival the only way she knew how: through education, discipline, and quiet resilience. She arrived with nothing but grit and the pressure to assimilate. Her Creole was tucked behind perfect French, her Caribbean softness pressed beneath Parisian expectations. She carried herself like a woman who knew the world was watching, and judging.

My father had been chasing survival long before her, through the chaos of World War II. Born in France on October 27, 1927, at the Gaston-Métivet Clinic on 48 Rue d'Alsace Lorraine in Saint-Maur-des-Fossés, the very same clinic I was born in, 57 years later, he came into the world during the shadow between wars. By the time he was a teenager, he had already known hunger, fear, and forced discipline. War made him rigid, proud, and unbending. It also made him silent. He didn't talk much about what he'd seen, only that it hardened him.

Together, my parents didn't just come to France, they *built* a life in France. My mother brought the warmth of the islands. My father brought the cold precision of survival. And somewhere between them, I was expected to find balance. To smile, sit still, and succeed. All while pretending I didn't notice the silence behind their eyes.

They didn't talk about racism openly, but it lived in our home like a quiet draft, under doors, in glances from strangers, in how polite they became in public, and how demanding they were in private.

We eventually landed in Lamerville, postal code 45210, a town so small it didn't have a single business. Just winding roads between farmland and forests. No sidewalks. No cafés. Only nature, silence, and isolation. I still don't know how my father found it. It felt like exile and sanctuary all at once.

That little town, however, sparked my imagination. It was the kind of place where your inner world became your main world. There weren't distractions. Just trees and thoughts and the occasional scream of a rooster echoing through the woods. Lamerville gave me quiet, but it also gave me disconnection. From others. From access. From the world I saw on TV. And maybe even from myself.

My mom was the only Black human for miles. I was the only Brown. As a Light-skinned Caribbean with tight curls it was impossible to blend in. My parents kept a strict household with polished shoes and fresh scents. You did not raise your voice. You did not speak unless spoken to. If you cried, it better be for blood. There was no space for emotional expression. That was a luxury, and luxuries were for other people.

One evening, my father turned to me mid-laugh and said in front of everyone:

*"Look at him! Why is he laughing? He doesn't even get the joke. He always does that. Smiling like an idiot."*

Everyone laughed.

I didn't.

I wanted to disappear. I wanted to slide beneath the table and melt into the floor. But I stayed. And in staying, I learned something that would follow me for decades:

**My joy was embarrassing. My instinct to connect made people uncomfortable. My natural smile was a threat.**

That night, I didn't cry. I stayed quiet. I internalized the lesson, as kids do. From that day forward, silence became a shield, and my smile became something to hide rather than share.

The cultural weight of this moment was enormous. In French and Caribbean culture, particularly the generations my parents came from, children who stood out, who were too loud, too emotional, too different, were seen as bringing shame to the family. My mother, who had immigrated to France with dreams of assimilation and respectability, couldn't afford a child who drew the wrong kind of attention.

My father, shaped by his own father's military background, believed that discipline and conformity were the keys to success in a world that was already skeptical of immigrants. A smiling child who didn't understand the social cues was a liability.

## Extended Family Dynamics

But even inside that pressure cooker, I had my anchors, my cousins.

Nina was the eldest, ten years ahead of me. Tiny frame, gentle energy, and hair so long and curly it touched her lower back. The first time I saw her sit cross-legged in our backyard, wrapped in a blanket, reading quietly with the birds chirping around her, something clicked. She wasn't flashy. She wasn't loud. She was still. A passive sun. Her pace, her voice, her presence, it all soothed me in a way I didn't quite understand yet. And her hair, wild, coiled, unapologetic, looked just like mine. I wanted what she had. Not just her hair, but her calm and her knowingness. Her peace. I didn't know it then, but she was my first model of spiritual regulation. Meditation in human form.

Fanny, on the other hand, was fire. Two years older than me, always steps ahead. She lived in the Alps, in a world of snowboards and architecture and mixtapes. To me, she was the Black Pocahontas, tall, athletic, radiant. She wore her identity like armor and fashion at once. Grungy one day, R&B queen the next. She could hang with anyone. Skate, hoop, climb, charm. She was what I wanted to be, cool without apology. Her twin brother and older siblings were like a crew from a Nike commercial. One could play guitar like Hendrix, cook like a Chef.. The other is launching a business school. They always had the latest game consoles and the freshest shoes. But more than the lifestyle, they gave me a glimpse of possibility. That you could be Black, French, and bold. That you didn't have to shrink or decode yourself to belong.

And then there was Pauline. We didn't grow up as close, but when I turned seventeen, she became everything.

I had just passed my Baccalaureate. I was newly single. So was she. We started hanging out more. She became the piece I didn't know I was missing. At nineteen, when I finally moved out of my parents' home, depressed, disoriented, but determined, she was the one who stayed close. She didn't need to say "I love you." She just showed it. She was warmth in human form. Soft when the world was hard. Constant when everyone else was temporary. I often wish I knew how to show her the same love she gave me. But I wasn't raised with emotional language. My affection gets caught behind the teeth. Still, I hope she knows, I love her more than words can say.

These women, these cousins, weren't just family. They were maps.

They each showed me a different way to exist: calm, radiant, compassionate. And in a world that constantly demanded I shrink, they gave me glimpses of what it looked like to simply *be*.

We were all Black. Light-skinned. Caribbean. Ethnically clear, visually misread.

And through them, I learned something that no French textbook ever taught me:

*Tchimbé Raid Pa Moli.*

Hold strong. Don't give in.

A Caribbean phrase whispered across generations. Said with love, but also out of necessity. Because life was hard, and harder for people like us.

That saying wasn't just encouragement. It was instruction. A command to survive when the system isn't designed for you. It was our creed. And deep down, I carried it in my bones.

But over time, I added my own line, one the world wasn't ready for:

**"Black is not a color. It's a flavor."**

Because people see the shade and miss the story. They confuse pigment with identity. But being Black isn't about tone, it's about legacy, resilience, rhythm, texture, pain, joy, and resistance.

We are cappuccino, vanilla, espresso, cocoa, honey-gold, burnt sugar.

We are not just Black, we are everything.

And no one taught me that in school.

That pattern extended beyond our immediate household. Family gatherings were exercises in performance and evaluation. Aunts and uncles would examine us children like inspectors, commenting on our behavior, our French pronunciation, our manners.

"Il faut qu'il apprenne à se tenir," they would say about me. "He needs to learn how to behave."

My cousins seemed to navigate these evaluations effortlessly. They knew when to speak and when to be silent. They could sense the adult mood and adjust accordingly. I felt like I was always a step behind, always missing some crucial signal that everyone else could read.

At Christmas dinners, I would watch my cousins perform, reciting poems, playing piano, and demonstrating their accomplishments. When my turn came, I would freeze. Not because I lacked talent or knowledge, but because the performance felt impossible to calibrate. How much enthusiasm was too much? How much was too little?

Often, the safest option was to mumble through whatever was expected and retreat to the margins as quickly as possible.

# When Sports Became My Language

Fortunately, I discovered that my body could do what my mind couldn't, communicate clearly.

Sports became my refuge when words failed me. It started with ping pong. My father was good, very good, and when he taught me how to play, something clicked. It wasn't about decoding instructions anymore. It was rhythm. Reaction. Repetition. It bypassed the thinking. It was movement and instinct.

Later came basketball. Then boxing. Then volleyball. These weren't just activities, they became tools to ground myself in the present moment. In sports, the rules were clear. The boundaries were visible. The feedback was immediate.

If you miss the ball, try again. If you don't move, you lose. No gray area. No decoding of hidden meanings.

I didn't have to ask myself: "Did I answer correctly?" "Did I say too much?" "Did I just embarrass myself?"

All I had to do was move. And for someone whose brain was constantly hijacked by doubt and noise, that kind of clarity was freedom.

The boxing gym became my sanctuary. There, aggression was not only acceptable but necessary. The hypervigilance that exhausted me in social situations became an asset. The ability to read micro-expressions and body language - skills I'd developed to survive family dinners - translated into reading opponents' tells and timing.

My coach, a gruff Marseillais named Marcel, never commented on my smile or my social awkwardness. He cared only about footwork, technique, and heart. In the ring, my intensity wasn't "too much." It was exactly what was needed.

"Tu as l'instinct," he would say. "You have the instinct."

For the first time, a trait that had been seen as problematic was being celebrated.

# School Experiences: The Laboratory of Difference

There were moments in school when I felt like a magician. When I answered a question no one else could. When I saw patterns others had missed. When I handed in an assignment with an interpretation so unique the teacher paused before marking it.

But those moments were rare.

Most of the time, I felt like a ghost inside a machine that refused to respond to my commands.

Classrooms were sensory battlefields. The scraping of metal chair legs across linoleum. The flicker of fluorescent lights. The chalk dust cloud hovering in the air. Teachers droning through explanations while my attention pulled toward the bird outside, the whisper behind me, or the vibration of my own heartbeat in my ears.

I couldn't concentrate unless I was fascinated. And I couldn't fake fascination.

Sometimes I would hyperfocus on something meaningless just to survive, like counting how many times the teacher said "alors" or watching the second hand of the clock make perfect circles, hoping the bell would save me.

When I got something wrong, I didn't just feel embarrassment. I felt annihilation.

The shame came fast and loud. One wrong answer and I could feel the whole class watching, waiting. My cheeks burned. My ears rang. I'd shrink into the chair, smile awkwardly, and stop participating for the rest of the day. Maybe the rest of the week.

And still, still, I tried to do well. I wanted to be good. To be impressive. To be safe. So I developed strange rituals: rewriting my notes in color-coded formats, even though it drained me. Creating elaborate outlines for simple assignments. Memorizing sentences verbatim instead of summarizing. My brain needed structure, but the structure was never provided. So I built my own. At a cost.

Sometimes, I'd raise my hand not because I had something to say, but because I wanted to prove I wasn't fading. That I was still there.

And sometimes, I didn't raise my hand at all. Even when I knew the answer.

Because silence felt safer than risk.

School presented a more complex challenge than family life. At home, the rules were clear even if they were difficult to follow. At school, the rules seemed to shift depending on the teacher, the subject, the time of day, even the weather.

In Madame Laurent's mathematics class, my tendency to see patterns differently was sometimes rewarded. I could solve problems in ways that surprised even her. But when she asked me to explain my method, I would stumble. The path from question to answer was intuitive, not logical. I couldn't show my work because the work happened in places I couldn't access or articulate.

"C'est correct, mais il faut expliquer comment," she would say. "It's correct, but you have to explain how."

But how do you explain intuition? How do you show work that happens in leaps rather than steps?

In literature classes, I would become hyperfocused on details that seemed irrelevant to others. While classmates discussed the main themes of a novel, I would be fascinated by a minor character's psychology or a specific word choice that appeared once. My observations were often insightful, but they didn't fit the lesson plan.

"Très intéressant, Fabien, mais ce n'est pas le sujet," teachers would say. "Very interesting, Fabien, but that's not the subject."

Physical education was a mixed experience. Team sports revealed my difficulty with social coordination, I could execute individual skills well but struggled to read the flow of group dynamics. Individual sports, however, allowed me to excel. In track and field, my hyperfocus became an advantage. I could run through discomfort that stopped others, not out of superior conditioning but because my brain would simply disconnect from the physical sensations and enter a flow state.

14

# Early Friendships: The Periphery Pattern

Making friends felt like solving a puzzle where the pieces kept changing shape. I developed a pattern of gravitating toward the edges of social groups, close enough to feel included, but far enough to avoid the intensive social navigation required at the center.

I was drawn to other kids who seemed different: the ones who read during recess, who had unusual interests, and who didn't quite fit the standard molds. But even among the outsiders, I often felt like an outsider to the outsiders.

There was Marc, who was obsessed with trains and could recite timetables from memory. There was Sandrine, who drew intricate fantasy creatures in her notebooks and rarely spoke above a whisper. There was Ahmed, who had immigrated from Algeria and understood the feeling of being between cultures.

With them, I felt less pressure to perform normalcy. But I also noticed that I processed friendship differently than they did. While they might develop intense one-on-one connections, I seemed to need more variety. I would become fascinated by someone for weeks, then suddenly lose interest and move on to someone else. It wasn't cruelty, it was more like my brain's need for novelty extended to relationships.

This pattern confused and sometimes hurt people. I would leave others feeling like I had used them up and discarded them, when in reality I was simply following my brain's need for stimulation and change.

# The Development of People-Pleasing

This peripheral positioning became my default, but it came with an unexpected cost: the constant work of reading rooms and managing impressions from the sidelines. What I didn't realize then was how much energy this edge-dwelling required—constantly calibrating my responses, watching for social cues I might miss. I wasn't the leader. I wasn't the loud one. I was the mirror.

I learned early on that if I could reflect what people wanted to see, they'd let me stick around. So I became a collector of social signals. I studied how people laughed, how they shared secrets, how they teased each other. I learned to mimic that rhythm in order to match their tone, their slang, and their preferences.

If one friend loved rap, I made it my favorite genre that week. If another was obsessed with skateboarding, I started carrying a board even if I couldn't ride. If someone made a joke, I laughed, even if I didn't get it. Even if it felt sharp, even if it landed in a way that made my stomach twist.

Because inclusion, even shallow, felt better than isolation.

The problem was, I didn't know how to stop mirroring once it started. I became a version of myself customized to the people around me. And then I'd walk home alone feeling hollow. Like I had spent the whole day puppeteering a version of Fabien that people liked, but who didn't really exist.

One time a group of friends called me "the easy one." As in, easy to be around. Not dramatic. Not complicated.

They meant it as a compliment.

But I remember going home and sitting with that phrase: *the easy one.*

I wasn't easy. I was exhausted. I was scared. I was analyzing every interaction in real time to make sure I didn't mess up. I was fighting to stay regulated. I was overperforming empathy so no one would see the chaos underneath.

Easy wasn't who I was. It was who I became when I didn't feel safe.

As I became more aware of my social difficulties, I developed sophisticated people-pleasing strategies. I learned to mirror others' interests and opinions. I became an expert at asking questions that would get others talking about themselves, thereby reducing the pressure on me to contribute original thoughts.

In group settings, I would identify the most socially successful person and study their behavior like a scientist. How did they know when to interject humor? When did they show interest versus when did they show skepticism? What made their stories engaging while mine seemed to fall flat?

I developed a repertoire of safe responses:

"That's so interesting!" "I never thought of it that way." "You're probably right." "What do you think?"

These phrases could buy me time to figure out what was expected while making others feel heard and valued.

But this strategy came with costs. The more I focused on giving others what they wanted, the less I knew about what I wanted. My preferences became secondary to my performance. I would find myself agreeing to activities I had no interest in, laughing at jokes I didn't find funny, expressing enthusiasm I didn't feel.

## Physical Manifestations of Hidden Stress

The effort of constant social navigation began to show up in my body. I developed chronic headaches that doctors couldn't explain. My jaw was often clenched from the effort of controlling my expression. I had frequent stomachaches before social events.

Sleep became elusive. My mind would race at night, replaying the day's interactions and analyzing them for signs that I had revealed too much of my authentic self or had failed to read a social cue correctly.

I began having what I now recognize as mild panic attacks, sudden onset of racing heart, sweating, and a feeling of impending doom. But at the time, I had no framework for understanding these episodes. They seemed to come from nowhere and disappear just as mysteriously.

My parents interpreted these physical symptoms as signs that I was trying to get out of school or seeking attention. The idea that academic and social environments might be genuinely overwhelming for some children wasn't part of their framework. In their experience, you endured difficulty and complained less, not more.

## The Science Behind the Smile

What I didn't understand then, what no one around me understood, was that my constant smile was neurological, not social. Studies show that approximately **6% of adults have ADHD**, with over **55% diagnosed only in adulthood**. Many of us went through childhood displaying behaviors that were misinterpreted as defiance, daydreaming, or emotional instability.

The smile, for many neurodivergent children, serves as a **nervous system regulator**. When overwhelmed by sensory input or social confusion, the brain sometimes defaults to familiar expressions, not because the child finds the situation amusing, but because smiling releases endorphins and can momentarily stabilize an overactive nervous system.

Dr. Russell Barkley, a leading ADHD researcher, notes that **"ADHD is not a disorder of knowing what to do; it's a disorder of doing what you know."** This disconnect between intention and execution often manifests in childhood as seemingly inappropriate responses, like smiling when being scolded or laughing during serious moments.

For children like me, growing up in the 1980s and 90s, this neurological reality was invisible to the adults around us. We were labeled as defiant, attention-seeking, or simply "different" in ways that made people uncomfortable.

## The Immigrant Experience: Double Outsider Status

The added layer of being the child of immigrants intensified every struggle. My parents had sacrificed everything to build a life in France. They worked multiple jobs, learned a new language, adapted to a culture that often looked down on them. The last thing they needed was a child who couldn't seem to follow basic social rules.

When I struggled in school, (forgetting homework, getting distracted during lessons, having difficulty sitting still) it wasn't just my failure. It was a reflection on my family's ability to raise a "proper" French child.

The pressure to assimilate was enormous. Speaking Creole at home but French at school, navigating between two worlds with different expectations, different definitions of respect and success. I was expected to be twice as good to get half the recognition, and I couldn't even manage to be normally good.

My parents' frustration wasn't cruelty, it was fear. Fear that their son wouldn't make it in a world that was already challenging for people who looked like us, sounded like us, and came from where we came from.

# The Slow Erosion of Self

As I moved through adolescence and into adulthood, the smile evolved. It became more selective, more calculated. But every once in a while, I'd forget. I'd show too much joy. I'd speak with too much passion. I'd share an idea too early or laugh at the wrong time.

The response was always the same: silence. A pause. A subtle pullback. A look that said: *You're too much.*

I began to learn the dance, the emotional math of social acceptance. **Tone it down. Hide the joy. Dim the light.** Because nothing, I discovered, scares people more than someone who doesn't know they're "supposed" to be ashamed.

Gradually, I retreated further inward. I became hyper-aware of how people perceived me, trying to mold myself in real time, adjusting my tone, my posture, my word choice. I used humor to disarm people, hoping they'd accept me. But deep down, I was afraid. And if I wasn't completely sure I'd be received well, I chose not to speak at all.

I stopped raising my hand in class. I stopped offering ideas at work. I stopped reaching out in friendships.

**The cost of that silence? Years of missed opportunity. Years of isolation. Years of pretending.**

This pattern nearly broke me. Because silence becomes a habit. A habit becomes a belief. And that belief becomes a prison, one I built for myself.

## Understanding the Why

It wasn't until my thirties that I began to understand what had been happening all along. The first person to suggest I might be on the autism spectrum wasn't a doctor, it was my barber. He mentioned that his brother was autistic and that something about my mannerisms, my intensity, the way I processed conversations, reminded him of that.

I laughed it off initially. But then a friend said the same thing. Then an osteopath. Followed by a therapist. Eventually, I couldn't ignore the pattern.

When I finally looked into it, everything clicked. Every memory of being misunderstood, of being "too much," of people being frustrated with me without knowing why, it all came into focus.

What psychologists describe as **executive dysfunction**, a core feature of ADHD and autism, explained my childhood struggles. It's not a lack of motivation or laziness. It's the inability of the brain to access the "start" button, even when the will is there. When you pair that with hypersensitivity, emotional, social, sensory, you get a cocktail of confusion, shame, and exhaustion.

That was me. That had always been me.

## The Turning Point

Six years ago, I got sober. Not because I hit rock bottom in the stereotypical way, but because I realized I had slowly been abandoning myself, night after night, drink after drink.

At first, sobriety was terrifying. I had to face the noise in my head without numbing it. I had to feel the shame I'd buried. But I also had to learn something I never truly grasped: how to live authentically.

I started small. Ten minutes of meditation in the morning, ten at night. Gratitude lists, writing down three things every day that I was thankful for, even if one of them was "the ceiling fan still works." I began affirmations:

- I am safe.
- I am not too much.
- I can take up space.

At first, they felt ridiculous. Like whispering spells to an indifferent universe. But slowly, very slowly, something in me softened. I didn't magically become a new person. I simply began listening to the one I had always been.

I woke up one day and realized: I'm still here. Still breathing. Still fighting. And maybe, just maybe, I wasn't cursed. Perhaps I had something to offer.

# Reclaiming the Smile

Somewhere along the way, my smile stopped being mine.

At first, it was a reflex. A social cushion. A way to say "I'm okay" when I wasn't. Then it became a defense, a way to disarm adults, diffuse conflict, and avoid questions. But eventually, it became something else entirely.

It became camouflage.

I smiled through confusion. I smiled through overstimulation. I smiled through betrayal. And because people saw the smile, they assumed I was fine.

"You're always smiling," they said, as if that proved something.

It did. It proved how well I had learned to hide.

The truth is, smiling became a survival strategy so effective that I forgot how to stop. Even when I was alone, I'd catch myself smiling at nothing, my body still performing safety cues to no one. And I began to wonder: if I wasn't smiling, who was I?

Did I know?

Because when you spend years making yourself digestible, palatable, pleasant, you lose track of your flavor. You become a blank slate for other people's comfort.

The smile was never fake. It just didn't belong to me anymore.

And losing your own expression, your own default state, is its own kind of grief.

I smile today not because I'm naive or unaware. I smile because I survived.

Because I'm learning that being too emotional, too reactive, too sensitive, too much, all the things they said were wrong with me, are also the things that help me connect, help me write, and help me feel deeply in a world that often feels surface-level.

This chapter isn't about blame. It's about context. It's about unlearning the lies that shame taught me. Lies like:

- You should be able to focus like everyone else
- You're too old to change
- You'll always be misunderstood

No. I believe in another truth now:

**Awareness is not a destination. It's a doorway. A moment of recognition that changes everything that follows.**

And this book is me, walking through that door.

My smile today is different from the one I wore as a child. It's not constant, but when it appears, it's genuine. It's not performed for others' comfort but rather, expressed from my own joy. It's not a shield against the world, but a bridge to those who understand that neurodivergent joy is not a mistake to be corrected. It is truly a gift to be celebrated.

The eight-year-old boy who was told to stop smiling like an idiot deserved better. He deserved to be understood, accommodated, and celebrated. I can't go back and give him that, but I can give it to myself now. And in doing so, I can help ensure that other neurodivergent children never have to accept that their natural expressions of joy are something to be ashamed of.

The smile that once betrayed me has become my emblem of resilience. It says: I am still here. I am still joyful. And I am unapologetically myself. Chapter 2: The Child Who Disappeared.

# Chapter 2: The Child Who Disappeared

## The Disappearing Act

The moment I realized I was different, I began editing myself.

It wasn't conscious. It wasn't dramatic. It was subtle, quiet, and surgical. I began to track reactions, teachers, parents, friends, and adjust in real time.

Too loud? Lower your voice. Too fast? Speak slower. Too excited? Look down. Too intense? Shrug like you don't care. Too curious? Pretend you already knew.

I didn't know I was *masking*. I just knew that every time I showed up as myself, something broke. A silence. A pause. A look. A shift in the air so slight, but devastating.

So I adjusted. And then adjusted again. Until one day, I wasn't even sure what version of me was real anymore.

Was I the one who asked too many questions? Or the one who laughed too hard? Was I the one who observed too much, or the one who retreated into silence?

I became a shapeshifter. A ghost of my own making. This is what masking does. It teaches you how to vanish in plain sight.

Middle school is where everything became louder, both inside and out.

My body changed before I was ready. Hair, height, hormones. New rules. New bathrooms. New social codes that no one explained, but everyone else seemed to understand. Boys became more aggressive. Girls became more mysterious. Teachers became less forgiving. Every hallway felt like a test I hadn't studied for.

I wasn't just masking anymore, I was auto-masking.

At that age, I didn't think, *How should I act?* I just did. I mirrored the tone of whoever I was talking to. If a group was laughing at something, I laughed too, sometimes a beat too late, sometimes too loudly. I watched how other boys walked, sat, and threw their bags over one shoulder. I copied it. Not to be cool, but to avoid being noticed for the wrong reasons.

But even copying had limits. Sometimes I'd forget who I was supposed to be. I'd say something "too enthusiastic" in class, or answer a question with too much detail, and suddenly the air would shift. A few chuckles. A side-eye. A teacher's long pause. I learned quickly: knowing too much was just as dangerous as knowing too little.

Puberty didn't just alter my body, it rewired the rules of engagement. My voice got deeper, but I didn't sound more confident. I got taller, but I didn't feel bigger. If anything, I felt smaller inside, more unsure of how to move through the world that expected me to already know the dance.

For neurodivergent youth, puberty is especially ~~privileged as~~ a trigger for masking. One study found masking, also called camouflaging, rises sharply between ages 11–14, as underlying differences collide with social expectations. That sudden pressure to blend became my full-time job. And it wasn't just social, my nervous system was fighting through sensory chaos. Classrooms buzzed like beehives. The fluorescent lights made my head throb. Group work drained me before it even started.

Puberty was already disorienting, but for someone neurodivergent and undiagnosed, it was chaos. Sensory overload mixed with emotional hypersensitivity. One day I'd feel like I could conquer the world, the next I'd be curled up in my room, unable to move. The smallest things, a sarcastic comment, a skipped invitation, a change in seating, could send me into a spiral.

I remember one day during science class, we were asked to pair up. Everyone moved fast, choosing their people. I hesitated for one second too long. That was enough. No one picked me. I laughed it off, pretending to help the teacher clean the sink, but I went home that night and stared at the ceiling for hours, feeling like I didn't exist.

I didn't tell anyone what was happening inside me because I didn't have the words for it. I just thought I was weird. Or wrong. Or broken in a way I needed to keep hidden.

So I smiled. I joked. I leaned into being "the nice one," "the chill one," "the funny one." But underneath, I was scanning every interaction, checking every mental mirror, adjusting constantly.

And the more I adjusted, the less I recognized myself.

This is what masking does. It teaches you how to vanish in plain sight. It wasn't just in class or with teachers that I vanished. It happened in my first romantic moments too, the awkward, quiet beginnings of desire that I didn't know how to name, let alone trust.

I remember having a crush on a girl in my class who smelled like vanilla and wore oversized hoodies. She had this way of dragging her pencil down the margin of her notebook while she listened. I wasn't sure if I liked her or if I just liked how I felt near her – safe, curious, invisible in a good way.

But I didn't know how to act on it. Not in a real, embodied way. So I did what I had seen in movies. I mimicked what the boys in magazines or R&B music videos did: say something cool, not too much, not too fast. I lowered my voice. I rehearsed a "casual" comment in my head ten times before delivering it. When she laughed, I thought it meant something. When she didn't look up, I thought it meant everything.

Every crush became a script. And I studied the lines obsessively.

The problem was, I wasn't sure what part I was playing. Romantic interest, for me, was performance first, emotion second. I watched how other kids flirted, touched arms, and passed notes. I copied it, even when it didn't feel natural. Not because I was pretending, but because I was trying to locate my real feelings through someone else's behaviors. I didn't trust my own instincts. I didn't even know if I had any.

When I liked someone, I mirrored their music tastes. I laughed harder at their jokes. I said "me too" even when it wasn't true. I didn't know how to show love, so I imitated what I thought affection looked like, until the energy shifted and I felt rejected, and then I shut down completely.

Sometimes I pulled away before they could. I'd ghost them or go quiet for weeks, not out of disinterest, but because I was overwhelmed. The closeness confused me. I didn't know how to hold it. I didn't know what I was supposed to *do* with it. Intimacy wasn't soothing. It was destabilizing.

And when I got hurt, when someone ignored me, chose someone else, or simply didn't understand me, I didn't cry. I shut down. I blamed myself. I thought: *Maybe I'm not built for love.* Maybe I feel wrong. Maybe I'm wired wrong.

But I never showed it. I smiled. I teased. I said "it's whatever."

On the outside, I was chill. On the inside, I was freezing.

School was where I both shined and suffered the most.

I was smart. That wasn't the issue. I absorbed information quickly, made connections others missed, and sometimes answered questions in ways that made teachers pause. But my intelligence was messy. It came in waves. I'd ace an essay, but forget to turn in the worksheet. I'd deliver an oral presentation that stunned the class, and then forget my homework three days in a row.

To most teachers, I was either brilliant or lazy. I was praised one week and punished the next. My report cards were a strange cocktail of excellence and disappointment. "He has so much potential if only he applied himself." I started to believe that sentence was a diagnosis.

But I *was* applying myself. Constantly. Behind the scenes, in ways no one saw.

I was overthinking every instruction. Rewriting notes to "make them perfect." Obsessively checking that my handwriting was neat enough, my headings underlined. I'd spend more time organizing my thoughts than writing them. My brain needed time, more time than the school system allowed. But instead of asking for it, I masked. I smiled. I told teachers, "No worries, I'll catch up," even when I was drowning.

In group work, I either took over everything, because I didn't trust anyone else to care, or I checked out completely. There was no middle ground. I didn't know how to collaborate without spiraling into control or overwhelm. But I never explained that. I didn't even know how to.

Parent-teacher conferences were a roulette wheel. Some teachers raved about me. Others described me as "inattentive," "disruptive," or "emotionally inconsistent." My parents couldn't make sense of it either. "You're smart, so why are you acting like a fool?" my father once said. I didn't have an answer. I just stared at the floor.

The truth was, I wasn't acting. I was surviving. Every assignment felt like a performance I had to overthink. Every test was a trigger for shame. Every compliment felt unstable, like it could be ripped away the moment I forgot something simple, like putting my name at the top of the page.

Eventually, I stopped trusting praise altogether.

I knew I was smart.

I just never felt understood.

I didn't call it depression back then. I didn't even know kids could be depressed. I just thought I was tired. Or lazy. Or broken in some unfixable way.

What I now recognize as my first major depressive episode came around age twelve. I would come home from school, drop my bag, and go straight to my room. Not to play or eat or talk. Just to sit. Or lie on my bed. Or stare out the window. I didn't cry, I just disappeared from the inside out.

Sometimes I would sit there for hours, not moving, not thinking. My mom would knock and ask if I was okay. I'd say "yeah," then go right back to silence. Other times I'd blast music, French rap, R&B, or ambient beats, and create little mental movies in my head where I was someone else. Stronger. Cooler. Understood.

I invented characters. Imagined elaborate futures. One where I moved to New York and became a fashion mogul. One where I lived in a cabin in the Alps with no one around. One where I was famous enough to be left alone. My imagination wasn't just escape, it was therapy. A self-built refuge.

When it got really bad, I'd fixate on a single object, like the corner of my desk or a crack in the ceiling, and just breathe into it, letting my body go numb. I didn't know then that this was dissociation. I thought it was just zoning out. But I wasn't zoning, I was fleeing.

I never harmed myself physically, but I often fantasized about disappearing completely. Not dying, just vanishing. Becoming invisible enough to stop disappointing everyone, including myself.

The scary part was, I could function. I could still get dressed, still go to class, still smile when someone waved at me. But inside, I was gone. And because I was still "doing okay," no one thought to ask if I was in pain.

So I escaped into fantasy. Into music. Into perfectionism. Into silence.

No one told me I was depressed.

No one told me I was grieving the loss of a self I never got to be.

No one told me it was okay to ask for help.

So I didn't.

I just sank quietly, one imagined life at a time.

## The Laboratory of Childhood

School became my laboratory for social experimentation. Every classroom was a new environment with different variables to test. Which teachers appreciated enthusiasm? Which ones punished it? Which classmates would accept my intensity? Which ones would use it against me?

I developed different personas for different contexts. There was Math Class Fabien, quiet, careful, always double-checking his work because mistakes meant humiliation. There was Playground Fabien, still quiet but watchful, learning the unspoken rules of games I never quite understood. There was Cafeteria Fabien, the one who sat on the periphery of conversations, laughing at jokes he didn't get, hoping to blend in.

Each version was carefully calibrated to avoid the dreaded response: the pause, the look, the sudden shift from acceptance to judgment.

## Middle School: Puberty Meets Neurodivergence

If elementary school was challenging, middle school was a nightmare. Not only were the social rules becoming more complex, but my body was changing in ways that added new layers of confusion and self-consciousness.

The onset of puberty seemed to amplify every neurodivergent trait I had. My emotional intensity increased. My sensory sensitivities became more pronounced. The social demands multiplied while my capacity to meet them felt diminished.

Other kids seemed to navigate this transition with some innate knowledge I lacked. They understood the new hierarchies, the importance of brand names, and the subtle art of flirtation. I felt like I was watching a play where everyone else had the script and I was improvising badly.

My voice changed unpredictably, cracking at the worst moments — like when I finally worked up the courage to answer a question in class. My body grew awkwardly, all elbows and knees, which made me feel even more self-conscious about my physical presence in space.

The emotional volatility of adolescence hit my already dysregulated nervous system like a hurricane. Small disappointments felt catastrophic. Minor social slights sent me into spirals of shame that could last for days. I had no framework for understanding that these reactions were both neurological and normal. Instead, they felt like evidence of my fundamental wrongness.

## First Romantic Interests and Social Confusion

When classmates began showing interest in dating, I felt completely lost. The social scripts for romantic interaction were even more mysterious than those for friendship. I could tell when I was attracted to someone, but I had no idea how to express it appropriately.

I would develop intense crushes that felt all-consuming. I would analyze every interaction with the object of my affection, looking for signs of reciprocal interest. But my ability to read social cues was so poor that I often misinterpreted neutral friendliness as romantic interest, or missed genuine signals because they were too subtle for me to detect.

When I did work up the courage to express interest, it usually went poorly. My approaches were either too intense or too indirect. I would either overwhelming someone with the force of my attention or be so subtle that my interest was completely missed.

The rejection felt devastating, not just disappointing, but like confirmation that there was something fundamentally wrong with me. I began to believe that I was destined to be alone, that whatever made other people attractive to each other was missing in me.

## The First Lie

I remember the exact moment I learned to lie, not with words, but with behavior.

It was during a family gathering. My cousin was being scolded harshly for talking back. I watched the fear flicker across his face and disappear behind a forced smirk. That smirk saved him.

That's when I understood: compliance earns safety. Authenticity earns punishment.

So I practiced compliance. Polite. Agreeable. Quiet. Smiling. Perfect.

But inside, I was loud. I was questioning. I was furious.

This duality became my first prison. On the outside: golden child. On the inside: chaos.

I learned how to make adults proud of me while simultaneously feeling like a fraud. And worse, believing I was one.

That was the first lie I told myself: "If they love the version of me I present, maybe I'll start to believe in him too."

# Academic Performance vs. Internal Struggle

The disconnect between my academic performance and my internal experience grew wider as I progressed through school. On paper, I was a good student. I got decent grades, rarely caused trouble, and participated when called upon. Teachers generally liked me.

But beneath the surface, I was drowning.

The effort required to maintain focus during lectures was exhausting. I would sit perfectly still, make appropriate eye contact, nod at the right moments, all while my mind wandered to completely unrelated topics. I became an expert at looking engaged while being mentally absent.

Note-taking was a particular challenge. I would either write down everything the teacher said, creating pages of illegible scrawl, or get so focused on making my handwriting perfect that I would miss large chunks of the lesson. There seemed to be no middle ground.

Homework was a nightly battle. Tasks that seemed simple when assigned would become overwhelming obstacles at home. I would sit at my desk for hours, staring at assignments I couldn't begin, paralyzed by a combination of perfectionism and executive dysfunction.

My parents would find me there, apparently studying, and praise my dedication. They had no idea I was trapped in a cycle of anxiety and avoidance, unable to start but unable to admit defeat.

## Teacher Conferences and Parental Frustration

Parent-teacher conferences became exercises in cognitive dissonance. Teachers would praise my behavior and effort while noting that I seemed to have "potential that wasn't being realized" or that I "could do better if I applied myself more."

My parents would leave these meetings frustrated and confused. If I was well-behaved and capable, why wasn't I excelling? The implication was always that I wasn't trying hard enough, that I was lazy or unmotivated.

The truth was more complex. I was trying extraordinarily hard, but my effort was being spent on maintaining my mask, regulating my nervous system, and navigating social complexities that others handled intuitively. By the time I got to actual academic work, I was often depleted.

But I had no words for this experience. When asked why I wasn't performing better, I would shrug and mumble something about needing to try harder. This response satisfied neither my parents nor my teachers, but it was safer than trying to explain something I didn't understand myself.

## School: A Stage, Not a Sanctuary

Every classroom I entered felt like a new test, not just academically, but socially, emotionally, energetically.

I watched how other kids moved through the world. How they knew when to speak, how to joke, how to sit just the right way to avoid attention or earn it. They had some internal script I wasn't given.

And when I tried to improvise, I got it wrong. Either I was too late to join the game, or too early with the answer. Too intense. Too weird. Too much.

I learned to play dumb. I learned to act chill. I learned to say "I don't care" even when I cared deeply. Because caring made me vulnerable. And vulnerability was a gamble I couldn't afford.

At school, I was praised for my potential and punished for my process. I remember a math class where I got every answer right on the final exam, but was docked points because I didn't "show my work." I didn't know how to explain what my brain had done. I just saw the solution.

The teacher told me that wasn't good enough.

That's when I started to believe that **being right wasn't enough**, you had to do it their way, in their language, in their format. And I just didn't know how.

# Friendship Patterns: Always on the Periphery

As I moved through my teenage years, I developed a consistent pattern in friendships. I would be the one who was included but never central, welcomed but never essential. I was the friend you could depend on to listen, to be supportive, to go along with whatever the group wanted to do.

This position had advantages. It was relatively safe, I rarely faced direct conflict or rejection. I could observe group dynamics without being responsible for managing them. And I genuinely enjoyed supporting my friends and being helpful.

But it also meant I was often invisible. My preferences weren't consulted because it was assumed I was flexible about everything. My opinions weren't sought because I had established myself as someone who went along rather than led. My needs weren't considered because I had trained people to see me as undemanding.

I told myself I preferred it this way, that I was naturally accommodating and didn't need to be the center of attention. But underneath, I felt empty and disconnected. I was so good at being what others needed that I had lost track of what I needed.

# The Science of Disappearing

What I was experiencing, this constant adaptation and self-editing, has a name: **masking**. Research shows that **masking is particularly common among neurodivergent children**, especially those who are gifted or high-functioning.

The National Autistic Society explains that **"some autistic people use a strategy called masking to hide or suppress their autistic traits. This means it is harder for others to tell they are autistic."** But the cost is enormous.

Studies indicate that **heavy masking in childhood contributes to higher rates of anxiety, depression, and identity confusion in adulthood**. One research project found that autistic individuals who masked extensively were **three times more likely to experience mental health crises** in their twenties and thirties.

For ADHD children, masking often looks different, suppressing hyperactivity, forcing attention on boring tasks, or hiding the emotional intensity that comes with rejection sensitive dysphoria. But the internal cost is the same: **the authentic self goes underground**.

## The Development of People-Pleasing Behaviors

By high school, my people-pleasing had evolved into a sophisticated art form. I could read a room and adjust my personality to match what was needed. With studious friends, I was intellectual and serious. With sporty friends, I was competitive and physical. With artistic friends, I was creative and emotional.

This adaptability made me well-liked across different social groups, but it also meant I never developed a stable sense of self. I was like a social chameleon, taking on the colors of my environment so completely that I lost track of my natural hue.

The exhaustion of this constant adaptation was immense, but I had no comparison point. I assumed everyone worked this hard at social interaction. I thought the headaches, the fatigue, the need to decompress alone after social events were normal parts of being a teenager.

## Early Signs of Anxiety and Depression

What I now recognize as anxiety and depression began manifesting in my teenage years, but at the time I had no framework for understanding these experiences. I thought the persistent worry, the difficulty sleeping, the periods of hopelessness were character flaws rather than symptoms.

I developed what I now know were panic attacks, sudden episodes of intense fear accompanied by physical symptoms like racing heart, sweating, and difficulty breathing. But without understanding what they were, I interpreted them as evidence that I was weak or crazy.

The depression was sneakier. It crept in gradually, like a fog that made everything seem gray and distant. I lost interest in activities I had previously enjoyed. Getting out of bed became difficult. I felt like I was watching my life from behind glass, present but not engaged.

My parents noticed I seemed tired and moody, but they attributed it to typical teenage behavior. And I had become so skilled at masking that I could still perform normalcy even when I felt like I was falling apart inside.

## Coping Mechanisms: Isolation and Fantasy

When the social world became too overwhelming, I retreated into isolation and fantasy. I would spend hours in my room, reading books or creating elaborate imaginary scenarios where I was competent and understood.

Video games became a particular refuge. In virtual worlds, the rules were clear and consistent. Success was measurable. I could control my environment and my interactions. Unlike real life, where I felt constantly off-balance, games provided structure and predictability.

I also developed rich fantasy lives. I would imagine myself as different people in different scenarios, confident, charismatic, successful. These fantasies weren't escapism so much as experimentation. They were ways of trying on different identities, exploring who I might be if I weren't constantly worried about being too much or not enough.

## The Cost of Hyper-Awareness

I became a master of reading people. I could feel tension from across the room. I could tell when someone was uncomfortable before they knew it themselves. I could sense danger not through action, but through vibe.

It sounds like a superpower. And sometimes it was. But mostly, it was exhausting.

Because instead of just being present, I was always tracking:

- Is she annoyed at me?
- Did I say something wrong?
- Did I come off too strong?
- Should I apologize?
- Do I need to leave?

I wasn't living. I was analyzing.

And the deeper tragedy? No one noticed. They just saw a quiet, polite boy with a charming smile and thought, "He's fine."

I wasn't.

## Unseen Wounds

There's a grief that comes from being misunderstood, not just once, but habitually. Chronically. It's like being trapped in a soundproof room, screaming your truth, while the world outside compliments your composure.

"You're always so calm." "You're so easygoing." "You're so mature for your age."

Inside, I was imploding. But I had learned to nod, to thank them, to take the compliment like a piece of stale bread handed to a starving man.

I didn't need to be praised. I needed to be understood.

But that never came. Not from school. Not from home. Not even from most of my friendships. I was praised for what I suppressed. Rewarded for the mask. And punished the moment it slipped.

## Identity Without Anchor

As I moved into my teens and twenties, I didn't know what I liked. I didn't know what I wanted. I didn't even know what my voice sounded like unless it was responding to someone else's expectations.

If someone liked rock music, so did I. If they smoked, I probably would too. If they loved a certain movie, I'd pretend I loved it too, even if it made no sense to me.

I had preferences. But I couldn't trust them. Because for years, I had trained myself to disconnect from my instincts in order to survive social interaction.

So I drifted. Friend to friend. City to city. Relationship to relationship. Not building a life, just trying on costumes.

# Meltdowns in Disguise

Here's the thing no one tells you: not all meltdowns look like crying or screaming. Some look like withdrawal. Some look like ghosting. Some look like calmness so complete, it's chilling.

Mine looked like silence.

There were moments when the weight of pretending became so heavy that I disappeared completely. I wouldn't text back. I wouldn't leave my room. I'd stare at walls for hours, unable to move.

Frozen, not out of laziness, but because the cost of pretending had overdrafted my nervous system.

This is called **autistic burnout**. Or **neurodivergent fatigue**. Or what I used to call "my shutdowns."

And it took me years to understand it wasn't weakness. It was my body begging me to stop hiding.

# The Research Spiral

When the word "autistic" was first suggested to me, by a barber, of all people, I brushed it off.

He wasn't diagnosing me. He was sharing something gentle and honest: "My brother's autistic," he said. "And you remind me of him. Not in a bad way, just... you feel things deeply."

I nodded, smiled, and changed the subject. But when I went home and Googled it. Then I couldn't stop.

What started as casual reading became an obsession. Not out of fear, but recognition. Every blog post, every video, every checklist, it was like reading my own diary, written by strangers who had never met me, but knew every single thing about me.

I discovered terms I'd never heard before:

- **Monotropism,** the tendency to hyper-focus on one interest at a time
- **Sensory sensitivity,** why I couldn't handle certain fabrics or loud environments
- **Masking,** the exact skill I had perfected since I was a child
- **Rejection Sensitive Dysphoria,** the electric jolt of shame I'd feel from the smallest comment

This wasn't some online rabbit hole. This was a reunion, with myself.

## My Childhood, Rewritten

I started replaying memories like a detective returning to the scene of the crime.

The tantrum I had at five in the shoe store? Sensory overload. The panic I felt during group activities? Poor executive function plus social decoding difficulty. The smile I couldn't wipe off, even when I was devastated? Autonomic regulation, it was my body protecting itself.

None of it was random. None of it made me weak.

I wasn't "overreacting." I wasn't "too emotional." I wasn't "difficult."

I was neurodivergent. Full stop.

And just like that, my past changed shape. The narrative of a weird, inconsistent, overly sensitive kid turned into the story of someone surviving the best they could in a world that didn't speak their language.

## The Grief That Follows Truth

But here's what they don't tell you about discovery: Even when it's freeing, it still hurts.

I grieved hard.

I grieved the child who thought he was broken. I grieved the teenager who hid his panic under cool silence. I grieved the twenty-something who drank to feel normal. I grieved every missed opportunity, every misread moment, every self-betrayal.

I wasn't just finding a label, I was reckoning with the lost time.

And I was furious. Not at my parents. Not at teachers. Not even at the systems that failed me. I was furious at how long I had been afraid of myself.

Because when you spend your whole life adapting, you forget what's yours and what's borrowed. I had worn so many masks, I didn't know what my real face looked like anymore.

## Reclaiming Myself, One Layer at a Time

Healing didn't come all at once. It came in fragments.

It came when I allowed myself to stim, to pace, to hum, to bounce my knees, all without shame.

It came when I stopped forcing myself into crowded rooms when I needed quiet.

It came when I created a wardrobe that felt good on my skin instead of chasing trends.

It came when I finally told a close friend: "I think I'm autistic."

And she didn't flinch. She just said: "That actually makes so much sense. I love you."

That moment cracked something open. Because when someone accepts your truth without hesitation, it rewires something deep. It tells the nervous system: **You're safe now.**

## The Power of Naming

Here's what I've learned: naming something doesn't limit it. It liberates it.

When I named my experience, I stopped needing to explain or justify or overperform. I didn't need to apologize for being overwhelmed. I didn't need to hide my routines or preferences. I didn't need to pretend that bright lights or noisy crowds were "no big deal."

Because now I had a map. And even if I was still learning how to read it, at least I wasn't lost anymore.

## The Smile, Reclaimed

These days, I still smile. But not for approval. Not to blend in. Not to defuse tension or beg for belonging.

I smile because I finally understand myself. Because I've stopped punishing the child I was. Because I've stopped apologizing for how I show up in the world.

And when I forget, and I still do, I come back to that boy. The one sitting at the dinner table, misunderstood but still hopeful. The one who laughed too hard and loved too loudly. The one who kept smiling, even when no one else did.

I come back to him, and I whisper: You made it. You didn't vanish. You were never the problem. You were just waiting for someone to see you.

And now, I do.

# Chapter 3: The Mask Becomes the Face

By the time I hit my mid-teens, I didn't think of myself as "hiding" anymore.

There was nothing conscious about it. No moment of decision where I said, *I'm going to become someone else.* It was more like sediment, layers of micro-adjustments built up over time until I was covered. A shell had formed. A personality. One that got approval. One that was consistent enough to pass inspection. One that could function.

I stopped noticing when I was masking because masking had become my default.

It wasn't that I didn't feel things. I just didn't let them reach the surface. They lived in the background like white noise, emotions I couldn't name, instincts I didn't trust, impulses I filtered before they made it to my face.

I started to confuse being liked with being safe.

I started to confuse achievement with identity.

I started to confuse external validation with internal truth.

On the outside, I looked like a kid figuring it out. Decent grades. Well-dressed. Respectful. Athletic. Friendly. But internally, I had no idea who I was when no one else was watching.

Every time I started to feel something real, like excitement, anger, attraction, confusion, I'd pause, scan the environment, and modulate myself accordingly. The real me didn't get expressed. He got edited. Compressed. Repackaged.

And over time, I stopped asking, *What do I think? What do I feel?*

I started asking, *What do they expect me to feel? What role am I supposed to play here?*

I became a full-time actor in my own life.

And the longer I stayed in character, the harder it became to remember what the original script even looked like.

By the time I reached high school, the mask wasn't something I wore.

It had become my face.

I had become a master of disguise. The careful social experimentation of my childhood had evolved into something more sophisticated and more dangerous: I had learned to become whoever the situation required me to be.

## High School: The Performance Intensifies

High school amplified everything. The social hierarchies were more complex, the academic demands were higher, and the pressure to figure out who you were going to become felt overwhelming. For someone who had spent years erasing himself to fit in, this pressure was particularly acute.

I navigated different social circles with the fluidity of a method actor. In AP classes, I was the serious student who discussed literature and philosophy with earnest intensity. In the weight room, I became the focused athlete who communicated primarily through shared effort and friendly competition. At parties, I was the easy-going guy who laughed at jokes and made others feel comfortable.

Each performance was flawless because I had studied my roles extensively. I knew which references would land with which groups, which humor was appropriate in which contexts, and which level of vulnerability was safe to reveal. I was like a social algorithm, constantly processing inputs and adjusting outputs.

But the more successful I became at these performances, the further I drifted from any authentic sense of self. I was succeeding socially by failing personally, gaining acceptance by losing myself.

## Dating and Romantic Confusion

Dating in high school presented particular challenges for my masked existence. Romantic relationships require a level of authenticity and vulnerability that my carefully constructed personas couldn't provide.

I learned to perform attraction and affection in ways that looked convincing from the outside. I could say the right things, make the appropriate gestures, hit the expected emotional notes. I studied romantic comedies and popular songs like textbooks, learning the language of love without understanding the experience.

My relationships felt scripted because, in many ways, they were. I was playing the role of a boyfriend rather than being one. I would mirror my partners' interests so completely that they would often comment on how much we had in common, not realizing that I had unconsciously molded myself to match their preferences.

The relationships inevitably ended when my partners began to sense that something was missing. They couldn't quite put their finger on it, but they felt like they weren't connecting with a real person. They were right, they weren't.

"I feel like I don't really know you," more than one girlfriend told me. "It's like you're always performing for me."

I would protest, but deep down I knew they were right. I had become so skilled at being what others wanted that I had forgotten how to be myself. The problem was, I wasn't sure there was a self underneath all the performances.

## Academic Performance vs. Internal Chaos

Academically, I had learned to work the system. I could produce the essays teachers wanted, give the answers they were looking for, and participate in discussions in ways that made me appear engaged and insightful.

But my academic success was as performative as my social success. I rarely pursued subjects out of genuine curiosity or passion. Instead, I became an expert at identifying what each teacher valued and delivering exactly that.

In English class, I learned that Mrs. Henderson loved when students connected literature to personal experience, so I became masterful at crafting fake personal anecdotes that illuminated the themes she wanted us to explore. In history class, Mr. Rodriguez rewarded students who could argue multiple perspectives on controversial topics, so I became a talented devil's advocate, taking positions I didn't necessarily believe but arguing them with convincing passion.

The grades were good. The teachers' comments were positive. But I felt like an academic fraud, succeeding through mimicry rather than genuine learning or insight.

The most troubling part was that I had lost track of what I actually thought about anything. My opinions had become so malleable, so dependent on context and audience, that I no longer had access to my own authentic responses to ideas.

## Part-Time Jobs and Workplace Difficulties

My first experiences in the working world revealed new challenges for my masked existence. Unlike school, where I had years to study the environment and develop appropriate personas, jobs required me to perform competence immediately.

I worked various part-time jobs throughout high school and college: retail clerk, restaurant server, office assistant, camp counselor. In each role, I encountered the same pattern: initial success followed by gradual difficulties as the demands of sustained performance took their toll.

I was often praised during training periods for being attentive, cooperative, and quick to learn. Managers would comment on my positive attitude and strong work ethic. But as the novelty wore off and the job became routine, my performance would begin to decline.

The mask required constant energy to maintain, and in work environments where I had to sustain it for eight-hour shifts, I would begin to crack. My attention would wander. My enthusiasm would feel forced. The careful politeness would slip into something that felt more like dissociation.

Coworkers would notice the change. "You seem different lately," they would say. "Is everything okay?"

I never knew how to answer these questions. Everything was not okay, but I couldn't articulate what was wrong. I was exhausted by being someone else, but I didn't know how to be myself.

# University: The Freedom That Felt Like Prison

College should have been liberating. For the first time, I was away from family, away from the social dynamics of my hometown, free to reinvent myself however I wanted.

But freedom felt terrifying when you didn't know who you wanted to be.

I approached college like an actor preparing for the role of a lifetime. I researched what college students were supposed to be like, how they were supposed to act, what they were supposed to care about.

I joined clubs based on what seemed most likely to make me appear well-rounded rather than what interested me. I chose classes that seemed appropriately challenging and diverse rather than following any genuine academic passion. I even selected a major (business) that seemed practical and respectable rather than pursuing subjects that captured my imagination.

The persona I developed for college was perhaps my most sophisticated creation yet: the well-adjusted, socially conscious, academically serious young man who was clearly destined for success. I had learned to perform thoughtfulness, ambition, and maturity so convincingly that professors, advisors, and fellow students all saw great potential in me.

But underneath the performance, I felt empty and lost. I was succeeding at being a college student while failing to actually get an education. I was learning to navigate academic and social systems while learning nothing about myself.

# Early Career Attempts

After college, I entered the professional world with the same approach I had taken to everything else: careful observation followed by strategic performance.

I got a job at a consulting firm, attracted by the promise of fast-paced work and frequent travel. I thought the constant variety would keep me engaged and the professional environment would reward the kinds of performances I had perfected.

For a while, it worked. I was good at client presentations, skilled at making complex information accessible, and talented at managing relationships. I could walk into a conference room and quickly assess the dynamics, identify the key decision-makers, and adjust my communication style accordingly.

But the work felt hollow. I was solving problems I didn't care about for companies I had no connection to. I was performing competence and enthusiasm while feeling increasingly disconnected from my own life.

The breaking point came during a particularly long project that required me to spend three months essentially living in hotels and client offices. The extended performance, with no safe space to decompress or be authentic, led to what I now recognize as a significant bout of depression and anxiety.

I would lie awake in anonymous hotel rooms, staring at ceilings and wondering who I was when no one was watching. The question scared me because I wasn't sure there was an answer.

## Social Drinking as Self-Medication

College had introduced me to alcohol as a social lubricant, but by my mid-twenties, drinking had become something more essential: a way to temporarily turn off the exhausting process of constant self-monitoring and performance.

When I drank, the careful calculations that governed my social interactions would quiet. I could be spontaneous, emotional, even vulnerable in ways that felt impossible when sober. For a few hours, I could feel like I was accessing something authentic within myself.

But alcohol was a crude tool for a complex problem. The relief it provided was temporary and often came with consequences. I would say things while drunk that felt true, but that I would have to walk back when sober. I would show emotions that felt genuine, but that didn't fit with the persona I had constructed.

The morning-after regret became a familiar feeling. Not just the physical hangover, but the emotional hangover of having let the mask slip and showing parts of myself that felt too raw, too real, too much.

I began to see alcohol as both a solution and a problem: it gave me access to authenticity, but only in ways that were ultimately destructive.

## Identity Confusion and the Crisis of Not Knowing

By my late twenties, I was facing a crisis that I couldn't name or understand. I had achieved many of the markers of success: good education, respectable job, active social life, romantic relationships, but I felt like I was living someone else's life.

The question "Who are you?" became paralyzing. I could tell you who I was in any given context, I was extremely good at that, but I couldn't tell you who I was independent of context.

I would try to identify my authentic preferences by process of elimination. Did I actually like the music I listened to, or had I just adopted the tastes of people I wanted to impress? Were my political opinions genuinely held, or were they positions I had taken to fit in with particular social groups? Did I enjoy the activities that filled my free time, or were they just ways of maintaining various social connections?

The more I examined my life, the more I realized how little of it felt genuinely chosen. I was living by default, following scripts I had internalized without conscious decision.

## The Exhaustion of Constant Performance

What I now understand as masking fatigue was becoming unbearable. The energy required to maintain various personas across different contexts was leaving me depleted and empty.

I would come home from social events and need hours of complete solitude to recover. Not just time to relax, but time to remember who I was when no one was watching. The problem was, I was increasingly unsure of the answer to that question.

Simple social interactions began to feel overwhelming. A casual coffee with a friend required the same level of preparation and energy as an important business presentation. I was analyzing every conversation, evaluating every response, constantly adjusting my performance based on real-time feedback.

The irony was that my performances were successful. People liked me, sought my company, and considered me a good friend and colleague. But I felt more alone than ever, surrounded by people who knew and liked elaborate fictions of myself rather than connecting with who I actually was.

## Moments When the Mask Slipped

Despite my best efforts to maintain perfect control, there were moments when the mask would slip. These moments terrified me because they revealed not just my authentic self, but how different that self was from the personas I had constructed.

Sometimes it would happen when I was overtired or overstressed. The careful emotional regulation would fail, and I would react to minor frustrations with an intensity that surprised everyone, including myself. These episodes would be followed by lengthy apologies and renewed efforts to maintain better control.

Other times, genuine enthusiasm would break through my careful composure. I would become animated about a topic that truly interested me, speaking with a passion and intensity that felt foreign to my usual measured responses. These moments felt both exhilarating and dangerous, like glimpses of an authentic self that I wasn't sure I could integrate into my social life.

The most painful slips were moments of vulnerability, times when genuine emotion would break through my carefully maintained emotional equilibrium. These moments felt like failures of self-control rather than expressions of humanity.

## Depression and Anxiety Manifestations

By my late twenties, the psychological cost of sustained masking was manifesting as clinical depression and anxiety. But because I had no framework for understanding the connection between my social performance and my mental health, I interpreted these symptoms as personal failings.

The depression felt like a gray fog that made everything seem distant and unreal. I could still perform my various roles, but it felt like I was watching myself from far away. The anxiety manifested as a constant low-level worry about whether I was managing my performances correctly.

I sought therapy, but I found myself performing for therapists too. I would present my problems in ways that seemed most likely to elicit helpful responses. I would edit my experiences to make them more coherent and less messy than they actually were.

Even in therapy, I was acting like the kind of patient I thought would be most successful rather than revealing the confusion and emptiness I actually felt.

## Seeking Therapy but Not Knowing What Was Wrong

My first attempts at therapy were frustrating for both me and my therapists. I could articulate that I felt unhappy and anxious, but I couldn't identify specific problems or traumas that might be causing these feelings.

From the outside, my life looked good. I had no obvious reasons for depression or anxiety. I had achieved academic and professional success, maintained friendships and romantic relationships, avoided major crises or traumas.

The problem wasn't what had happened to me, it was what hadn't happened. I had never developed a stable sense of self. I had never learned to identify and trust my own authentic responses to the world. I had become so skilled at being what others needed that I had lost track of what I needed.

But this kind of problem is difficult to address in traditional therapy models that focus on specific symptoms or traumatic events. How do you treat someone whose primary issue is that they don't know who they are?

## The Moment of Recognition

The beginning of change came not through therapy or self-help, but through an unexpected moment of recognition. I was at a party, performing my usual role of the charming, easy-going guy who made others feel comfortable.

I was talking to someone I had just met, adjusting my personality in real-time based on their responses, when I suddenly had a moment of startling clarity: I had no idea who I was when I wasn't performing for someone else.

The realization was both terrifying and liberating. Terrifying because it revealed the extent to which I had lost myself. Liberating because it finally gave me a framework for understanding what was wrong.

I wasn't depressed because of something that had happened to me. I was depressed because I had spent so many years being someone else that I had forgotten how to be myself.

The question became: who was I underneath all the performances? And was it too late to find out?

## The Slow Process of Unmasking

Recovery from a lifetime of masking couldn't happen overnight. The personas I had developed weren't just costumes I could take off, they had become integrated into my identity and my survival strategies.

The first step was simply becoming aware of when I was masking versus when I was being authentic. This required developing a kind of internal observer who could monitor my social interactions and identify moments when I was performing versus moments when I was genuine.

Initially, this awareness was more disturbing than helpful. I realized that I was masking almost constantly, even in relationships I thought were authentic. The gap between my performed self and my authentic self was much larger than I had realized.

But awareness was the prerequisite for change. I couldn't stop masking until I could recognize when I was doing it.

## The Fear of Authenticity

As I began to experiment with being more authentic, I discovered that my fear of revealing my true self was not entirely irrational. Some people did respond negatively when I stopped performing for them.

Relationships that had been built on my ability to be what others needed began to strain when I started expressing my own needs and preferences. Some friendships couldn't survive the transition from performance to authenticity.

This was painful but necessary. I was learning that relationships built on masks are ultimately unsustainable, both for the person wearing the mask and for those who believe the performance is real.

## Finding Glimpses of the Real Self

Recovery involved learning to recognize and trust moments of genuine feeling and authentic response. These moments were often subtle, a spontaneous laugh, a genuine opinion, a natural gesture that wasn't calculated for effect.

I began to pay attention to activities and experiences that generated authentic engagement rather than performed enthusiasm. Reading certain books, listening to specific music, having particular kinds of conversations, slowly, I began to map the territory of my genuine interests and responses.

The process was like archaeology, carefully excavating an authentic self that had been buried under years of performance and adaptation.

## The Gift of Crisis

What I initially experienced as a crisis of identity eventually became a gift. The painful awareness that I had lost myself created the motivation necessary to begin the long process of recovery.

Many people live their entire lives wearing masks without ever recognizing what they're doing. The consciousness of performance, however painful, was the first step toward choosing authenticity.

The mask had become my face, but faces can change. The question was whether I had the courage to let mine.

# Chapter 4: Chasing Normal

## Part 1: Fixing the Outside – Jobs, Moves, and Self-Help Obsession

For most of my twenties, I was in a full-time relationship with self-improvement.

Not the gentle, grounded kind rooted in self-love. No. This was high-speed, high-stakes, all-consuming. A desperate, obsessive campaign to become someone better. Someone normal. Someone who didn't fall apart when the routine changed or ghost friends when their nervous system shut down.

The problem was not that I didn't try. I tried everything.

### The Career Chameleon

My résumé looked like ambition. In reality, it was panic.

I went from marketing to retail management to freelance writing to launching my own fashion line. I convinced myself each pivot was part of a larger arc, that I was "discovering my path." But really, I was running. Not from laziness. Not from failure. But from a quiet truth I didn't yet have words for:

I didn't know how to function sustainably in any environment built for neurotypical brains.

The first few months of every job were golden. I'd show up early, overdeliver, offer ideas in meetings, and make everyone laugh. I'd become obsessed with optimizing workflows. My managers would call me a "rising star."

But eventually the novelty would fade, and with it, my ability to mask at full volume. I'd forget deadlines. Avoid team lunches. Ghost Slack channels. Small changes, like a schedule tweak or a surprise meeting, would send me into a tailspin. The expectations never changed, but my ability to meet them vanished.

So I'd quit. Or they'd "mutually part ways" with me. And I'd convince my-self the job wasn't the problem. I just hadn't found the right fit yet.

## The Geography of Escape

Every city I moved to felt like a reset button.

Paris. New York. Toronto. LA. Each one a promise: *This time will be different.* I'd imagine the new version of myself I'd become, the structured, focused, high-performing Fabien who worked out every morning, sent thank-you emails, and meal-prepped on Sundays.

I'd study maps, tour apartments, curate playlists for "the new chapter." I treated every move like a spiritual rebirth.

But the same patterns followed me.

In every city, I'd unpack with intensity, furniture arranged just so, workspace optimized, books lined up by theme. I'd spend the first few weeks exploring cafes, joining coworking spaces, and building a rotation of social spots. I'd talk about my goals with enthusiasm that bordered on evangelical.

And then… the fog would return. My routines would unravel. I'd forget appointments. I'd stay up too late and wake up exhausted. I'd start canceling plans with vague excuses. The adrenaline would wear off, and I'd realize: I brought my brain with me.

It didn't matter where I was. I couldn't outrun my wiring.

## The Productivity Hustle

Around that time, I discovered productivity YouTube.

Notebooks. Pomodoro timers. Notion dashboards. The gospel of discipline. It all made sense, at least intellectually. If I just found the right system, I could finally align my life with my ambition.

I bought planners. Downloaded apps. Tried "time blocking" and "habit stacking" and "mindful scheduling." I color-coded my Google Calendar until it looked like a Pride flag during a heatwave.

I followed creators who woke up at 5 a.m. and meditated in cold showers. I believed the problem was that I hadn't committed hard enough. So I committed harder. I set ten goals for the week. Then I burned out by Tuesday.

I became addicted to the idea of discipline, but not the practice of it. The systems weren't bad, but they weren't built for me.

Because no productivity hack can fix a nervous system in constant fight-or-flight.

## The Self-Help Spiral

Self-help books became my religion. Every week I was reading something promising to change my life: *Atomic Habits, The Power of Now, Getting Things Done, Deep Work, The Four Agreements*. I highlighted sentences like prayers. I believed if I just underlined the right sentence, something would finally click and I'd wake up normal.

I journaled. I vision-boarded. I tried guided meditations that left me more anxious than centered. I signed up for webinars, joined online masterminds, took courses with titles like "Discipline Without Guilt" and "Own Your Time, Own Your Life."

It wasn't that these things were useless. Some helped. But I was treating the symptoms, not the root.

I didn't know then that I was navigating executive dysfunction, sensory overload, rejection sensitivity, and chronic masking. I thought I was just lazy. Undisciplined. Weak.

So I doubled down. Hustled harder. Made more vision boards. Pushed through more fatigue. And each time it didn't work, the shame deepened.

It wasn't just that I was failing. It was that I believed I shouldn't be failing. That other people made it look easy. That I had all the tools and still couldn't make them stick.

## The Normal I Was Chasing

The normal I was chasing didn't even exist.

I thought normal meant:

- Getting up at 6 a.m. and crushing a workout

- Focusing on one task for hours without distraction

- Calling friends back on time

- Having a five-year plan

- Never missing appointments or losing keys or zoning out mid-conversation

But what I actually wanted wasn't normalcy. I wanted peace. I wanted to stop feeling like I was at war with myself every day. I wanted to stop apologizing for being late, or tired, or overwhelmed. I wanted a system that fit *me*, not one I had to contort into.

But I didn't know that yet. I just kept running. Trying. Fixing the outside. Hoping one day, it would fix what was broken inside.

Only nothing was broken. I just didn't know that yet.

# Part 2: Relationship Patterns and Self-Abandonment

I didn't just chase normal through career pivots and city moves. I chased it in relationships too, though I wouldn't have called it that at the time.

What I craved wasn't just love. It was legitimacy. I thought if I could just find the "right" person and be the "right" partner, maybe I'd finally feel whole. Maybe I'd finally feel real.

Instead, I kept abandoning myself.

## The Mirror Effect

Looking back, every relationship I entered in my 20s had one thing in common: I mirrored the other person.

If she liked indie films, so did I. If she wanted to go vegan, I went vegan. If she talked about hiking, I suddenly owned boots. I was a social chameleon, but in romance, here again I became a shapeshifter.

It wasn't manipulation, it was survival. I didn't know who I was, so I borrowed traits that seemed appealing, admirable, or "dateable." I adjusted how I spoke. What I wore. What I listened to. How I expressed affection. I studied what made people feel seen, and I gave it to them.

The problem was, I didn't know how to receive the same in return. I didn't give people a real version of me to love. I gave them a curated one. A highlight reel. And when I sensed they loved the mask, not the me beneath it, I spiraled.

# Hyperfocus Love and Sudden Withdrawal

There's a term in ADHD circles: *love bombing.* It's often used in the context of manipulation, but that wasn't what I was doing.

For me, it was more like emotional hyperfocus.

When I fell for someone, I fell hard. I wanted to talk to them constantly. Send them poems. Take them to my favorite places. Study their voice and smile and habits like they were sacred texts. I wanted to make them feel worshipped, chosen, understood.

But then… something would shift.

The routine of the relationship would set in. The stimulation would fade. The structure of intimacy would become confusing. I didn't know how to stay. How to keep showing up when the dopamine wore off and vulnerability took its place.

So I'd pull back. Not cruelly. Not intentionally. Just… less present. Slower to respond. More emotionally distant.

And the worst part? I didn't know why I was doing it. I didn't feel like I was choosing to detach. It felt like something was slipping away, and I couldn't hold it.

Partners would ask: "Did I do something?"

And I didn't know how to say: *No, it's not you. I just don't know how to sustain anything once the mask starts cracking.*

## The Shame Loop

I carried a deep fear: that once someone really saw me, they'd leave.

So I worked overtime to be impressive. To be desirable. To be interesting. I read the room. I remembered their coffee order. I made playlists. I remembered their childhood stories and quoted them back like prayers.

But the moment I felt like they were pulling away, or worse, that I'd been too much, I panicked. I'd either overcompensate with grand gestures, or I'd ghost entirely out of fear of being rejected.

And every time something ended, I'd tell myself it was because I was too intense. Too clingy. Too distracted. Too sensitive.

The truth? I was too disconnected from myself to give anyone something real.

I hadn't built a relationship with myself, so every romance became a borrowed identity.

## When You Don't Know What You Want

Most people can name their preferences in relationships: emotional availability, shared values, physical affection, trust.

For me? I didn't know what I wanted. I only knew what I thought would make me "good enough" to be chosen.

So I made myself agreeable. Easygoing. Chill. I'd say "sure" when I meant "I'm exhausted." I'd agree to plans I didn't want. I'd go along with dynamics that confused me. I let the other person set the emotional tone, and then blamed myself when I felt lost in it.

One partner once asked me, "What do you need from me?"

And I remember blinking.

Not because I didn't have needs, but because I hadn't been asked. Not like that. Not directly. And I didn't know how to answer.

So I said, "I don't know."

But inside, I was screaming: *I need permission to stop performing. I need to be able to fall apart without being discarded. I need someone to see the pieces and still stay.*

But I didn't say that. Because I hadn't said it to myself yet either.

## Performing Stability

In every relationship, I tried to be the one who had it together.

I played therapist. Gave pep talks. Showed up calm and regulated even when I was falling apart inside. I'd take care of their emotions, their goals, their insecurities, meanwhile ignoring my own.

Because if I could be useful, maybe I'd be loved.

Because if I made myself needed, maybe they wouldn't leave.

Because if I could carry their weight, they wouldn't notice mine.

But all that emotional labor came with a cost: I began resenting people for not seeing my exhaustion, when I'd gone to great lengths to hide it. I wanted them to read my silence as a cry for help, even though I said "I'm fine" with a smile.

No one can save you from a mask they don't know is there.

## The End of Self-Abandonment

Eventually, the pattern became undeniable. Love didn't make me feel safer, it made me feel more exposed.

And somewhere around age thirty, I reached a threshold. A relationship ended not with a bang, but with a quiet ache. With another partner saying, "I just don't know who you really are."

I remember sitting alone on my bed, not angry, not heartbroken, just empty. And for the first time, I didn't blame them. I didn't blame myself either.

I just saw it clearly: *I had built my entire romantic life on a foundation of self-abandonment.*

I wasn't dating people, I was dating their approval.

And as long as I kept chasing love through performance, I'd keep losing myself.

That was the beginning of a new kind of longing. Not for a partner, but for a self. Not for validation, but for clarity. Not to be chosen, but to choose myself.

## Part 3: The Wellness Obsession – Diets, Meditation, Fitness & Control

When career reinventions didn't fix the fog, and relationships couldn't fill the emptiness, I turned inward.

If I couldn't control the world around me, I'd control my body. My mind. My breath. My habits. I would fine-tune my vessel like a machine, optimize it into stillness, focus, and stability.

I called it wellness. But in hindsight, it was a quiet form of war.

## The Rituals of Discipline

I became obsessed with biohacking.

MCT oil. Intermittent fasting. Cold plunges. Sleep trackers. I listened to Huberman podcasts like sermons. I studied cortisol like scripture. I began every morning with warm lemon water, no sugar, full fasted cardio, and a list of micronutrients I couldn't pronounce.

I wasn't trying to be trendy, I was trying to be okay. To silence the static in my head. To focus. To calm down. To find the version of myself that didn't need caffeine and chaos to function.

I kept thinking: *Maybe I'm not broken. Maybe I'm just inflamed.*

*Maybe I'm not neurodivergent, maybe I'm just deficient in magnesium.*

I didn't know yet that these rituals weren't healing me, they were distracting me from the deeper wound: that I still believed my worth was conditional on how well I could perform "balance."

## Exercise as Proof

The gym became my church.

I lifted. I ran. I boxed. I logged every session. I posted progress. I tracked macros, then cut carbs, then tried paleo, then keto, then Mediterranean.

On the outside, I looked disciplined. Healthy. Even inspiring.

But my body was a battlefield, one I was trying to dominate into submission.

If I felt chaotic, I trained harder. If I felt foggy, I fasted. If I felt tired, I forced movement anyway. Because rest felt like failure. Because stillness meant facing myself. Because I believed sweat could flush out my shame.

The mirror wasn't about vanity. It was about evidence. I needed proof that I could change. Proof that I was in control.

But I wasn't in control. I was terrified.

## Meditation as Warfare

When the world started talking about mindfulness, I leaned in hard.

I downloaded Headspace. I sat cross-legged for ten minutes every morning, trying to breathe my way into clarity. I joined a yoga studio where the teacher said things like "you are not your thoughts" while I silently judged myself for having so many of them.

I wanted to master my mind.

But my mind wouldn't cooperate.

I'd sit in stillness, trying to focus on my breath, and instead I'd think about laundry, or the message I forgot to send, or whether my posture looked "mindful enough."

Afterward, I'd open Instagram and see people meditating on beaches, looking serene. I didn't feel serene. I felt like a fraud.

I kept trying, but every failed attempt felt like confirmation: *Even peace requires discipline, and I couldn't even do that right.*

## The Clean Eating Spiral

Food became math.

Every bite was weighed, logged, considered. I followed meal plans like they were moral codes. Green juice meant I was good. Sugar meant I was slipping.

I bought books about inflammation and gut health and adrenal fatigue. I convinced myself that if I could just find the perfect diet, I'd unlock the version of myself that didn't forget appointments or freeze during conversations or wake up tired even after eight hours of sleep.

I wasn't nourishing myself, I was managing myself. Policing myself. Trying to avoid the fog, the crash, the overwhelm.

But no matter how much chia I ate or how many supplements I took, my brain didn't change. I still lost time. I still got overstimulated in grocery stores. I still spiraled after small rejections. I still couldn't focus unless I was obsessed.

Eventually I realized: my problem wasn't that I was unhealthy. My problem was that I thought health meant erasing who I was.

## When Wellness Becomes a Distraction

All of it, the workouts, the breathwork, the fasting, the supplements, it wasn't useless. Some of it helped. Temporarily.

But it also distracted me.

I didn't have to face my identity confusion if I was focused on my body fat percentage. I didn't have to process childhood trauma if I was in the sauna four days a week. I didn't have to admit I was lonely if I was training for a half marathon.

Wellness became my newest mask, cleaner, shinier, socially praised. But a mask all the same.

Because behind the cold plunges and collagen smoothies was a boy who still didn't know why his brain didn't work like everyone else's. Who still didn't know how to sit with his emotions without needing to fix or explain them away.

# Optimizing Myself into Oblivion

The more I optimized, the worse I felt.

Because even after the transformation, after I looked the part, moved the part, ate the part, I was still waking up with dread. Still missing emails. Still zoning out in conversations. Still forgetting simple things and overanalyzing everything else.

That's when the wellness obsession began to collapse.

Not because I gave up, but because I burned out.

And in that burnout, I found the first tiny thread of truth:

*What if I don't need another protocol?*

*What if I just need to understand myself?*

# Part 4: The Pattern Break – Realizing It Wasn't You, It Was the System

There's a kind of heartbreak that comes not from losing a person, but from losing a belief.

For years, I believed that if I just tried harder, I'd figure it out. That somewhere on the other side of all this effort, jobs, fitness, meditation, romance, there was a version of me who didn't struggle. Who woke up clear-headed. Who flowed through routines. Who was "finally better."

But that version never arrived.

And one day, standing in the middle of a tidy kitchen I'd optimized to death, drinking a magnesium latte from a $70 frother, I realized:

*I am doing everything right, and I still feel like I'm failing.*

So maybe the problem... isn't me.

## A System That Was Never Built for Me

That was the beginning of the break.

Not a breakdown. A pattern break. A cognitive rupture. A moment where the coordinates snapped into focus and I saw, for the first time, that I had been trying to thrive inside a system that had never been built with me in mind.

School wasn't designed for kids who think in constellations instead of straight lines.

Work wasn't designed for people who need silence, novelty, and deep rest between bursts of brilliance.

Relationships weren't designed for those who need time to decode their own emotions before they can express them.

Even wellness spaces, yoga studios, health apps, clean eating blogs, weren't built for people who stim, who mask, who have nervous systems that misfire under bright lights and constant notifications.

Every framework I'd tried to squeeze into, academic, professional, romantic, spiritual, had asked me to contort just a little too much. And every time I bent myself to fit, I lost a piece of something essential.

## The Invisible Curriculum

It's not just the systems, it's the expectations.

There's an invisible curriculum we all inherit. A silent syllabus for "how to be human." And if you're neurodivergent, you spend your life failing exams you were never taught how to take.

You're expected to:

- Sit still and pay attention (even when your mind races)
- Interpret tone and body language instinctively (even when your brain processes social data differently)
- Wake up at the same time every day with no variation in energy
- Process emotions neatly, without disruption or delay
- Be consistent, even when your executive function is episodic

I internalized all these expectations as proof that I was failing.

But I wasn't failing. I was speaking French in a room full of people pretending not to hear me.

## When Your Best Still Isn't Enough

One of the hardest truths to face was that I wasn't underachieving. I was overachieving just to appear average.

I was working overtime, behind the scenes, in the margins, in my mind, just to maintain the illusion that I was okay. And when that performance cracked, the shame was instant.

Because when you've convinced everyone you're doing fine, the moment you fall apart, no one understands why.

"You seemed so on top of it."

"I thought you were thriving."

"You're one of the most disciplined people I know."

No one sees the panic behind the calendar. The shutdown behind the silence. The executive dysfunction buried under productivity hacks.

When I said I was tired, I didn't mean I needed sleep. I meant I was carrying my life like a backpack filled with bricks, everyday tasks loaded with invisible weight.

## Borrowed Identities, Fragmented Self

The most painful realization wasn't that the system didn't work for me.

It was that I didn't know who I was without it.

I had built an identity entirely from the outside in. Built from feedback, praise, performance. Built from being "the ambitious one," "the fit one," "the creative one," "the deep thinker."

But none of those labels came from internal clarity. They were masks I tried on until one stuck. And the more I succeeded, the more I felt like an imposter.

Because deep down, I knew: if I stopped performing, would there be anything left?

I hadn't built a self. I'd built a brand. One I had to maintain constantly or risk unraveling.

## First Clues of Neurodivergence

The first time I saw the word *neurodivergent*, it was in a tweet.

Someone wrote, "It's wild how many neurodivergent adults are out here thinking they're lazy and broken when they've just been trying to live without accommodations their whole life."

I stared at the screen.

Then I read it again. And again.

I didn't retweet it. I didn't bookmark it. I just sat with it, quiet.

Because something inside me stirred, not dramatically, not instantly. But something shifted.

*Neurodivergent? Could that be me?*

*But I'm not... autistic. I don't... have ADHD. Do I?*

I didn't know. But I couldn't unsee the question.

And once the question arrived, it refused to leave.

## The Mismatch is the Message

I began tracing the pattern.

Why was I exhausted after every social event, even ones I enjoyed?

Why did I spend hours in silence recovering from small talk?

Why did I remember tiny details about people's voices but forget what they just said?

Why did I thrive in chaos but collapse in routine?

Why did every productivity system feel like a suit I could wear but never breathe in?

The more I asked, the clearer it became: I wasn't disorganized, I was unaccommodated. I wasn't emotionally volatile, I was unregulated. I wasn't lazy, I was depleted. I wasn't inconsistent, I was context-sensitive.

What if everything I thought was a character flaw… was actually a coping mechanism?

## When "Enough" Is Redefined

Eventually, I stopped trying to become someone else and started trying to become curious.

What if the question wasn't "How do I fix myself?"

What if the question was "How do I work with myself?"

What if the goal wasn't productivity, but alignment?

I started moving slower. Listening more. Not to podcasts, to my body. My attention. My emotions. My exhaustion. My sparks.

I began asking:

- What environments help me feel regulated?

- What routines are mine, not copied from influencers or coaches?

- What sensory needs do I have that I've been overriding for years?

- What relationships allow me to be unmasked without fear?

And slowly, gently, the chasing stopped.

Because the version of "normal" I was chasing had never been mine. It was someone else's blueprint. Someone else's mask.

I didn't need to chase anymore. I needed to rest. Reflect. Rewrite the story.

## The Seed of Truth

Here's the truth I wish I had known a decade earlier:

You can't optimize your way into authenticity.

You can't self-help your way out of being neurodivergent.

You can't fix a system mismatch by fixing yourself.

I wasn't broken. I wasn't weak. I wasn't behind.

I was *misunderstood*. By others, yes, but more painfully, by myself.

And once I started telling the truth, quietly, shakily, imperfectly, that's when things began to shift.

Not because I had arrived.

But because I had finally stopped running.

By my mid-twenties, I had identified the problem: I wasn't normal. The solution seemed obvious: become normal. What I didn't understand was that my entire conception of "normal" was based on observing other people's performances rather than understanding their genuine experiences.

I embarked on a decades-long quest to fix myself, to optimize myself, to transform myself into the kind of person who could navigate the world with the ease and confidence I observed in others. It was the most expensive and exhausting education of my life, and ultimately, the most futile.

## Career Pivots: Searching for the Right Fit

My first strategy for achieving normalcy was finding the right career. I reasoned that my feelings of disconnect and emptiness were the result of being in the wrong professional environment. If I could just find work that aligned with my strengths and interests, everything else would fall into place.

The problem was that I didn't really know what my strengths and interests were. I had spent so many years performing enthusiasm for whatever was expected that I had lost track of what genuinely engaged me.

I left the consulting firm and tried marketing at a tech startup. The fast-paced, creative environment seemed like it might be a better fit for my scattered energy and tendency toward novelty-seeking. For a few months, I was energized by the change and convinced I had found my calling.

But the same patterns emerged. The initial excitement wore off as the job became routine. The personality I had constructed for that environment: creative, ambitious, digitally native, began to feel as performative as any other. The work itself, despite being more interesting than consulting, still felt disconnected from any deeper sense of purpose or identity.

I tried nonprofit work, thinking that a meaningful mission might provide the engagement I was missing. I tried freelance writing, thinking that creative work might unlock some authentic part of myself. I tried sales, thinking that my people-reading skills might translate into financial success and social validation.

Each transition followed the same pattern: initial optimism, brief improvement in mood and energy, gradual return to emptiness and dissatisfaction, followed by the conviction that the next change would be different.

## The Entrepreneurial Venture: Fashion as Identity

Perhaps my most ambitious attempt at transformation came when I decided to start a fashion company. Fashion seemed like the perfect intersection of creativity, business, and personal expression. I convinced myself that building something from scratch would force me to develop the authentic vision and leadership skills I seemed to lack.

I threw myself into the project with characteristic intensity. I studied fashion blogs, attended industry events, networked with designers and manufacturers. I developed elaborate business plans and brand concepts. I created social media presences and pitched investors.

For a while, the project consumed all my energy and attention in a way that felt almost like hyperfocus. I told myself this total absorption was evidence that I had finally found my passion. The truth was more complex: starting a business gave me a socially acceptable reason to obsess over details and systems while avoiding the deeper questions about what I actually wanted from life.

The fashion company became another sophisticated form of performance. I was playing the role of Creative Entrepreneur, complete with the aesthetic choices, networking strategies, and lifestyle modifications that role required. I moved to a hipper neighborhood, updated my wardrobe, and began frequenting the kinds of establishments where creative professionals gathered.

When the business failed, as most startups do, I was devastated not just financially but existentially. I had invested so much of my identity in the project that its failure felt like confirmation of my fundamental inadequacy. I was back to square one, but now with additional debt and the shame of public failure.

### *"My First Dream Wasn't to Be Normal, It Was to Be Seen"*

I wasn't trying to be normal. I was trying to be *seen*.

Back then, I didn't have the words for what I was feeling. I just knew something was off. I was tired of performing in real life, pretending I wasn't sensitive, pretending I understood jokes I didn't get, pretending I wasn't overwhelmed by textures or sounds or expectations. So I walked into a theater class.

I didn't know what I was doing. But I knew I needed to be there.

The room was nothing fancy. A few chairs scattered against the walls. A tall instructor in a scarf with a voice like thunder and a strange silence in his eyes. He looked at us and said, "I don't want you to act. I want you to *listen*."

At first, I thought he meant to listen to him. But what he meant was something else. Listen to the breath. Listen to the tension in your body. Listen to the silence between words.

Theater was the first place where I was allowed to move without being corrected. Shake without being told to stop. Yell without being scolded. Feel without being punished.

Every exercise became a tiny revelation. One day we did a walking drill, just walk across the room, but feel each step. The weight. The intention. I realized I had never really *walked* in my own skin before. I had been marching to survive, sprinting to fit in, posing to protect myself.

Here, I wasn't faking it. I was inhabiting it.

In one class, I had to perform a monologue from *Caligula*. A powerful man unraveling in madness. As I let the words out, something cracked open. I wasn't pretending to be crazy, I was releasing something that had been buried under years of control.

The teacher didn't say much afterward. Just nodded. And I remember, as I walked back to my seat, a few classmates whispered my name. "That was strong." "Damn." "Fabien, you got something."

For the first time in my life, I didn't feel broken, I felt dangerous. In a good way.

That stage wasn't a mask. It was a mirror.

## Theater as a Bridge for Neurodivergent Minds

What wasn't clear at the time was that research was quietly backing up what I felt. Drama therapy and inclusive theatre have been shown to reduce social anxiety and improve communication in people on the autism spectrum grateful-careaba.com. A study of youth with autism found theater-based interventions helped them develop emotional insight and better self-control ijessnet.com. Programs like Michigan State University's "neurodiverse theatre" are explicitly designed for inclusive, sensory-sensitive storytelling artsmuseumsmanagement.cal.msu.edu.

Coming back to myself in that rehearsal studio was more than encouragement, it was therapy by another name. I was finding order in chaos. I was learning structure, rhythm, and connection. I was learning to listen, to others and to my own body. That monologue was a release valve and a spotlight. It signaled I wasn't just surviving. I could *thrive*.

Around that same time, someone told me I should model.

"You have presence," they said. "An edge. You walk like you know something the rest of us don't."

I was 17, still in Paris. I didn't have much, just a beat-up pair of sneakers, a black jacket I wore everywhere, and a head full of curls I barely knew how to manage. But I had a dream now.

So I did it. I walked into an agency.

Actually, I walked into a few: Ford Models, People Agency, others whose names I don't remember. But that moment I'll never forget.

One casting director, sharply dressed and sharper tongued, asked me to do a walk. "Just across the room and back," he said.

I did it. Calm. Controlled. The way they showed me on TV. The way I practiced in mirrors, on metro platforms, in the apartment when no one was home.

He nodded slowly. Then said something that stuck with me forever.

"Turn around. Look at that wall."

Behind me was a massive photo wall, stretching maybe eight meters. Rows and rows of headshots. All men. All *white*.

Strong jaws. Blue or hazel eyes. Slicked-back hair or buzzcuts. A mix of Tom Cruise, Brad Pitt, Leonardo DiCaprio clones.

"Where do you fit in?"

I didn't know what to say.

"Do you see anyone who looks like you?"

I scanned. My heart sank.

"No," I said. "I guess not."

He nodded. "Stylists don't know what to do with your curls," he added. "They're unpredictable. They frizz. They fight the shoot."

I tried to argue, my curls weren't even that tight. I was mixed, not fully African. "They're not hard to manage," I said. "You just need the right product."

He smiled in that polite way people smile when they've already made up their mind. "We do have ethnic models," he said, pointing to a corner.

There they were. Four or five Black men. All shaved heads. Abs chiseled by Michelangelo. No curls. No softness.

He looked back at me. "You've got presence," he said. "A walk. Confidence. But I wouldn't have work for you."

That moment burned into me. Not because I was rejected. I've been rejected before.

But because I saw, for the first time, the invisible architecture of the industry.

It wasn't about beauty. It wasn't about talent.

It was about **belonging**.

And I didn't.

## Curly Hair as Discrimination

I didn't understand it then, but there's a word for what I experienced: **texturism**, the bias against curly or kinky hair. Research has shown that tightly coiled hair is often deemed "unprofessional" or "unattractive" in Eurocentric beauty standards hbr.org. A Perception Institute study found natural hair is associated with anxiety and workplace penalty, though positive media representation can shift perceived norms self.com. Laws like the CROWN Act were passed to prevent such discrimination en.wikipedia.org.

So when I entered that room, I wasn't just fighting for a job, I was fighting for my identity. My hair was not a prop. My presence wasn't a trend.

That day, I realized the game wasn't broken. It was never built for me.

But I didn't stop.

I still got a few castings. One for Nintendo's new Wii console. I landed the job. A print ad at the Virgin Megastore on the Champs-Élysées. My face, my body, right there in the middle of Paris. I brought my friends to see it like a kid showing off his first trophy.

"C'est moi," I'd say, grinning.

I got background work in films. I show up in *ELLE*, pushing a stretcher in a hospital scene. The lead actresses would nudge me, "Fabien, come closer." They liked my energy. I stood out, even when I was supposed to fade into the background.

I almost booked a Dior campaign when Galliano was still designing. But they said I was "too short."

I'm 5'11". One meter eighty. In what universe is that short?

Oh right. In *that* universe.

My biggest almost-break was for Diesel's first fragrance. I nailed the casting. I could feel it. But at the last moment, they gave it to Common, the American rapper.

You can't fight that.

You don't beat a name.

But each near-miss didn't discourage me. They revealed something: the blueprint wasn't broken. It just wasn't built for me.

So I started thinking: what if I built my own?

I didn't become rich. I didn't become famous. Not in the way I dreamed.

But that fire from Theater, that edge from the street, that sense that *I belonged somewhere*, even if the world couldn't see it yet, that never left.

Now I'm building my own stage.

Not for applause.

But for freedom.

Now I'm creating a brand that looks like me. A nonprofit that thinks like me. A platform that *feels* like us.

Because someone has to make space for the kids who never fit the wall.

For the ones who don't see themselves in the mirror, not because they're broken, but because the mirror was built wrong.

I used to chase the dream of being seen.

Now, I'm making sure *we* can see *ourselves*.

## Geographic Solutions: Fresh Starts

When career changes failed to provide the transformation I sought, I turned to geographic solutions. I became convinced that my problems were environmental rather than internal. Perhaps I was just in the wrong city, surrounded by the wrong people, embedded in social and professional networks that brought out the worst in me.

I moved from my college town to a major metropolitan area, thinking that a bigger city would provide more opportunities for authentic self-expression and meaningful work. When that didn't work, I moved to a smaller city, thinking that a more intimate community would provide the connection and belonging I was missing.

I tried the East Coast and the West Coast. I tried places known for outdoor recreation, thinking that proximity to nature would ground me. I tried cities known for arts and culture, thinking that creative environments would unlock hidden aspects of my personality.

Each move was accompanied by elaborate planning and optimistic projections. I would research neighborhoods carefully, imagining how different living situations might facilitate different versions of myself. I would arrive in new places with carefully constructed plans for reinvention.

And for a few months, each move would feel successful. The novelty would energize me, the process of establishing new routines would provide structure, and the opportunity to present myself to new people would feel like a chance to start fresh.

But inevitably, the same patterns would emerge. The new environment would become familiar, the initial excitement would fade, and I would find myself facing the same internal emptiness in a different geographic location. The problem, I slowly realized, was not where I was but who I was, or rather, who I wasn't.

## Relationship Patterns and Serial Searching

My romantic relationships followed similar patterns of searching and disappointment. I approached dating like a research project, convinced that finding the right person would provide the missing piece of my identity puzzle.

I was drawn to partners who seemed to possess the authenticity and confidence I lacked. I dated artists who appeared to have clear creative visions, activists who seemed driven by genuine conviction, professionals who navigated their careers with apparent certainty and purpose.

In each relationship, I would attempt to absorb some essential quality from my partner that I felt I was missing. I would mirror their interests, adopt their perspectives, integrate their social circles into my own. For a while, this would feel like growth and self-discovery.

But the relationships would inevitably collapse under the weight of my projections and dependencies. Partners would become frustrated with my apparent lack of independent identity. They would complain that I seemed to agree with everything they said, that they never knew what I actually wanted, that I seemed more interested in becoming them than in being myself.

"I feel like you're a different person depending on who you're with," one girlfriend told me. "I never know which version is real."

She was right, but I didn't know how to explain that none of the versions felt entirely real to me either.

## The Self-Help Obsession

When external changes failed to provide transformation, I turned inward. I became obsessed with self-help books, personal development seminars, productivity systems, and life coaching. I approached self-improvement with the same intensity I brought to everything else, convinced that the right techniques and insights would finally unlock my authentic self.

I read voraciously about habit formation, goal setting, time management, emotional intelligence, and mindfulness. I attended weekend workshops on everything from leadership development to spiritual awakening. I tried meditation retreats, therapy intensives, and various forms of alternative healing.

Each new system or technique would generate initial enthusiasm and apparent progress. I would implement elaborate routines for morning pages, gratitude journaling, exercise tracking, and personal reflection. I would create detailed plans for achieving greater authenticity, deeper relationships, and more meaningful work.

But like everything else, these systems would eventually become performative rather than transformative. I was excellent at following programs and implementing strategies, but I struggled to identify what I actually wanted these changes to accomplish beyond making me more "normal."

The self-help obsession became another sophisticated form of avoidance. Instead of facing the fundamental questions about who I was and what I wanted, I could focus on optimizing systems and following expert advice. I was performing self-improvement rather than actually improving.

## Fitness and Wellness: Attempts to Feel Normal

Physical fitness became another avenue for attempted transformation. I reasoned that many of my problems, the anxiety, the scattered energy, the emotional volatility, might be solved through better physical conditioning and health optimization.

I threw myself into various fitness regimens with characteristic intensity. I tried bodybuilding, thinking that physical strength might translate into emotional resilience. I tried distance running, thinking that endurance training might teach me patience and persistence. I tried martial arts, thinking that discipline and focus in physical practice might carry over into other areas of life.

For periods, these pursuits would provide genuine benefits. Exercise helped manage anxiety and provided structure to my days. The measurable progress in physical capabilities gave me concrete evidence of improvement and growth. The communities that formed around different fitness activities provided social connection with less pressure for complex emotional navigation.

But I approached fitness the same way I approached everything else: as a solution to fundamental problems rather than as an activity with intrinsic value. I was trying to exercise my way to normalcy, to physically train myself into being the kind of person who could handle life with greater ease and confidence.

When fitness failed to provide complete transformation, I expanded into broader wellness optimization. I experimented with various diets, convinced that the right nutritional approach would finally give me the energy and mental clarity I was seeking. I tried elimination diets, Mediterranean diets, ketogenic diets, intermittent fasting, and various forms of nutritional supplementation.

I tracked sleep meticulously, invested in expensive mattresses and blackout curtains, experimented with different sleep schedules and pre-sleep routines. I tried light therapy, meditation apps, breathing exercises, and cold exposure therapy.

Each intervention would produce some benefits, but none provided the comprehensive transformation I was seeking. I was optimizing around the edges of my life while avoiding the central question of who I actually was beneath all the optimization.

## The Cycle of Hope and Disappointment

What emerged across all these attempts at change was a painful cycle that would repeat itself with minor variations. I would identify a new approach, career change, geographic move, relationship, fitness regimen, self-help system, and become convinced that this was finally the solution I had been seeking.

The initial period would always be energizing. The newness would provide temporary relief from the underlying emptiness, and the process of change would create a sense of forward momentum. I would feel hopeful, optimistic, even excited about the future for the first time in months or years.

But inevitably, the new situation would normalize. The initial excitement would fade, the novelty would wear off, and I would find myself facing the same internal landscape in a different external context. The disappointment was crushing not just because the solution had failed, but because I had invested so much hope in it.

Each failed attempt at transformation left me more convinced that I was fundamentally broken in some way that couldn't be fixed through normal means. The problem wasn't just that I was struggling, it was that all the solutions that seemed to work for other people failed to work for me.

## Burnout Patterns: The Cost of Constant Trying

The relentless pursuit of normalcy was exhausting. I was constantly in some phase of transformation: researching new approaches, implementing new systems, monitoring progress toward ill-defined goals. I never allowed myself to simply exist as I was, because I was convinced that who I was wasn't acceptable.

This constant effort to become someone else created a particular kind of burnout. It wasn't just the tiredness that comes from working hard, it was the deeper exhaustion that comes from never being able to rest in your own identity.

I would have periods where I would abandon all self-improvement efforts and sink into depression and inactivity. These weren't conscious decisions to take breaks, they were system crashes where I simply couldn't maintain the energy for continued transformation efforts.

During these burnout periods, I would often fall into unhealthy patterns: excessive sleeping, binge-watching television, ordering takeout instead of cooking, avoiding social contact. These episodes would generate additional shame and self-criticism, which would eventually motivate renewed efforts at change and optimization.

## Substance Use as Enhancement

As my transformation efforts became more sophisticated, I began experimenting with various substances as tools for acceleration or enhancement. This wasn't recreational drug use motivated by pleasure-seeking, but strategic substance use aimed at overcoming perceived limitations.

I tried microdosing psychedelics, convinced that small amounts might unlock creativity and emotional insight. I experimented with nootropics and cognitive enhancers, hoping to optimize mental performance and focus. I used cannabis strategically for anxiety management and creative work.

Even my relationship with alcohol evolved from social lubrication to performance enhancement. I would drink specific amounts at specific times to achieve particular mental states: just enough to reduce social anxiety without impairing performance, or precisely the right amount to enhance creative thinking without causing next-day impairment.

This approach to substances reflected the same mindset I brought to everything else: the belief that the right intervention, precisely applied, could solve fundamental problems with my basic functioning. I was trying to chemically optimize my way to normalcy.

## The Comparison Trap

Throughout all these efforts, I was constantly comparing myself to others who seemed to navigate life with greater ease and success. Social media amplified this tendency, providing curated glimpses into lives that appeared more authentic, more purposeful, more satisfying than my own.

I would study successful people obsessively, trying to identify the secrets to their apparent happiness and effectiveness. I would read biographies, follow their social media accounts, attend their talks and workshops. I was convinced that if I could just decode the formula for their success, I could replicate it in my own life.

But this approach was fundamentally flawed because I was comparing my internal experience to others' external presentations. I was seeing their highlight reels and comparing them to my behind-the-scenes struggles. I had no way of knowing how much effort they were putting into maintaining their apparent ease, or what private struggles they might be facing.

More importantly, I was trying to become someone else rather than discovering who I actually was. I was so focused on achieving an external standard of normalcy that I never stopped to question whether that standard was appropriate for my particular brain and circumstances.

## Professional Help: Therapy Attempts

I tried therapy multiple times during this period, but my approach to therapy was contaminated by the same mindset I brought to everything else. I wanted therapists to help me identify what was wrong with me and provide tools for fixing it. I was looking for more sophisticated techniques for self-optimization.

I tried different therapeutic modalities: cognitive-behavioral therapy to change negative thought patterns, psychodynamic therapy to understand unconscious motivations, mindfulness-based approaches to develop greater self-awareness. Each approach provided some insights and benefits, but none addressed the fundamental issue.

The problem was that I was presenting a curated version of myself even in therapy. I would edit my experiences to make them more coherent and less messy than they actually were. I would perform the role of the insightful, motivated client who was making good progress and implementing therapeutic recommendations.

Even in therapy, I was trying to be the kind of person who would be successful at therapy rather than simply being honest about my confusion and struggles.

## Growing Sense of Fundamental Wrongness

As each transformation attempt failed, I developed an increasingly strong conviction that something was fundamentally wrong with me in a way that couldn't be fixed through normal means. I began to see myself as uniquely flawed, possessing some essential deficit that prevented me from achieving the kind of life satisfaction that seemed accessible to others.

This sense of wrongness was different from typical low self-esteem or depression. It was more existential, a feeling that I was somehow operating with the wrong instruction manual for life, that other people had access to information or capabilities that I lacked.

I would have moments of clarity where I could see that my expectations were unrealistic, that perfect happiness and complete self-knowledge weren't actually achievable goals. But these moments of rationality would be overwhelmed by the emotional conviction that everyone else had figured out something essential that remained mysterious to me.

# The Moment of Questioning

The beginning of real change came not from finding a new solution, but from questioning the entire premise of my search. After years of failed transformation attempts, I began to wonder whether the problem wasn't that I was broken, but that my understanding of "normal" was fundamentally flawed.

What if other people weren't actually navigating life with the ease and confidence I perceived? What if everyone was struggling in their own ways, but some were better at hiding it? What if the standards I was trying to meet were themselves artificial constructions rather than natural human states?

This questioning didn't provide immediate relief or solutions, but it opened up new possibilities for understanding my experience. Instead of asking "How can I become normal?" I began asking "What if there's nothing wrong with me?"

It would take several more years and the discovery of neurodivergence for me to fully develop this line of thinking. But the seed was planted: maybe the problem wasn't me, but the expectations I was trying to meet.

# The Expensive Education

Looking back, I can see that my decades of chasing normalcy provided a valuable education, even though it didn't achieve its intended goals. I learned enormous amounts about psychology, productivity, health optimization, business, and personal development. I developed resilience and adaptability through constant change and experimentation.

Most importantly, I learned what didn't work for me. Each failed attempt was data that helped narrow the field of possibilities. By process of elimination, I was moving closer to understanding what might actually be helpful.

But the cost was enormous, financially, emotionally, and temporally. I had spent years and thousands of dollars trying to become someone else instead of learning to understand and work with who I actually was.

## The Setup for Discovery

All of this searching and striving set the stage for the real breakthrough that would come later: the discovery that I was neurodivergent. But that discovery would only be meaningful because I had exhausted so many other explanations for my struggles.

When I finally learned about ADHD and autism in adulthood, the information landed with such impact because I had already tried everything else. I couldn't dismiss neurodivergence as just another self-help trend or excuse for not trying hard enough, because I had demonstrated to myself that trying harder and different approaches weren't sufficient.

The years of chasing normal had taught me that the problem wasn't lack of effort or wrong techniques. Something more fundamental was going on, something that required a different framework for understanding my experience.

But I wouldn't discover that framework for several more years. In the meantime, I had to live with the growing awareness that all my efforts at transformation were failing to address something essential about my relationship with myself and the world.

# PART II: AWARENESS

## Chapter 5: Sitting in the Fire

I thought that once I knew the truth, I'd be free.

I imagined clarity would feel like relief. That naming what I was, neurodivergent, masked, misread, would untangle the knots inside me like pulling a single thread from a sweater.

But that's not what happened.

Knowing was only the first step. Awareness was something else entirely. Awareness was the heat. It was the moment after the mask came off, and I had to sit with the raw skin underneath. It was feeling everything I had pushed down, loud, messy, undeniable.

And it burned.

Sobriety wasn't a straight path, it felt like walking into a furnace.

I thought sobriety meant turning off the tap, removing alcohol, weed, distraction, and breathing again. Instead, I was met with flame. Every buried fear, disappointed hope, and shame-soaked secret surged back, roaring.

One evening, barely three weeks into recovery, I found myself at an AA meeting. Among the slogans and stories, a phrase struck me:

"This isn't about stopping alcohol. It's about sitting in the fire and not running."aa-edinburgh.org.uk amethystrecovery.org

That line sank into my bones. Because that's what sobriety asked of me, for the first time in years, I wasn't allowed to escape. I had to stay. I had to feel.

I learned that early sobriety isn't clarity, it's confrontation. Research supports this instant flood: many recovering people report rediscovering painful emotions and memories once substances fade, and are often surprised by the sudden identity crisis it triggers.

My own confrontation came in the clutter of my tiny studio apartment. There was one shelf I had ignored for years, a dust-covered monument to half-finished self-help, worn-out vitamins, and photos of me "smiling on the outside." During a one-on-one with my life coach, he said simply:

"Clean that shelf."

It was a test. I stared at that mess like it was a puzzle I didn't have the code for. But as I cleared each item, wiped each surface, I felt the weight shift. I cried, not because of tidiness, but because I was finally clearing emotional debris too. That shelf embodied everything I'd swept under the rug, and for once, I looked.

This wasn't just metaphor, it mirrored psychological research connecting cleaning behavior to emotional shame and forced separation from self burningtree.com Wikipedia.

Sobriety didn't heal me. It left me exposed. Vulnerable. With no distractions, and nowhere to hide.

So I learned to sit in the fire. I showed up to AA meetings daily, repeating slogans like:

"One day at a time.

"Easy does it."

"Progress, not perfection."amethystrecovery.org

These slogans weren't cliché, they were lifelines. They taught me that recovery isn't about strength. It's about consistency, community, and courage. That the "miracle" comes amid discomfort, like one speaker said: *"Don't leave five minutes before the miracle."* Medium

Through daily meetings, I began to see sobriety not as absence of substance, but as presence of self. Research into recovery frameworks describes this shift, a "reoriented identity" that brings connectedness, empowerment, and everyday meaning PMC.

When somebody asked me why I had cleaned that shelf, I said:

"Because I wanted to see the man underneath the mess."

It was small. It was simple. And yet it was everything.

After the fire of early sobriety, I thought therapy would be the balm.

Sobriety stripped away the numbing, but it didn't provide the answers. If anything, it amplified the questions. Who was I without substances to smooth my edges? What lay beneath years of chemical cushioning? That's when I turned to therapy, not for answers, but for a witness to whatever I might find.

I imagined a wise, compassionate professional who would help me put everything back in order, someone who would hand me a framework for my pain, then teach me how to walk out of it. But instead of clarity, therapy offered confusion. And instead of relief, it often triggered shame.

My first therapist smiled too much. She nodded politely as I described my life in fragments, childhood, identity loss, the room I couldn't clean. She suggested I try gratitude journaling. I left the session feeling like I'd just shared open-heart surgery and been handed a Band-Aid.

The second therapist told me I might struggle with low self-esteem. She said I needed to "be more gentle" with myself, but when I asked *how*, she blinked and moved on. I started wondering if I was doing therapy wrong. Like maybe I was too complicated to be helped.

By the third attempt, I had stopped bringing my full self to the room. I edited my words. I spoke in summary. I smiled when I was hurting. I downplayed the shutdowns, the spirals, the moments where I dissociated mid-conversation and forgot where I was. I didn't want to seem *too much*, even to someone I was paying to hold space for me.

And each time I walked out, I felt worse. Because now, on top of the pain, I had disappointment.

I began to internalize the silence in those rooms. The flat responses. The note-taking without recognition. I told myself:

*You're too smart for therapy.*

*You're too complicated.*

*You're too hard to help.*

But what I really meant was:

*You're too broken.*

The shame came in quietly, like fog. I told people I was working on myself, that therapy was going well. I posted quotes on my social media stories. I probably said "healing isn't linear." But deep down, I was afraid it wasn't linear because it wasn't even possible.

My life coach, the one who told me to clean the shelf, was the only one who saw past the performance. He didn't analyze me. He asked questions I couldn't dodge. He challenged me to stop outsourcing my worth to people who didn't know how to see me.

He said,

"You're not too much. You've just been in the wrong rooms."

That line cracked something open.

Because he didn't try to fix me. He just witnessed me. Fully.

And in doing that, he reminded me that I wasn't too broken for help. I was just too masked to be helped by people who couldn't see through it.

What I didn't understand at first was that my body had been trying to speak to me for years.

Long before I ever used the words "neurodivergent" or "bipolar" or "burnout," my body was already sounding the alarm. But I didn't listen, because I was too busy managing everyone's expectations. Too busy surviving my own brain.

It started with fatigue. Not tiredness, *fatigue*. A kind of heaviness that sat behind my eyes and in my bones. I'd sleep for nine hours and still wake up exhausted. Coffee barely scratched the surface. No amount of sleep or smoothies or supplements gave me back the energy I had lost just by pretending to be okay.

Then came the stomach. Bloating, acid reflux, cramps that would show up without warning. I'd cut foods, reintroduce them, try fasting, try meal plans. I told myself it was diet, stress, or "just aging." But deep down, I knew it was something deeper, like my gut was holding emotions I refused to digest.

The worst was the panic.

Not the movie-style version, no screaming, no flailing. Just a quiet hijack. My heart racing in the middle of a conversation. My chest tightening while waiting in line at a grocery store. My vision narrowing while sitting still at a café. I'd grip the table and pretend I was just cold. But I wasn't cold, I was barely there.

**Clinical reviews note neurodivergent burnout includes chronic exhaustion, sensory sensitivity, and cognitive shutdowns.** One overview describes symptoms as "loss of skills" and "reduced tolerance to stimulus," often triggered during puberty or major life transitions. medicalnewstoday.com.

Sometimes I'd shut down entirely. Couldn't answer a text. Couldn't return a call. Couldn't remember what I had just read. My brain would fog so thick I felt like I was swimming through air. And the more I fought it, the worse it got.

Doctors ran bloodwork. Said things like, "Everything looks normal." But nothing felt normal. I started to wonder if I was imagining it. Gaslighting myself into thinking I was being dramatic.

But I wasn't.

I was inflamed. Not just physically, but emotionally. Mentally. Energetically. I had spent years absorbing tension and pain and expectations. And now my nervous system was revolting.

**Stress hormones are literally burning your body.** Chronic activation of the HPA (stress) axis floods your system with cortisol and adrenaline, responses that trigger panicky chest tightness, digestion issues, brain fog, and inflammatory markers en.wikipedia.org.

My body wasn't betraying me.

It was begging me to stop betraying it.

## Awareness Isn't a Lightbulb. It's a Slow Flame.

People talk about awareness like it's this spark of brilliance, this aha moment that solves everything.

But for me, it was more like waking up in a room slowly filling with smoke. Not enough to choke you, but enough to make you cough. Enough to sting your eyes. Enough to make you realize: I've been living in this for years, and I called it normal.

That's the thing about survival mode. You don't realize you're in it until something breaks. And when it finally does, what you feel first isn't peace.

It's grief.

## The Grief I Didn't See Coming

No one prepared me for the grief that followed clarity.

I didn't just grieve the years I had masked. I grieved the relationships I sabotaged, the jobs I left too early, the dreams I never pursued because I thought I wasn't capable. I grieved how many times I played small to avoid being called "too much." I grieved every "no" I said to myself before the world ever got the chance.

And the worst part? I grieved in silence. Because once you realize how long you've abandoned yourself, it's hard to know where to start coming back.

The grief came in waves. Some days it felt like sadness, mourning for the confused child I was, the struggling teenager, the lost young adult. Other days it felt like rage, fury at the systems that failed me, the people who labeled me without understanding, the years of unnecessary suffering.

## The Stages of Neurodivergent Grief

I went through something like the classical stages of grief, but with a neurodivergent twist:

**Denial**: "I'm probably not really ADHD/autistic. I'm just making excuses."

**Anger**: "Why didn't anyone see this? How many other kids are suffering right now?"

**Bargaining**: "If I just work harder, maybe I can overcome these traits."

**Depression**: "I've wasted so much time. It's too late to change."

**Acceptance**: "This is how my brain works, and that's okay."

But these stages weren't linear. I cycled through them daily, sometimes hourly. I could accept my neurodivergence in the morning and be furious about it by afternoon.

## The Body Keeps the Truth

There were days my body screamed before I did.

My chest would tighten in rooms that felt unsafe. My jaw would clench during conversations I didn't know how to leave. My legs would shake when I was "calm."

I wasn't crazy. I was out of alignment.

Even if your mind learns to lie, your body won't. I began to realize that my nervous system had been fighting for its life long before I ever noticed. That my migraines, stomach aches, muscle tension, and fatigue weren't random, they were messages. They were symptoms of internal dissonance.

And the longer I ignored them, the louder they became.

**Bessel van der Kolk**, author of *The Body Keeps the Score*, writes: **"The body keeps the score: if the memory of trauma is encoded in the viscera, in heart-breaking and gut-wrenching emotions, then we can also change trauma symptoms through body-based interventions."**

For neurodivergent individuals, the trauma isn't always a single event, it's the accumulation of years feeling wrong, misunderstood, or fundamentally broken. Our bodies hold this history, and healing requires listening to what they're trying to tell us.

## The Somatic Experience of Masking

I began to understand that masking wasn't just a mental or emotional process, it was physical. Years of suppressing stims, forcing eye contact, controlling my natural expressions had created a kind of bodily armor.

My shoulders were permanently raised, ready for the next criticism. My breathing was shallow, afraid to take up too much space. My hands were often clenched, holding back the movements that wanted to come naturally.

When I finally began to unmask, my body had to relearn how to be itself. The first time I allowed myself to flap my hands when excited, it felt like stretching a muscle that had been cramped for decades.

## Emotions I Had No Name For

I used to think I was good at feeling. I cried during movies. I felt other people's pain like it was my own. I wrote poetry. I loved deeply.

But emotional awareness? That's different. It's not about *feeling a lot*. It's about *feeling clearly*.

It's about naming the difference between disappointment and devastation. Between fear and fatigue. Between abandonment and overstimulation.

When I got overwhelmed, I'd shut down. When I got triggered, I'd get loud, or I'd disappear. When someone hurt me, I'd pretend I didn't care. When I hurt someone, I'd spiral into guilt so deep I couldn't speak.

No one had taught me the language of emotional regulation. So instead, I developed fluency in avoidance.

## The Emotional Vocabulary of Neurodivergence

Learning about neurodivergence gave me new words for experiences I'd had my whole life:

**Rejection Sensitive Dysphoria**: That crushing, disproportionate pain from criticism or perceived rejection.

**Emotional Dysregulation**: When feelings become so intense they overwhelm my ability to function.

**Sensory Overload**: When the world becomes too much input for my nervous system to process.

**Executive Dysfunction**: When I know what I need to do but can't make myself start.

**Masking Fatigue**: The exhaustion that comes from performing neurotypicality all day.

Having words for these experiences was revolutionary. Instead of "I'm overreacting again," I could say "I'm experiencing RSD." Instead of "I'm lazy," I could say "I'm having executive dysfunction."

## The Challenge of Mindfulness for the Neurodivergent Mind

Traditional mindfulness practices were often difficult for me. "Just observe your thoughts" is challenging when your thoughts move at hyperspeed. "Focus on your breath" is hard when your breathing patterns are part of what triggers anxiety.

I had to adapt mindfulness to my neurodivergent needs:

- Moving meditation instead of sitting still
- Focusing on external sounds rather than internal breath
- Using guided meditations with specific structure rather than open awareness
- Accepting that my mind would wander and that was okay

## The Discomfort of Slowing Down

In survival mode, speed feels like control.

If I kept moving, I didn't have to feel. If I kept helping others, I didn't have to look inward. If I kept laughing, no one would hear the panic under my breath.

Stillness was terrifying. It forced me to face the parts of myself I had labeled as weak or shameful. The anger. The fear. The longing.

But when I finally let myself slow down, when I turned off the noise, when I stopped running, I realized something wild: I wasn't fragile. I was just buried. Beneath all that survival was someone strong, intuitive, and still alive. Still here.

## The Inner Critic: My Oldest Voice

I used to think my self-talk was honest. Brutal, maybe, but honest.

"You're lazy." "You're overreacting." "You should've known better." "No one else struggles with this."

I thought these were motivational truths, hard medicine I needed to swallow. But over time, I realized these weren't truths at all. They were inherited voices.

Some from childhood. Some from school. Some from culture. And all of them lies disguised as discipline.

The voice that told me to smile while I was hurting? That was survival. The voice that told me not to speak unless I was perfect? That was trauma. And the voice that said, "You're too broken to be loved"? That wasn't mine. It was implanted. Rehearsed. Internalized. And it was time to evict it.

## Tracing the Voices

I began to identify where different critical voices came from:

My mother's voice: "Why can't you just focus?" My father's voice: "Stop being so sensitive." Teachers' voices: "You're not trying hard enough." Peers' voices: "You're weird." Society's voice: "Normal people don't act like this."

Recognizing these as external voices that I had internalized was the first step in questioning their authority over my life.

## You Can't Heal What You Won't Feel

I didn't want to feel anything at first. Not the sadness, not the fear, and definitely not the rage. I thought if I opened the door, even a little, I'd get swallowed whole.

But here's what I've learned: **Avoided pain doesn't disappear. It shapeshifts.** Into anger. Into addiction. Into distraction. Into perfectionism. Into a life that looks good on the outside but feels hollow inside.

So eventually, I gave in. Not because I was brave, but because the weight of avoiding it became heavier than the weight of holding it.

## The Practice of Feeling

Learning to feel my emotions without being overwhelmed by them became a practice. I developed strategies:

**Emotional Temperature Taking**: Regular check-ins with myself throughout the day. "What am I feeling right now? Where do I feel it in my body?"

**The RAIN Technique:**

- Recognize what's happening emotionally

- Allow the experience to be there
- Investigate with kindness
- Non-attachment, let it pass without clinging or pushing away

**Emotional Granularity**: Getting more specific about feelings. Instead of "bad," was I anxious, frustrated, disappointed, overwhelmed, or something else?

# Naming Emotions = Releasing Them

I started small. I would literally sit with a journal and ask myself:

- "What am I feeling?"
- "Where do I feel it in my body?"
- "What is this emotion trying to protect me from?"

Some days I didn't have answers. Other days I found the same word scribbled over and over again like a child tracing a shape: **abandoned, invisible, confused, unworthy**.

And every time I named it, something softened. Because unspoken emotions don't disappear, they calcify. They build fortresses in your body. In your jaw, your stomach, your posture. They harden your voice and shape your decisions without you even realizing.

But when you name them? They move. They cry. They scream. They whisper. And then, eventually, they pass.

# The Neuroscience of Emotional Labeling

Research shows that the simple act of labeling emotions can reduce their intensity. When we name what we're feeling, activity in the amygdala (the brain's alarm system) decreases while activity in the prefrontal cortex (responsible for thinking and reasoning) increases.

For neurodivergent individuals, who often experience emotions more intensely, this labeling practice can be particularly powerful.

## The Tools That Helped Me Sit With It

**Movement** When I felt too much, I moved. Boxing. Running. Even walking in circles. Anything to let my body metabolize what my brain was too overwhelmed to handle. Some people journal. Some meditate. I punched bags. That's still prayer.

**Breathwork** I learned to breathe on purpose. Slowly. Deeply. Four seconds in, four seconds hold, four seconds out. Not for calm. For presence. Because when your brain spirals, the breath brings you back.

**Safe Witnessing** I found one friend. One person I could be messy with. No advice. No fixing. Just space. And in that space, I realized: **Being seen while you're in pain and not being shamed for it is one of the most healing things on Earth.**

**Music** I made playlists that matched my mood. Sometimes I needed sad French rap. Sometimes I needed gospel. Sometimes I needed silence between songs that felt like prayer.

**Saying It Out Loud** Even alone. Even if it sounded ridiculous. "I'm angry." "I'm terrified." "I feel abandoned." "I need to feel safe again." It didn't fix anything, but it made the experience real. And that alone changed everything.

## The Sensory Toolkit

As a neurodivergent person, I learned that my sensory environment significantly affected my emotional regulation. I developed a toolkit:

**For Overwhelm**: Noise-canceling headphones, dimmer lights, soft textures, weighted blankets.

**For Anxiety**: Fidget toys, chewing gum, cold water on my wrists, peppermint oil.

**For Sadness**: Specific music playlists, photos that brought comfort, favorite foods.

**For Anger**: Physical exercise, punching a pillow, writing letters I'd never send.

## Letting Go of the "Good Victim" Myth

At some point, I had to confront my anger. Not just the sadness of being misunderstood, but the rage of being misdiagnosed, mishandled, and minimized for decades.

And I felt guilty for feeling it.

Because society teaches us that only *perfectly wounded* people are allowed to be angry. If you're polite, broken, quiet, you're allowed sympathy. But if you raise your voice? If you speak up? If you're messy or loud or furious? You become "difficult."

Let me say this clearly:

**You can be angry and worthy of love. You can be furious and healing. You can rage and still be good.**

There is no prize for being a quiet victim. Your pain doesn't need to be palatable to be valid.

## The Righteousness of Rage

My anger, I learned, was information. It told me:

- This system failed me
- This treatment was wrong
- This person crossed a boundary
- This situation is unsafe

Instead of suppressing it, I learned to listen to what my anger was trying to teach me and then channel it constructively, into advocacy, into boundaries, into changes that could help prevent others from experiencing the same harm.

## When Old Patterns Come Back

Even in the thick of awareness, the old patterns return. I'd still mask without realizing it. I'd still freeze in conversations. I'd still feel guilty for saying what I needed.

And I used to see those moments as proof that I wasn't healing. Now I see them as proof that I am.

Because healing isn't a straight line. It's a spiral. You revisit the same wounds, but each time, with more wisdom. More breath. More tools. More grace.

You don't heal by never falling. You heal by learning how to catch yourself when you do.

I didn't become an advocate overnight.

At first, it was just a whisper. A soft *no* when someone pushed too hard. A decision not to attend something that would drain me. A boundary made without fanfare, not announced, not defended, just lived.

But the first time I truly used my voice, it surprised even me.

It happened in a team meeting. A colleague joked about "ADHD types" being late and flaky. I would've normally forced a laugh. Instead, I looked up calmly and said,

"I have ADHD. And I've worked harder than most here just to function in a system that doesn't accommodate me. That joke isn't funny, it's exhausting."

The room stilled. Not in anger, just recognition. Someone muttered, "Sorry." The conversation moved on, but I didn't.

For the first time, I hadn't swallowed it. I didn't internalize it. I didn't shove it down until it burned me from the inside.

I had spoken, not as a mask, but as a person.

That moment shifted everything. I started sharing pieces of my story in everyday moments. When people asked why I wore noise-cancelling headphones at lunch, I said, "I get overstimulated in big groups." When friends noticed I took days to text back, I explained executive dysfunction. Slowly, I stopped translating, and started existing.

And something remarkable happened: people listened.

Not everyone understood. Some didn't care. But others leaned in. They thanked me for giving words to what they'd felt but never named. They asked questions, not to challenge me, but to connect.

Because self-advocacy works.

Research shows neurodivergent self-advocates report better mental health, increased confidence, and stronger social connections teenvogue.com otservices.wustl.edu. One study of workplace culture found that employees who spoke openly about neurodiversity felt safer and more productive, just from taking that one step of disclosure.

But I wasn't chasing perfect disclosure or cure-all explanations. I was chasing permission to be messy. To have needs. To exist with nuance.

I still relapsed, into old patterns of self-erasure and perfectionism. But now I noticed. I could pause mid-pattern and ask: *Who am I performing for?* It didn't always happen. But it happened often enough.

Each interruption was a victory.

I began to mentor others. A coworker once told me: "Hearing your story helped me ask for a day off." Another whispered, "I've been diagnosed my whole life, but I never told anyone until you did."

We were building momentum, incremental, ripple by ripple.

Self-advocacy isn't shouting. It's whispering truth.

"You're not responsible for your first reaction. But you are responsible for your next."

My first reaction was always fear. Minimize. Apologize.

My second? That became my fire.

That's where I started building something real, not just for me, but for the people watching. The teen who hid behind a smile. The professional who wore a mask. The person learning that the world changes fastest when you speak.

## The Practice of Self-Compassion

**Dr. Kristin Neff's** research on self-compassion became crucial to my healing. She identifies three components:

1. **Self-kindness**: Treating yourself with the same gentleness you'd offer a good friend
2. **Common humanity**: Recognizing that struggle is part of the human experience
3. **Mindfulness**: Observing your experience without being overwhelmed by it

For someone who had spent decades being his own harshest critic, learning self-compassion was like learning a foreign language.

## Learning to Stay

That's what this stage of awareness taught me most: **How to stay.**

To stay in the room when the truth gets uncomfortable. To stay in the conversation when my instinct is to shut down. To stay with myself when shame rises. To stay present, even when I want to disappear.

Because leaving was once a skill I mastered. But staying, staying is the muscle I'm learning to build.

And every time I choose to stay, I reclaim something. A breath. A moment. A truth. Myself.

## The Practice of Presence

Staying present required developing new skills:

**Grounding techniques**: 5-4-3-2-1 (naming 5 things I can see, 4 I can touch, 3 I can hear, 2 I can smell, 1 I can taste)

**The pause**: Taking a breath before reacting to difficult emotions or situations

**Curious questioning**: Instead of "Why am I so messed up?" asking "What is my nervous system trying to tell me right now?"

## The New Voice

Somewhere along the way, a new voice emerged. It's quieter than the critic. Softer than the judge. But it's there. And it says things like:

- "You did your best."
- "You're allowed to rest."
- "You're learning."
- "This is what growth feels like."

It doesn't shout. It doesn't punish. It doesn't demand performance. It invites me to return to myself. And I'm finally learning to listen.

## Cultivating the Inner Ally

This new voice required cultivation. I practiced:

**Reframing internal dialogue**: Instead of "I'm so stupid," trying "I made a mistake, and that's how I learn."

**Celebrating small wins**: Acknowledging progress even when it felt insignificant.

**Speaking to myself as I would to a friend**: Would I tell a friend they were worthless for struggling? Then why was I telling myself that?

## What Awareness Looks Like Now

Awareness today isn't always poetic. Sometimes it's sitting on the floor, drinking water, and texting a friend: "Today's heavy. Just letting you know I'm still here."

Sometimes it's canceling plans because my body said no, even when my brain said "just push through." Sometimes it's laughing at a trigger instead of collapsing under it. Sometimes it's collapsing and knowing I can get back up.

Awareness isn't pretty. It's honest. And it's enough.

## The Daily Practice of Awareness

Awareness became a practice, not a destination:

**Morning check-ins**: How is my nervous system today? What do I need?

**Midday recalibration**: Am I staying true to my needs, or am I sliding into old patterns?

**Evening reflection**: What did I learn about myself today? What can I appreciate about how I showed up?

## The Bridge to Action

Awareness is the bridge between identity and choice. It's where you stop lying to yourself. Where you stop outsourcing your value. Where you stop negotiating your worth.

It's not the end. But it's where the third stage begins. Because once you know, and once you feel, it's time to do something with that truth. To build. To risk. To rise. To act.

The fire of awareness burns away what no longer serves while forging what remains into something stronger. Sitting in that fire isn't comfortable, but it's necessary. It's where transformation happens.

And on the other side of that fire, I discovered something unexpected: the very sensitivity that I had been taught to hide was actually my greatest strength. The emotions that felt like too much were precisely what allowed me to connect deeply with others, to create meaningful work, to live with authenticity and purpose.

The fire didn't destroy me. It revealed me.

And yet, the weight of change was still heavy. Owning my voice didn't make the world lighter, it made it real. Real meant turbulence, adjustment, resistance, and breakthroughs I hadn't imagined. Chapter 6 unfolds the next stage of the journey: *The Weight of Change*, when doing the hard internal work forces shifts in relationships, beliefs, and boundaries. It's the moment when reframing turns into reconstruction, and the work gets realer still.

# Chapter 6: The Weight of Change

## Losing People When You Start to Change

Change isn't just about becoming someone new. It's also about grieving who you used to be, and who people thought you were.

No one warns you how lonely transformation can be. They talk about growth, breakthroughs, and clarity. They tell you, "Keep going, you're doing the work." But they don't tell you what it feels like when your phone stops ringing. When the group chat goes quiet. When someone you love starts calling you "distant" just because you've stopped abandoning yourself to keep them comfortable.

That's the first real weight of change: loss.

When I got sober, when I started speaking more honestly, saying no, setting boundaries, the losses came fast. Some were subtle: texts that went unanswered, invitations that stopped coming. Others were direct: friends who told me I'd "changed too much," or said I wasn't "fun anymore."

I used to take pride in being the one who could hang. Who could drink all night and still make you laugh. I had friends who only knew me in that context. I was the flexible one, the spontaneous one, the one who'd say yes even when I meant no. I was high-functioning until I wasn't. I was generous until I was resentful. And when I stopped performing that role, it didn't just confuse people, it exposed them.

Because my change reflected their stagnancy.

They didn't want to see me heal. They wanted the version of me who validated their denial.

One of the hardest friendships to lose was someone I had known for years. We used to talk daily, exchange memes, and share voice notes about how "crazy life was." But when I started naming things, trauma, ADHD, boundaries, he pulled away. Slowly at first, then completely. I reached out a few times, wondering if I had done something wrong. I blamed myself. But the truth is: I had started telling the truth, and he wasn't ready to hear it.

Change doesn't just scare you. It scares the people who benefited from your silence.

When I stopped laughing at certain jokes, stopped minimizing my needs, stopped volunteering for roles I didn't want to play, some people left. Not because they were evil or cruel. But because they were invested in a version of me that made their life easier.

The funny thing is, I used to fear abandonment more than anything. I shaped my entire personality around preventing it. But the more I grew, the more I realized: staying small to be loved is its own kind of abandonment. And I had been abandoning myself for years, just to avoid making someone else uncomfortable.

That's the second weight of change: guilt.

I felt guilty for evolving. Guilty for setting limits. Guilty for no longer being available 24/7. Guilty for not showing up in the ways I used to, at 2am, mid-breakdown, during every emotional emergency that wasn't mine to carry.

There's a phrase they use in recovery rooms: *"You can't save people at the expense of yourself."* I didn't fully understand that until I started changing and saw how many people only knew how to relate to the broken version of me. The version who would drop everything to rescue them, while silently drowning.

I remember standing in my kitchen one night, phone in hand, staring at a message I didn't want to send. A boundary. A truth. Something simple like: *"I can't be that person for you anymore."*

I didn't send it right away. I stared at it for nearly an hour.

Because here's the thing no one says out loud: when you stop performing the role people assigned you, they grieve. But sometimes, they don't grieve silently. They punish.

They accuse.

They ghost.

They guilt-trip.

They tell other people that you "think you're better than them now."

They'll say you're selfish, for finally taking care of yourself.

And if you're not grounded, you'll believe them.

But I didn't believe them that night.

I pressed send.

Not because I was fearless. But because I was finally tired of being afraid of my own truth.

And in that moment, quiet, ordinary, unspectacular, I took one more step toward becoming someone I could trust.

I used to think change was a decision.

Just do it. Start. Commit. Push.

But that was a lie I inherited, from self-help books, gym ads, teachers, hustlers, even trauma. The idea that change is a straight line. That once you "know better," you must immediately "do better."

But the truth? **Change is not a decision. It's a process of grieving everything you'll lose when you finally stop lying to yourself.**

Because real change costs something. Time. Comfort. Familiarity. Identity. Relationships. Your version of success. Your former self.

And that's why most people don't change. Not because they don't want to, but because they're not ready to lose what change demands.

## The Grief of No Longer Fitting Your Old Life

There's a grief that no one talks about, the grief of realizing you no longer fit into the life you built.

Not because something dramatic happened. But because, slowly, you start to feel like a stranger in your own story. The things that used to feel like milestones start feeling like monuments to someone you no longer are.

That's what happened in New York.

On paper, I had "made it." I had my own champagne lounge in Manhattan. A sleek space with dim lighting, curved glassware, and 100 different bottles lining a glowing bar. People came to celebrate. To perform sophistication. To be seen.

And I was the man who built it.

I wore the right shoes. Knew the right names. Spoke in the right tone. I curated a world that looked effortless, and exclusive. From the outside, it was a success. From the inside, it was theater.

Every night, I played my role: host, connector, taste-maker, "visionary." I smiled, nodded, poured, pivoted. I was fluent in social currency. I knew how to light up a room and disappear inside of it.

But somewhere in the rhythm of opening bottles and managing payroll and shaking hands with "important people," I started to feel like I was ghostwriting my own life. I was showing up, but I wasn't present. I was admired, but I wasn't seen.

The grief hit me slowly, like a delayed emotional injury.

It didn't come in tears. It came in the silence between events. In the empty walks home after closing. In the moment when I looked out across a packed room and felt completely alone.

At first, I told myself I was just tired. That it was part of being a business owner, part of the grind. But that wasn't it.

The truth was: I had built a life around a version of me I no longer wanted to be.

And once that awareness landed, it hurt in a different way. Because it meant the relationships I had formed in that identity, the status I had chased, the attention I had performed for, weren't just fading.

They were never really mine.

That's what no one prepares you for when you start healing. That moment when you look around your life and realize: this house, this relationship, this dream, this version of success, it was all built by the masked version of you. The survival version. The one who thought, *If I'm impressive enough, they'll love me. If I'm useful enough, they'll stay.*

Letting go of that life felt like betrayal. Not just of others, but of the younger me who worked so hard to build it. The kid who believed that achievement would finally equal safety.

I didn't just lose friends when I changed. I lost whole identities. Entire chapters of my life that no longer made sense. Outfits that no longer fit. Roles I could no longer play.

I'd open Instagram and see people still performing the lifestyle I had walked away from, rooftop parties, velvet ropes, luxury dinners. It looked glamorous. It also looked like a costume I had outgrown.

**Research shows nearly 46 % of entrepreneurs experience chronic loneliness,** and over 30 % report burnout due to lack of support and life consistency cleelia.medium.com. That statistic hit me. I had built a life of "success," only to find myself isolated behind a velvet rope.

And some nights, that realization made me ache.

Not because I wanted it back.

But because I missed the illusion that it had ever been enough.

I missed the comfort of pretending.

I missed the social fluency of knowing what people wanted me to be and giving it to them.

I missed the lie.

**Studies in identity grief** show that losing a successful identity, like founder or connector, is a deep form of ambiguous loss, similar to mourning a relationship that's physically present but psychologically absent en.wikipedia.org. That grief felt like a wound I didn't even have words for.

But I knew I couldn't go back.

Because once you've tasted the truth, performance becomes poison.

## Boundary-Setting as an Emotional Earthquake

Real change isn't just about saying no. It's about weathering the emotional aftermath afterward.

Setting boundaries is not a one-time action, it's an emotional earthquake. You stand your ground, and the world trembles. And if those tremors hit too close, your world can collapse.

When I committed to change, I knew I'd have to say no. But I didn't expect what it would cost, how much it would feel like breaking things I never meant to break.

The first big boundary was saying no to overwork. In New York, late nights weren't the exception, they were the rule. I was in back-to-back meetings, hosting the champagne lounge until 3 a.m., checking emails at 6 a.m., midweek. My body was shouting at me via panic flares, migraines, collapsing energy, but my mind said: *Push through. Hustle harder.*

Until one morning, I didn't.

I didn't open my laptop. I didn't grab my notebook. I just didn't. I sat in silence. I paid my coach the hour fee and said, "I'm done." I wasn't quitting business. I was quitting my own self-abandonment.

That day, I learned boundaries can land physically. My heart raced. My stomach flipped. The familiar ache of guilt rose. I worried I was letting down investors, employees, and friends. My voice trembled when I said the words out loud.

A boundary set, yes. But the earthquake afterward was harder than the action itself.

It didn't stop there.

I told my best friend I needed space from her late-night venting sessions, and that I wasn't going to host big parties anymore. And when I stopped reaching out for group outings, some of them complained, saying I was abandoning them. Each "no" felt like defusing a bomb. Each cost me relationships I didn't expect to lose.

They weren't big fights. They were small betrayals.

- She cried.
- He said I was "too sensitive."
- They joked that I was "ghosting," "seen it, did nothing."
- Each reaction widened the emotional tremor radius. I expected pushback. But I didn't expect *how loudly* the boundaries would echo in my life's structure.

People didn't just feel disappointed, they felt betrayed.

I felt like I was betraying my own story. My role. The guy who said yes, who made sure no one crashed alone. The guy who'd clean up the mess, literal and emotional. And I wasn't that guy anymore.

Psychological research confirms it: setting healthy boundaries has profound mental health benefits, but not without stress. Studies in behavioral health note that boundary-setting reduces anxiety and burnout, but only if you're willing to risk backlash and discomfort elitedna.com Real Simple. And burnout? It's linked directly to saying yes when you mean no.

For neurodivergent people, it's even harder. We often struggle with interoception, feeling what we actually need Wikipediamysoulbalm.blog. When you don't know you're crossing your own line, others don't know to respect it.

But I learned to honor my crisis points.

When my coach pointed out that I hadn't eaten, or showered, in three days, that was a flashpoint. I listened, because saying yes to rest was suddenly more radical than saying no to demands.

When I told my therapist I'd stopped attending a social group, she asked two simple words: "Why not?" My answer wasn't about dislike. It was exhaustion. I said, "My nervous system can't re-charge in a group of 10." That admission felt dangerous, but it was necessary.

Only later did I see the data: people who set consistent boundaries report higher life satisfaction, stronger relationships, and lower stress reddit.combg-hc.com mayoclinichealthsystem.org. Boundaries aren't walls, their healthy versions are gates. Gateways into peace, not prisons.

Still, they shook everything.

One morning I woke up and realized my weekend calendar was empty. I hadn't booked coffee. I hadn't RSVP'd. I hadn't scheduled a thing. And I felt... good. But also guilty. Was this freedom, or abandonment?

I looked at the quiet, at the emptiness, and I understood: solitude doesn't have to mean loneliness. And saying no doesn't mean you're unloved, it means you're honest.

I breathed into that truth.

I started to say yes differently, not to events, but to moments.

"Yes, I'll call you in the morning when I have energy."

"Yes, I'll support you, but only when I can show up fully."

"Yes, I'll attend the event, but I leave at 9 p.m."

"Yes, I respect your crisis, we can talk later."

These aren't radical statements. But after years of disappearing when others needed me, they felt like liberation.

Because boundaries aren't just walls. They're scaffolding.

They hold up your self-respect, your time, your energy. They teach others how to treat you, or how not to.

That, more than any milestone, is what change demands.

**Setting and maintaining personal boundaries is a recognized form of self-care**. The Mayo Clinic notes it helps protect against stress and fosters healthy relationships.

**Studies confirm that saying no reduces burnout and promotes well-being**, as long as you're prepared for the emotional pushback that usually follows.

## Aloneness vs. Loneliness – The Silent Gain

In the wake of boundaries and loss, a curious thing began to arise: **aloneness**, not loneliness.

At first, the empty weekends felt like punishment. Unwanted silence. No texts, no plans, no noise. A void where I expected echoes. My anxious mind whispered: *You're alone. You're abandoned. You're invisible again.*

But through that unsettled space, something unexpected emerged.

I started noticing the difference between **loneliness**, that ache of disconnection, and **aloneness**, a quiet, chosen stillness.

Research defines these separately:

*"Loneliness is a distressing feeling of social disconnection; aloneness is a neutral or even positive state of being apart."* PLOSWikipedia

I began to see that solitude isn't a void, it can be a **gateway**.

Psychologists call it **positive solitude**: a calm, creative, self-respecting state. Even just 15 minutes can reduce anxiety and spark clarity New York Post.

# Alone ≠ Lonely

One night in New York, I sat on my couch, TV off for once, no music, no phone. Only moonlight reflecting off the dark brown floor and the rooftops of Queens beyond the glass. I felt dizzy at first, like the Earth was spinning beneath me.

Then, I felt still.

I took a deep breath and simply *existed*.

No one was texting. No one was calling. No one was needed.

And yet,

I needed me.

My chest softened. I felt a surge of presence. It reminded me of lying in the grass in Lamerville, France, the kind of meditation that's both quiet and infinite.

I sensed the universe shift.

Earth was my spaceship.

My body knew the pulse of galaxies.

In that moment, I realized: I was alive. Present.

A car passed outside. The sound slid past like a wave.

A siren echoed somewhere far off.

I felt my heartbeat, my tension, my breath. **And for the first time in a long time, I was not noise. I was the rhythm. The music.**

A quiet awakening. Empowered. Humble. Alive.

## Rituals Reborn in Solitude

Before sobriety, my self-care felt like a religion: gym, boxing, motorbike rides, Netflix nights, brunches, day drinking, smoothies, hustle, repeat. It was a loop without truth.

But during my healing, something deeper bloomed.

I walked, first with my Best friend through snowstorms, then with Paul (a friend I used to party with, who became a peer from my recovery group, actually the one who took me into my first recovery group) around Central Park, and later alone. NYC became a moving sanctuary.

I journaled and meditated. I lit incense, cooked nourishing meals, and felt my kitchen's warmth. I discovered Korean sheet masks, deep-tissue massages in Chinatown, smoothies with turmeric and ginger, tea, vitamins, hydration creams. I drank it in, self-care like oxygen.

Audible became my companion. I finally revisited the books I never finished. I repeated positive affirmations as I walked or waited at Starbucks, catching scraps of clarity along with my latte.

Yet, my ADHD brain still forgot routines. A day would pass, and suddenly I realized: I hadn't done *any* of it. I smiled, because even the absence of habit reminded me I'm still here, still learning.

## When Silence Speaks with Friends

Some nights, the silence felt heavy. A text didn't come. A friend stopped replying. I felt the sting of voices pushed away. I tried explaining, awkwardly: *"I've been imploding, not ignoring."*

Fanny called. We talked. She listened.

A friend in London said: *"I miss the wild you."*

Another said, *"You've become a Buddha or something."*

I heard it: people had grown accustomed to a version of me that made them feel safe or special. And when that version changed, some felt cheated.

They didn't realize that they were missing a mask, an act, not me. It hurt. But I couldn't go back.

## Mantras of Solitude

I held onto words that steadied me.

My aunt Geneviève, who passed away during my first year in NY, once said: *"I thought you were stronger than this. Even strangers don't knock you down."* Her voice taught me that foreign pain is still valid, and that I didn't owe it dismissal.

In early recovery, I found the **Serenity Prayer**:

> *God, grant me the serenity to accept the things I cannot change,*
>
> *The courage to change the things I can,*
>
> *And the wisdom to know the difference.*

I recited it on walks, at Starbucks lines, on the treadmill, sometimes fifty, a hundred times, until it seeped into my bones.

## The Silent Treaty

Eventually, I made a pact with myself:

- Solo dinners with candlelight and a journal.
- Early-morning solo walks through empty streets.
- Silence as ritual.

I wasn't secluding. I was *selecting presence*.

Each moment became a promise: *I choose me. I honor this self, even if no one else does.*

## When Aloneness Brings Loneliness Back

Aloneness wasn't perfect. Some nights, bipolar lows or doubt crept in.

Research shows solitude benefits are brightest when chosen, not imposed pmc.ncbi.nlm.nih.gov verywellmind.comnature.com. So, I learned balance:

- **Social loneliness**, when real connection is gone.
- **Emotional loneliness**, when unseen amid the noise.

When the void got loud, I texted Fanny. Or called a friend who said I ghosted. I let humanity back in, to remind me it wasn't abandonment; it was sanctuary.

## From Aloneness to Anchored Self-Respect

I realized aloneness and connection aren't opposites. They *coexist*.

I wasn't erasing myself. I was honoring my edges.

Research shows autonomy, self-regulation, and self-care strengthen mental health and resilience PLOSmcpress.mayoclinic.org.

I was no longer chasing approval, I was cultivating integrity.

## The Myth of Motivation

People ask me, "How did you change your life?"

They want to hear about vision boards. Journaling. Cold showers. Discipline.

But what changed me wasn't motivation. It was grief. And boredom. And anger. And the realization that if I didn't do something, anything, I would drown in the weight of my own unspoken life.

Motivation is a myth. It shows up when it wants, usually after the hard part is already over. The truth is, I changed because staying the same became more painful than the fear of what might come next. Not because I felt ready. But because I couldn't bear my own silence anymore.

# The Neurodivergent Challenge of Change

For neurodivergent brains, change is particularly complex. We often struggle with:

**Executive dysfunction**: Knowing what needs to change but being unable to initiate action.

**Hyperfocus and routine dependence**: Being so attached to familiar patterns that any change feels destabilizing.

**Rejection sensitive dysphoria**: Fear that changing might lead to criticism or loss of relationships.

**All-or-nothing thinking**: Believing we must change everything perfectly or not at all.

Understanding these challenges helped me approach change differently.

# The Resistance Is Real

There's a moment after awareness, after the lightbulb, after the clarity, after the tears, when everything inside you resists movement.

This is what therapists call **homeostasis**: the brain's deep desire to keep you exactly where you are, even if it's miserable, even if it's unsafe, because it's *familiar*.

And familiarity feels like safety to a brain shaped by trauma, masking, or neurodivergence.

It's why we go back to relationships that hurt. It's why we binge on habits that numb us. It's why we keep saying "I'll start tomorrow." Because our bodies are trying to protect us from the unfamiliar. Even when the unfamiliar is freedom.

# The Neurobiology of Resistance

Research shows that our brains are wired to resist change. The anterior cingulate cortex, the part of the brain that monitors for errors and conflicts, becomes hyperactive when we encounter anything unfamiliar.

For neurodivergent brains, which are already dealing with heightened sensitivity and irregular neurotransmitter function, this resistance can be even stronger.

Understanding this helped me have compassion for my own resistance instead of judging it as weakness.

## Fear Wears Many Faces

When I tried to change, I thought I was lazy. But laziness was just the mask that fear wore.

Fear said:

- "What if you fail again?"
- "What if people think you've changed too much?"
- "What if this version of you isn't lovable either?"
- "What if you're wrong about who you are?"

So instead of risking the unknown, I stayed. In relationships. In cities. In jobs. In thought loops. In shame.

Because failure felt terrifying, but so did becoming someone new. No one tells you that when you change, you don't just lose comfort. You lose *familiar reactions. Predictable rejection. Scripted self-worth.* And part of you mourns that loss, even when you know it's killing you.

## The Catalog of Fears

I began to name my specific fears about change:

**Fear of exposure**: What if people see who I really am and reject me?

**Fear of incompetence**: What if I can't succeed in this new way of being?

**Fear of loss**: What if changing means losing relationships that matter to me?

**Fear of responsibility**: What if success brings obligations I can't handle?

**Fear of impostor syndrome**: What if I'm not really capable of this transformation?

# The Invisible Contracts We Make

I had made invisible contracts with people:

- "I'll stay broken, so you don't feel insecure."
- "I'll stay silent, so you can stay comfortable."
- "I'll keep the peace, even if it costs me mine."

No one asked me to make these promises. But I made them anyway. Because I thought they were necessary to be loved.

So when I began to change, when I began to speak, to take space, to ask for clarity, to say no, the people around me felt the shift. Some cheered. Some vanished. Some tried to drag me back into the old dance.

And I had to decide, over and over again, if I loved myself enough to break those contracts.

# The Social Ecosystem of Dysfunction

I realized that my dysfunction served a purpose in my social ecosystem. Being the "helpful one" meant others could be less responsible. Being the "easy-going one" meant others could be more demanding. Being the "broken one" meant others could feel superior.

When I started changing, I disrupted these dynamics, and not everyone was pleased about it.

# Change Feels Like Loneliness Before It Feels Like Freedom

Let's be honest. Change doesn't feel good at first.

It feels like isolation. Like second-guessing. Like waking up in a new country where you don't speak the language yet. You look around and wonder: "Was it really that bad before?" Your brain romanticizes the past, not because it was safe, but because it was predictable.

I remember nights where I cried because the silence of healing was louder than the chaos I left behind. But here's the secret:

**Loneliness is not proof you made the wrong choice. It's proof that you've outgrown your old cage.**

And it takes time for your new life to find you.

## The Geography of Loneliness

Loneliness during change has a specific geography:

**The loneliness of being misunderstood**: When people can't understand why you're changing.

**The loneliness of outgrowing relationships**: When you no longer fit in spaces that once felt like home.

**The loneliness of being between identities**: When you're no longer who you were but not yet who you're becoming.

**The loneliness of high standards**: When you can no longer tolerate what you used to accept.

## Action Without Applause

No one prepares you for how quiet real change is. You expect fireworks. Applause. An obvious turning point.

But most days, change sounds like:

- A deep breath before you speak your truth
- A shaky "no" on the phone
- Silence where you once begged
- A choice to stay home with your peace instead of chasing someone who ghosts you

It's not dramatic. It's not cinematic. It's not Instagram-worthy. But it's sacred. Because real action doesn't start in the spotlight. It starts in the dark, where only you can see it.

## The Unglamorous Nature of Growth

Real change is:

**Boring**: The same small choices made repeatedly over time.

**Invisible**: Internal shifts that don't show up in before-and-after photos.

**Uncomfortable**: Sitting with difficult emotions instead of numbing them.

**Uneven**: Good days and bad days, progress and setbacks.

**Unwitnessed**: Most of the work happens in private moments no one sees.

## Small Acts Are Big

There were days I couldn't change everything. But I could change something.

So I made my bed. I washed one dish. I said no without explaining myself. I turned off my phone at night. I walked instead of drinking. I left one text unread.

And every one of those tiny acts said the same thing: **I'm not abandoning myself today.**

That's how real change starts. Not with a grand gesture. But with small truths, repeated. Until they're no longer acts of rebellion, but habits of self-respect.

## The Compound Effect of Small Changes

I learned that small changes compound exponentially:

**Day 1**: Made my bed. Felt 1% better about my space.

**Day 30**: My room became a place I enjoyed being.

**Day 90**: My improved environment supported better sleep, which improved my mood and energy.

**Day 365**: Better sleep, mood, and energy had transformed my relationships, work performance, and self-image.

One small change created a cascade of improvements.

## Discipline Isn't Punishment. It's Protection.

For years, I associated discipline with shame. It was something that punished me. Corrected me. Made me "better."

But that was survival-based discipline. That was: "You're lazy, so try harder." That was: "You're broken, so fix yourself." That was: "You're weak, so stop whining."

What I needed wasn't punishment. It was protection.

Discipline, at its core, is a boundary between who you are and what tries to pull you back into who you're not anymore. It says:

"No, we're not texting them again." "No, we're not abandoning ourselves just to feel chosen." "No, we're not rushing through this grief just to look productive."

That kind of discipline doesn't shrink you. It shields you. It says: "I know who I'm becoming, and I'm willing to show up for them today."

## Redefining Discipline for the Neurodivergent Brain

Traditional discipline relies on willpower and consistency, two things that neurodivergent brains often struggle with. I had to develop a different approach:

**Systems over willpower**: Creating environments and routines that make good choices easier.

**Flexibility over rigidity**: Allowing for neurodivergent rhythms and cycles.

**Self-compassion over self-criticism**: Treating setbacks as information rather than failure.

**Interest-based motivation**: Connecting changes to things I genuinely cared about.

## You Don't Need to Be "Fixed" to Start

There's this dangerous idea that you have to wait until you've healed to take meaningful action.

But some of the most transformative decisions I've made happened while I was still unraveling. Still unsure. Still shaking. Still grieving.

The truth? **Clarity doesn't always come before the decision. Sometimes it's the result of it.**

You don't need to be finished. You just need to be honest. You don't need a plan. You just need a pulse. You don't need to feel brave. You just need to move.

## Taking Action from Brokenness

Some of my best decisions came from my worst moments:

- I got sober not from a place of strength, but from exhaustion with my own patterns
- I started therapy not from wisdom, but from desperation
- I began setting boundaries not from confidence, but from the pain of having none
- I pursued my neurodivergent diagnosis not from clarity, but from confusion

Action doesn't require perfection. It requires willingness to move toward something better, even when you can't see the destination clearly.

# The Fear of Doing It Wrong

Every time I tried to act, I'd freeze, not because I didn't care, but because I was terrified of getting it wrong.

- What if I mess up?
- What if I embarrass myself?
- What if they laugh?
- What if I fail?

But healing taught me this truth: **Doing something imperfectly is how you build the strength to do it with confidence later.**

Action is a language. You learn it by speaking it. Badly at first. Awkwardly. Stumbling through syllables of self-worth and shaky boundaries. And over time, if you keep showing up, you become fluent.

# Some Days, Action Looks Like Stillness

Let's redefine action. It's not always big. It's not always loud.

Sometimes, it's:

- Not responding to the text
- Walking away from the drama
- Saying "I don't have the capacity today"
- Letting the dishes wait so your breath can come first

That is still action. That is still resistance. That is still growth.

Because for people like us, who have been praised for performance and punished for pause, rest is not laziness. It's rebellion.

# When the World Doesn't Reward Your Growth

Here's something no one tells you: The world might not reward your growth. In fact, it might resent it.

- You'll set boundaries, and people will call you cold

- You'll stop people-pleasing, and they'll say you've changed
- You'll heal, and some people will treat you like you've betrayed them

That's okay. Your healing is not a community project. Your alignment is not up for debate. Your growth is not meant to be approved, it's meant to be lived.

Let them misunderstand. You're not here to make everyone comfortable. You're here to make yourself whole.

## The Longevity of Small Promises

Change isn't about intensity. It's about consistency. It's the promises you make when no one's watching. The little rituals you keep even on your worst days.

- One glass of water before the caffeine
- Five minutes of journaling before the scrolling
- A single truth spoken out loud, even in a whisper

You don't need to overhaul your life overnight. You just need to stay in relationship with the version of you that's trying to grow. That version doesn't need grand gestures. They just need proof you haven't forgotten them.

## Identity as a Verb

You are not a fixed point. You are not who you were five years ago, or five weeks ago, or five minutes ago. You are an unfolding.

So stop waiting until you feel "fully healed" to act like your true self. Be your true self now. Messily. Tenderly. Imperfectly.

Because your identity isn't a noun. It's a verb. It's something you do. Something you live. Something you breathe into, each time you act with integrity.

## Creating Your Own Rituals

You don't need to wait for permission to make your life sacred. You can turn your mornings into ceremony. Your silence into prayer. Your workouts into therapy. Your food into gratitude. Your routines into declarations of who you're becoming.

One of my favorite rituals? Lighting a candle when I'm lost. Not because it fixes anything. But because it reminds me: Even small flames hold power. Even small choices carry light. Even small acts, done with intention, become legacy.

## The Quiet Wins That Matter Most

The biggest changes in my life didn't happen when someone clapped. They happened when no one noticed:

- When I paused before reacting
- When I said "I need time" instead of rushing to fix it
- When I asked myself what *I* wanted, instead of guessing what others expected
- When I chose rest over performance

These moments didn't go viral. They didn't earn applause. But they rewrote my story. Because every time I honored my own voice, I broke a curse. A curse of silence. Of self-erasure. Of generational fear. And those are the wins that matter.

Action is not a destination. It's the next breath you choose. It's the small truth you refuse to swallow. It's the life you create, not when you feel ready, but when you feel responsible for your own becoming.

Because the real revolution is staying consistent when the world is chaotic. And that's where we go next.

Aloneness became my quiet victory, not absence, but reclamation.

Not rejection, but resurrection.

I began to cherish the space where I could finally hear my own voice again; steady, sober, and sacred, even if no one else was listening.

It wasn't isolation, it was **empowerment**.

# Chapter 7: The Diagnosis Journey

The word "autism" first entered my vocabulary not through medical literature or clinical assessment, but through casual conversation in a barbershop in downtown Toronto.

I was thirty-three years old, getting my hair cut by Marcus, a soft-spoken Master Barber from Jamaica who had been cutting hair for years. We often talked during these sessions, about sports, about life, about his family. On this particular afternoon, our conversation had drifted to the topic of his younger brother.

"My brother's autistic," Marcus mentioned as he worked. "Smart as hell, but different, you know? Sees the world in his own way." He paused, studying my reflection in the mirror. "Actually, you remind me of him sometimes. Not in a bad way, just... you feel things deeply. You notice stuff other people miss."

I nodded politely and changed the subject. But something about that moment stuck with me.

## The Suspicion – Realizing Something Deeper Was Going On

There's a specific kind of confusion that feels like drowning in clear water.

Everything looks "fine." You're smart. Capable. People laugh at your jokes, trust your instincts. And yet, you're struggling. Not with life itself, but with the rhythm of it. The transitions. The invisible stairs that others seem to walk up without tripping.

That's what it felt like before the suspicion took hold.

I was "doing fine." Functioning. But only just. My life had turned into a patchwork of masking, exhaustion, moments of brilliance followed by total collapse. I'd power through a week, then disappear for two. I thought it was burnout. Or maybe I was just sensitive. Maybe I was broken in a poetic, French kind of way.

But deep down, a whisper had started forming.

Something else is going on.

It wasn't a therapist who planted the seed. It wasn't a diagnosis or a book. It was a moment.

I was watching a podcast, one of those clips that appear at 2 a.m. when your body won't let you rest, but your mind refuses to stay still. The guy on screen was talking about ADHD. About forgetting basic tasks. About time blindness. About waking up with a million dreams but forgetting to eat.

I sat up.

It wasn't just the symptoms, it was the tone. The *way* he spoke about reality. Like time was water. Like thoughts moved like wind. Like intensity was normal. Like the system wasn't designed for minds like ours.

I didn't feel seen.

I felt *recognized.*

That's the difference. Being seen is external. Being recognized is spiritual. Cellular. Like something dormant in your DNA just nodded quietly and said:

*"You're not lazy. You're built different."*

That night, I couldn't sleep. I fell into the rabbit hole. Articles. Reddit threads. YouTube videos. Instagram therapists. TikTok checklists. I laughed. I winced. I cried.

Because it was all there.

Every quirk I had minimized.

Every meltdown I had shamed.

Every "Why can't I just..." that echoed through my 20s.

I remember thinking: *How have I lived this long not knowing this?*

But the answer came fast: Because I survived.

Because I masked.

Because I was high-functioning enough to be impressive, but not sustainable.

Because I was the "smart kid" who couldn't finish paperwork.

Because I was charming in interviews and overwhelmed on day two.

Because I was a man. Black. French. Articulate. With good taste and good posture.

People don't ask those people if they're neurodivergent. They ask if they're tired. If they're too busy. If they've tried meditating. If they've tried harder.

So I tried harder.

But something in me was done trying.

I started whispering it to myself in private: *What if I'm autistic? What if I have ADHD? What if I'm bipolar? What if I'm not crazy, I'm coded differently?*

I whispered it, like a secret prayer.

Not because I wanted a label. But because I wanted relief. I wanted a bridge between the language of pain and the language of pattern.

I wanted the moment of recognition to mean something. I wanted to stop editing every sentence in my head before I spoke. I wanted to stop calculating my energy like a dying phone battery. I wanted to feel like my brain belonged to me, and not the other way around.

The suspicion didn't free me.

It haunted me.

Because once you see it, you can't unsee it. You start reviewing your entire life with new eyes:

- That time in school when you panicked during a group project and took over everything.
- The girlfriend who said you were intense and emotionally unavailable, on the same day.
- The way you never knew what to do with your hands at parties.
- The way you melted down after a joke landed wrong.
- The way your room stayed clean for six hours, then exploded again.
- The perfectionism. The self-hate. The all-or-nothing drive that left you sleepless at night and empty in the morning.

It was all there.

I hadn't been making it up. I hadn't been weak.

I had been operating on a system no one ever taught me how to run.

That was the beginning.

Not of the diagnosis. Not of acceptance.

But of *curiosity*.

And curiosity, when guided by pain, is the most honest teacher I've ever had.

## The Search – Late-Night Research, Self-Testing, Obsession

I dove into the rabbit hole at 2 a.m.

It started after that podcast moment. I opened my phone, hoping the speaker would disappear by morning. But he was still there. Articles, YouTube, Reddit, Instagram, each scroll seeded something deeper.

Then I saw the meme: *"ADHD is more than losing your keys because you had a beer."* I laughed, but something snapped. I hated that myth. I hated people reducing our nuance to hangovers or forgetfulness. ADHD is more than misplacing your keys, it's missing your own life.

Because I did.

Two days after first suspecting something was up, I already forgot the revelation. I forgot the checklists. Forgot the acronym. I sat at Starbucks, reciting the Serenity Prayer in my head:

*"God, grant me the serenity...."* over and over until Starbucks became a temple to presence.

My former colleagues often told me something that stuck with me: "The remarkable thing about you, Fab, is that we can share our most private struggles with you. You have this ability to help us navigate through the worst situations we've created for ourselves. And then the next day, it's as if you've wiped the slate clean, no judgment, no lingering awkwardness, just a fresh start. The challenge is getting you to slow down and really tune in to what we're saying. But once we have your attention, you lock in with such intensity that you won't let go until the problem is solved."

Now it all made sense, the intensity, the tunnel vision, the rupture that followed.

I hunted ADHD signs: hyperfocus, emotional spikes, executive dysfunction, time-blindness. Calmly jotting DSM-5 (The Diagnostic and Statistical Manual of Mental Illnesses) presentation bullet points: inattention, procrastination, forgetfulness, organizational invisibility, hyperfocus, emotional dysregulation, impulsivity. I saw it all.

Reddit threads snapped flame:

"That moment when you forget you discovered ADHD yesterday."

"I need to speak to myself out loud to remember, like my mom does."

That last line stopped me cold.

Because my mom was the expert. I'd finally understood something about her. She forgot her keys, didn't speak until she formulated every thought loud and clear, built a life blueprint in conversation. She never internalized. She externalized. Engineering life aloud, and it worked.

It wasn't disorder. It was strategy.

And suddenly it clicked: maybe that's my mechanism too.

I stumbled on stats:

- ADHD isn't just kids, it's about **self-regulation**, emotion, executive function.
- It's **neurodevelopmental**, not a character flaw.
- And that blowing-out-of-proportion myth? Debunked everywhere.

I learned genetics matter, nearly 70–80% heritability. I saw the brain-scans showing executive function differences. It wasn't me, it was structure. It was wiring.

On YouTube, I watched adults say the quiet part out loud:

"I've maxed out at every point, until I burned out."

"I could lead a global team, but not a 10-line email chain."

"It's not clumsy. It's disconnection."

Every confession felt like confession and communion.

I took online self-tests. The Adult Self-Report Scale (ASRS) lit up. I scored high in inattentive type. I paused. *I knew I could zone in, but I knew forgetting a plan was not about laziness.*

I followed podcasts where Black men said the quiet part:

"We're told to be calm. To be strong. To just handle it. But that's code for 'don't show your wiring.'"

It was as if every hidden narrative inside me was screaming: *Yes. That's it. Finally, yes.*

But the deeper the research, the more overwhelming it got.

This was not just me.

It was structure. It was adaptation. It was an architecture I'd been living inside without the manual.

Some nights, I broke down. The realization that certain patterns weren't failures, they were signals, felt both freeing and terrifying.

Because admitting it meant change.

Change meant revealing.

Revealing meant risk.

I sat in my apartment, pages of notes lying around, my mind buzzing. I cross-referenced OCD traits, my perfectionism, my internal checklist voice. I'd always said I was methodical. But OCD isn't discipline, it's compulsion. It's a trap.

Now I saw it: my mother repeating aloud. My misplacing things. My super focus and freeze. It was a constellation.

But I still hadn't named it out loud.

There was a quiet magic in self-naming. Like an incantation.

After a week of research, I wrote on my mirror: **"I am ADHD. I am working with a brain that is built differently."**

I stared at it. My eyes burnt. My truth was written in marker.

And for the first time in forever, I felt the ground shift beneath the word.

Recent research shows that ADHD in adults is still drastically underdiagnosed, especially in women, people of color, and individuals who appear "high-functioning." A 2023 Yale School of Medicine report noted that **Black adults are disproportionately mislabeled** with conduct disorders or personality issues instead of being screened for ADHD or bipolar traits (YaleMedicine.org). That felt eerily familiar.

Another article described ADHD as a "disorder of regulation, not intelligence", a mismatch between how we're wired and what the world expects from us.

That hit me hard.

Because I was always told I was intelligent, "ahead of my time," even brilliant. But I couldn't remember the dentist appointment I booked yesterday. I couldn't send the email I'd drafted four times.

And still, I kept going.

It wasn't dysfunction. It was *overcompensation.*

A constant masking act I didn't know I was performing.

And the realest freedom came the moment I stopped asking: *What's wrong with me?*

And started asking: *What's strong about me that no one ever taught me how to use?*

## The Diagnosis – Formal or Informal, Therapy, Internal Collapse & Rebuild

The diagnosis didn't come with a lightning bolt. There was no movie moment, no dramatic therapist reveal.

It came slowly, like mist lifting from a field you didn't even know was fogged.

I don't even remember the exact day. I just remember the feeling:

*This is it. This is what's been happening to me all along.*

It wasn't one diagnosis; it was a convergence.

ADHD. Bipolar. OCD. Traits that lived inside me for decades without a name, because no one thought to ask. No one thought to look deeper than performance.

It wasn't my behavior that confused people, it was the contradiction.

I was articulate, stylish, educated. I could lead teams, coach friends through crises, charm entire rooms. But I couldn't sit still. I couldn't remember my own deadlines. I couldn't function in silence. I couldn't go a week without burning out.

The system didn't flag me because I looked like I was succeeding.

And for a long time, I thought I was too.

When I first heard the word *bipolar*, I flinched.
I thought of extremes. Of psych wards. Of spirals I had only seen in films.
But then I looked back:

The times I stayed up all night building a business plan, only to abandon it by morning.

The fights I started over something I couldn't explain, then cried alone in the shower with no idea why.

The weeks where I felt electric, invincible.

The mornings I couldn't get out of bed.

The charm. The collapse. The silence that followed the storm.

No one had explained that bipolar could be high-functioning.

No one told me it could be silent and still destructive.

That it could look like success on the outside, and feel like chaos inside.

I started speaking to therapists with more confidence. Not asking for answers, naming patterns.

I said: "I don't want a diagnosis for pity. I want it so I can stop hating myself for things I couldn't control."

I told them I wasn't broken. I was *tired*.

Tired of rebuilding my life every three months. Tired of not trusting my own mind.

Tired of waking up with a plan and ending the day ashamed.

Some therapists listened. Others gave me the "functioning adult" test:

"Well, you're doing okay in life, right?"

But I wasn't doing okay. I was surviving behind glass.

Eventually, someone heard me fully.

They mirrored back my language. They didn't just ask about behavior, they asked about **energy**. About **sensory sensitivity**. About **shame** and **shutdown**. They didn't separate the medical from the emotional. They saw the whole story.

That was the moment it became real.

They said the words. ADHD. Bipolar II. OCD tendencies.

And I didn't feel labeled.

I felt *translated.*

At first, I grieved.
I thought: *Why didn't anyone see this earlier? Why didn't I see it earlier?*
But then I remembered, I *did.* I lived it. Every day. For years. I was surviving symptoms without a map.

And now, I had one.

The most important shift wasn't in how I saw myself.

It was in how I *stopped* blaming myself.

I stopped calling myself lazy.

I stopped calling myself inconsistent.

I stopped calling myself dramatic, disorganized, unstable.

I started calling myself by my name.

Fab.

Neurodivergent. Resilient. Relentlessly adaptive.

I wasn't cured. I wasn't transformed. I was *oriented*.

Later, I told a friend. They paused, then said, "Are you sure?"
I nodded.
"Because you don't seem bipolar."

Exactly. That was the point.

Bipolar doesn't always look how you think it does.

ADHD doesn't mean bouncing off the walls.

Autism doesn't mean robotic.

None of these things mean broken. They mean *different*.

And difference isn't a defect.

That's what this chapter of my life has taught me:

A diagnosis doesn't define you.

But it gives you a compass.

And sometimes that's all you need, to finally walk toward yourself instead of away from your truth.

I came across a study from Duke University showing that **nearly 30% of adults with ADHD are misdiagnosed or undiagnosed**, especially if they've learned to mask. The message was powerful: *you don't have to look like a stereotype to need help*.

Reading that, I realized how much I had internalized shame. Culturally, men, especially Black men, aren't supposed to admit they struggle. We're supposed to be *ok*. Yet here I was, sitting in silence, rebuilding myself one therapy session at a time.

Then came the financial planning test. I shared with my therapist how I excelled at big-picture strategies, raising funds, inspiring teams, but I couldn't balance a personal budget. I couldn't plan a grocery list. She asked gently:

"What if these aren't weaknesses, but symptoms?"

At that moment, I paused.

*Of course.*

I remembered my mom again, this time as my blueprint. Smart, methodical, charismatic, and yet, if she didn't speak it out loud, it didn't stick. That awareness became part of my diagnosis identity. It wasn't a flaw, it was *heredity meeting environment*. It was me meeting a history.

I also discovered Colin, a Black ADHD advocate, who wrote about **"twice exceptional"**: gifted and neurodivergent. That phrase hit like a revelation. Giftedness and hyperfocus gave me results. But the regulation part? That I lacked tools for.

I researched bipolar II, remitting depression, hypomania, not the full manic episodes. I recognized the writing sessions I stayed up late to complete. I saw the collapse the next day, apathy, exhaustion, flatness. Every swing back and forth suddenly had context.

I won't pretend it wasn't scary to say it out loud. A label felt like a tether.

But then I remembered something else: **labels are tools**. They give you language. They give you advocacy. They give you the ability to explain without apology.

Because neurodivergence isn't secret. It's structural. It's ancestral. It's chemical. It's real.

It's not about fixing yourself, it's about understanding yourself.

So when the therapist paused and said:

"Fab, this is who you are."

I didn't feel broken. I felt *found*.

## The Declaration – Speaking Your Truth, Sharing with Others, Integrating It

Telling the world you're neurodivergent isn't a press release. It's not a "coming out" video or a color-coded infographic.

Sometimes it's just a pause in conversation.

A choice not to lie.

A single sentence said in your own voice:

"I actually have ADHD."

"I'm bipolar, diagnosed."

"I'm neurodivergent."

No build-up. No preamble.

Just truth, offered like breath.

The first time I said it aloud to someone outside my inner circle, I didn't know how they'd respond.

It was a friend I hadn't seen in years. Someone from the "old life." They were asking why I didn't do nightlife anymore, why I didn't throw events, why I was "so zen now."

And instead of deflecting, I just said:

"Because I burned out. And because I'm neurodivergent. Diagnosed. I'm learning how to live without betraying myself."

Silence.

Then:

"Damn, I had no idea."

"I didn't either. Not for a long time."

That became my soft declaration strategy. Not the whole story. Not the full trauma. Just the doorway.

I noticed how people responded. Some leaned in. Some nodded, confused. Others changed the subject. And a few looked down, like they recognized something in themselves they weren't ready to say yet.

I didn't need validation. I wasn't seeking applause. But the more I said it, the more I heard myself say it.

And each time I did, it settled deeper.

Not an excuse. Not a brand.

Just a part of me I no longer had to hide.

The hardest people to tell were the ones who loved the older me.

The wild Fab. The night owl. The fixer. The one who always showed up even when he couldn't breathe.

I tried to explain. Gently. Clumsily. Sometimes through voice notes, sometimes over tea. Sometimes not at all.

One of them said:

"You think everything's neurodivergence now. Maybe you're just growing up."

It hurt. Because yes, I was growing.

But not *out* of something.

*Into* something.

Growing into awareness. Structure. Language.

Growing into the ability to say: *I need time. I need space. I can't do crowds right now. I need to stim. I need silence. I need music that doesn't hurt my skin.*

Declaring a diagnosis isn't just about telling others.

It's about telling yourself: *I'm allowed to design my life around my needs.*

I stopped trying to cram myself into environments that drained me.

I created structure where I could. Soft lighting. Scent. Routines. Headphones in public. Timers. Meal prep. Breaks between tasks. Less caffeine. More deep breathing. And with a journal always near.

I still forget things. I still lose days. I still freeze sometimes.

But now I recognize it for what it is:

A system glitch, not a character flaw.

There was a moment, standing in line at the pharmacy, waiting for my prescription refill, when a guy behind me said loudly:

"Man, everyone's ADHD these days. Nobody wants to just focus and grow up."

I didn't respond. I didn't need to.

But something in me softened. Because a year ago, that comment would have sent me spiraling.

Now? I just whispered the Serenity Prayer in my head and kept breathing.

Because the real declaration isn't public. It's private. It's internal. It's knowing who you are when no one else is watching.

I wrote myself a new affirmation one night, lit by candlelight:

I am not my symptoms.

I am not my productivity.

I am not my reputation.

I am not someone's projection.

I am a rhythm.

I am a pattern.

I am a full song, sometimes dissonant, sometimes harmonic.

And every note belongs to me.

Declaring your diagnosis doesn't mean living inside it.

It means holding it like a compass, checking direction when needed, but not mistaking the map for the journey.

There are still days I want to erase the label. Days I miss the mask. Days I resent the complexity of my brain. But I wouldn't go back. Not for a second.

Because the cost of hiding is always greater than the price of being seen.

And in the end, what I gained wasn't just a word or a file in a clinic.

What I gained was **a home inside myself**.

A place I could finally rest.

Recent studies underscore the ripple effects of declaring a neurodivergent identity. A 2024 publication in the *Journal of Occupational Health Psychology* found that **professionals who openly embrace their neurodiversity report 25% lower**

**workplace stress and 30% higher job satisfaction**, compared to peers who mask continuously. Disclosure isn't just speaking, it's liberation. It reshapes your environment, subtly signaling to others: *This is who I am.*

Another piece in *Mind & Brain* notes how **self-affirmation practices**, like writing your own diagnostic confirmation or affirmation statements, can significantly reduce rejection and threat brain responses. In one experiment, subjects who recalled personal affirmations showed lower cortisol levels during stressful social tasks. In my case, candlelit affirmations aren't just poetic, they're neurological reset buttons. (neuroscience study)

I also found research on the concept of **"identity-confirming speech"**, the act of saying a truth about yourself and actually believing it. This simple act fosters greater self-congruence and less internal conflict. When you declare yourself neurodivergent, your brain begins to rewire old pathways of self-criticism and shame. (Psychology Today summary)

Finally, remember this: a 2022 meta-analysis in *PLOS One* tracked over 15,000 participants across 12 countries. It found that **people with visible or declared mental health conditions experienced 45% better access to community support and 50% higher recovery rates**, not because of treatment alone, but because the community knows you and holds space.

So when you say:

"I am ADHD. I am bipolar."

You're not just naming symptoms.

You're opening a door, to support, to self-love, to belonging.

That's the true power of declaration.

## The Seed of Recognition

Marcus's comment planted a seed that would take months to germinate. At first, I dismissed it entirely. Autism was something that happened to other people, people with more obvious differences, people who needed significant support, people who fit the narrow stereotypes I carried in my mind.

But the seed was planted nonetheless. And over the following weeks, I found myself paying attention to conversations about neurodivergence in ways I never had before. A podcast interview with an autistic adult. A friend mentioning ADHD. Articles about late diagnosis that would pop up in my social media feeds.

Each exposure created a small crack in my assumptions about what autism and ADHD looked like. Slowly, I began to realize that my understanding of these conditions was based almost entirely on outdated stereotypes and media representations.

## The Google Rabbit Hole

The real journey began on a quiet Sunday evening when I found myself alone with my laptop and a growing sense of curiosity. I can't remember exactly what prompted me to type "adult autism symptoms" into the search bar, but once I did, there was no going back.

What I found was simultaneously shocking and familiar. Blog posts written by late-diagnosed autistic adults describing experiences that felt like reading my own diary. Checklists of traits that seemed to have been compiled by someone who had been following me around my entire life. Videos of people explaining their inner experiences in ways that made me feel less alone than I had in years.

I discovered terms I had never heard before:

**Masking**: The practice of camouflaging autistic traits to appear neurotypical.

**Stimming**: Self-stimulatory behaviors used for regulation and comfort.

**Sensory processing differences**: Atypical responses to environmental stimuli.

**Executive dysfunction**: Difficulties with planning, organization, and task initiation.

**Special interests**: Intense, sustained focus on particular topics or activities.

Each new piece of information felt like a puzzle piece clicking into place. The childhood experiences that had confused and frustrated my parents. The social difficulties that had made adolescence so painful. The workplace challenges that had led to multiple job changes. The relationship patterns that had left me feeling perpetually misunderstood.

For the first time in my life, I had a framework that made sense of experiences I had never been able to explain.

## Initial Resistance and Denial

Despite the recognition I felt while reading about autism, my first reaction was resistance. I couldn't possibly be autistic. I had friends. I had maintained relationships. I had been successful in school and work. I could make eye contact and carry on conversations.

All of my preconceptions about autism were rooted in outdated understanding of the condition. I thought autism meant being nonverbal, intellectually disabled, or completely unable to function independently. I thought it was something that would have been obvious from early childhood, something that teachers and parents would have immediately recognized.

I had no idea that autism, particularly in girls and intellectually gifted individuals, often went undiagnosed well into adulthood. I didn't understand that many autistic people become incredibly skilled at masking their differences, developing sophisticated strategies for appearing neurotypical while struggling internally.

The idea that I might be autistic challenged fundamental assumptions about my identity and my understanding of my life experiences. It was easier to dismiss the possibility than to confront the implications of what recognition might mean.

## The Pattern of Suggestions

But Marcus's comment wasn't an isolated incident. Over the following months, other people began making similar observations.

My osteopath, during a session where I was describing my chronic muscle tension and tendency toward overwhelm, mentioned that some of her clients with similar presentations had found relief after being diagnosed with autism or ADHD.

A friend I had known for years, after watching me navigate a crowded restaurant with obvious discomfort, suggested that I might want to look into sensory processing differences.

My therapist, who had been working with me on anxiety and depression for several months, began asking questions about my childhood that seemed designed to explore neurodivergent traits.

Each suggestion on its own might have been easy to dismiss. But the pattern was becoming impossible to ignore. Multiple people, independently and without consultation with each other, were seeing something in my behavior and experience that I had been blind to.

## Finding Healthcare Providers

When I finally decided to pursue an evaluation, I discovered that finding qualified healthcare providers who understood adult autism was more challenging than I had expected. Many psychologists and psychiatrists had limited experience with autism presentations in adults, particularly those who had learned to mask effectively.

I was fortunate to live in a major metropolitan area with access to specialists, but even so, the wait lists were long and the costs were significant. Many insurance plans didn't cover autism evaluations for adults, treating them as elective rather than medical necessities.

I spent weeks researching practitioners, reading reviews, and trying to find someone who had specific experience with late-diagnosed adults. I wanted someone who would understand that my presentation might be subtle, that my masking skills might be sophisticated, and that my struggles might not fit traditional diagnostic criteria.

Eventually, I found Dr. Sarah Chen, a psychologist who specialized in autism assessments for adults and had particular expertise working with intellectually gifted individuals. Her practice focused specifically on people who had "fallen through the cracks" of childhood diagnosis.

# The Evaluation Process

The evaluation process was more comprehensive than I had anticipated. It began with an extensive intake interview that covered my entire developmental history, from early childhood through the present day.

Dr. Chen asked detailed questions about my sensory experiences, my social development, my patterns of behavior and interest, and my emotional regulation throughout different life stages. She wanted to understand not just how I appeared to others, but how I experienced the world internally.

One of the most challenging aspects of the evaluation was reconstructing my childhood behavior. Autism symptoms need to be present before age 12 for an adult diagnosis, but my memories from that period were filtered through decades of reinterpretation and masking.

Dr. Chen encouraged me to contact family members who could provide external perspectives on my early development. She also gave me structured questionnaires to complete and similar forms for people who had known me well during different life periods.

## Psychological Testing

The formal assessment included several standardized psychological tests designed to evaluate autism-related traits and rule out other conditions that might present similarly.

The **Autism Diagnostic Observation Schedule (ADOS-2)** involved structured social interactions and communication tasks designed to observe autistic behaviors in a controlled setting. As an adult who had developed sophisticated masking strategies, I found this test both fascinating and anxiety-provoking.

I completed the **Autism Spectrum Quotient (AQ)** and other self-report measures that asked about my experiences with social communication, sensory processing, and restricted interests. Some questions were easy to answer; others required careful consideration of behaviors I had never consciously analyzed.

The **Wechsler Adult Intelligence Scale (WAIS-IV)** provided a comprehensive assessment of my cognitive abilities, including areas where autistic individuals sometimes show distinctive patterns of strengths and weaknesses.

Additional tests explored executive functioning, attention, and emotional regulation to provide a complete picture of my neuropsychological profile.

## Family Involvement and Childhood History

One of the most revealing aspects of the evaluation process was involving my family in providing historical information about my development. Dr. Chen asked my parents to complete questionnaires about my behavior as a young child, focusing on areas that might indicate early autism traits.

These conversations with my parents were emotionally complex. They were being asked to remember and report on behaviors they had experienced as problems or challenges, without necessarily understanding the clinical significance of what they were describing.

My mother recalled my intense sensitivity to clothing textures and food temperatures. My father remembered my tendency to become completely absorbed in particular activities for hours at a time. Both parents described my difficulty with transitions and changes in routine, my literal interpretation of language, and my tendency to have emotional meltdowns over seemingly minor frustrations.

What had been characterized as behavioral problems or personality quirks in my childhood were being reexamined through the lens of neurodevelopmental differences. This reframing was both validating and painful, validating because it provided explanation for experiences that had never made sense, painful because it highlighted years of misunderstanding and missed opportunities for support.

## The Wait for Results

The period between completing the evaluation and receiving results was agonizing. Dr. Chen had explained that she needed several weeks to review all the testing data, interview transcripts, and historical information before reaching a diagnostic conclusion.

During this waiting period, I found myself oscillating between hope and fear. Part of me desperately wanted a diagnosis that would finally explain my lifelong struggles and provide a framework for understanding myself. Another part of me was terrified of receiving a label that might change how others saw me or how I saw myself.

I continued researching autism and connecting with online communities of late-diagnosed adults. Reading their stories helped me feel less alone in the uncertainty, but it also raised new questions about what an autism diagnosis would mean for my life going forward.

## The Moment of Diagnosis

The call came on a Tuesday afternoon in March. Dr. Chen asked if I could come in that week to discuss her findings. The careful neutrality in her voice gave nothing away, but I knew that positive results were rarely delivered over the phone.

Sitting in her office three days later, I listened as she explained her conclusions. Based on the comprehensive evaluation, she had determined that I met criteria for Autism Spectrum Disorder, Level 1 (requiring support). She also identified significant traits consistent with ADHD, though the autism diagnosis was primary.

"This explains a lot about your experiences," she said gently. "The social challenges, the sensory sensitivities, the intense interests, the need for routine and predictability, these are all consistent with autism. You've developed remarkable coping strategies, which is why it took so long to be recognized."

I felt a strange mixture of relief and disorientation. Relief because finally having an explanation for my lifelong struggles. Disorientation because this new information required me to reinterpret my entire life story.

## Understanding the Diagnosis

Dr. Chen spent considerable time helping me understand what the diagnosis meant and didn't mean. Autism Spectrum Disorder encompasses a wide range of presentations, and my particular profile was characterized by:

**Strengths**: Strong verbal abilities, intellectual giftedness, developed masking skills, capacity for independence in most areas of life.

**Challenges**: Sensory processing differences, executive function difficulties, social communication differences, emotional regulation challenges.

**Support needs**: Primarily around sensory accommodations, social energy management, and strategies for executive function challenges.

She emphasized that being diagnosed with autism didn't mean I was "more disabled" than I had been the day before. It meant I finally had accurate information about how my brain worked, which could guide more effective strategies for managing challenges and building on strengths.

## Processing the News

The days immediately following my diagnosis were emotionally intense. I felt like I was grieving and celebrating simultaneously.

I grieved for the child who had struggled without understanding why. I grieved for the teenager who had felt alien and alone. I grieved for the young adult who had spent enormous energy trying to fix problems that weren't actually problems but differences.

At the same time, I felt profound relief and even joy. The diagnosis provided a coherent explanation for experiences that had never made sense. It connected me to a community of people who shared similar experiences. It gave me language for communicating my needs and challenges to others.

## Telling Friends and Family

One of the most challenging aspects of receiving an autism diagnosis in adulthood was deciding how and when to share the news with important people in my life.

I started with close friends who had been supportive during my evaluation process. Most responded with warmth and curiosity, asking questions about what the diagnosis meant and how they could be better friends and allies.

Some responses were less supportive. A few people expressed skepticism about the validity of the diagnosis or suggested that I was "looking for excuses" for ordinary life challenges. These reactions were painful but not entirely unexpected.

Telling my family was particularly complex. My parents had lived through my childhood struggles without understanding their cause. The autism diagnosis invited them to reexamine memories and possibly feel guilt about responses that hadn't been helpful.

To their credit, my parents were ultimately supportive and curious. They asked thoughtful questions and began educating themselves about autism. They also shared stories from my childhood that took on new meaning in light of the diagnosis.

## Insurance and Healthcare Navigation

Dealing with insurance coverage for adult autism evaluation and support services proved to be another challenge entirely. Many insurance plans treat autism as a childhood condition and don't provide adequate coverage for adult diagnostic services or ongoing support.

I was fortunate to have insurance that covered most of the evaluation costs, but many adults seeking diagnosis face significant financial barriers. The evaluation process can cost several thousand dollars, making it inaccessible to many people who might benefit from it.

Finding ongoing healthcare providers who understood adult autism was another challenge. Many therapists and psychiatrists had limited experience working with autistic adults, particularly those who had been diagnosed later in life.

## The Medication Decision

During my evaluation, Dr. Chen had also identified significant ADHD traits that were impacting my daily functioning. While autism itself isn't treated with medication, the ADHD symptoms could potentially be managed pharmacologically.

The decision to try medication was difficult. I had internalized stigma about psychiatric medications and worried about changing my personality or becoming dependent on drugs to function.

Dr. Chen referred me to a psychiatrist who specialized in neurodevelopmental conditions in adults. Dr. Martinez explained that ADHD medications don't change personality, they help the brain access executive functions that are already there but harder to reach.

After careful consideration and extensive discussion about potential benefits and risks, I decided to try a low dose of methylphenidate, a stimulant medication commonly used to treat ADHD.

## First Experiences with Medication

The first time I took ADHD medication, the change was subtle but profound. Tasks that usually required enormous willpower suddenly felt manageable. The constant background noise in my mind quieted to a whisper. I could choose what to focus on instead of being at the mercy of whatever was most stimulating.

It wasn't a dramatic transformation, I was still myself, just with better access to my own capabilities. I could sustain attention on important but uninteresting tasks. I could remember to complete multi-step processes. I could regulate my attention and energy more effectively.

## Full Integration: Mind + Body + Breath Healing Journey

Medicine isn't cheating, it's *tuning*. Just like protein fuels muscle recovery, the right brain and body strategies help you rebuild stronger. I learned that firsthand.

### The Day I Became My Own Doctor, Mental Tuning

I'd always known something was off, brain fog, hypersensitivity, and stubborn fatigue no matter how much I slept. My labs showed creatinine at 1.3 mg/dL and borderline high cholesterol labeled as "mixed hyperlipidemia." But the doctors just said, "Looks okay, let's monitor."

That day I took action. I uploaded my lab results, creatinine, cholesterol, "mixed hyperlipidemia", into ChatGPT:

**"What does mixed hyperlipidemia mean?"**

*"It can indicate kidney dysfunction and contribute to brain fog, fatigue, inflammation."*

Finally, answers. I said,

**"What can help brain fog from this?"**

*"Magnesium L-threonate crosses the blood–brain barrier and supports memory, clarity, sleep, ADHD symptoms."*

ChatGPT also explained that only L-threonate crosses into the brain; glycinate helps muscles and citrate supports digestion verywellhealth.com. I'd assumed "magnesium is magnesium," but now I understood.

- That evening, I ordered:
- 2 g magnesium L-threonate (Magtein®)
- Rhodiola rosea
- MSM + amino-ATP
- Hydroxyzine to reset sleep

I added a cold face plunge and a high-protein, dairy-free carrot smoothie.

For the first time, instead of waking into a storm, I woke with clarity. The chest-jumping fog was still there, but I could *push through it.*

**Science backs this.** Magnesium L-threonate raises brain magnesium and boosts cognition and memory in adults within 30 daysglobalrph.com Aetnaeurjther.com mdpi.com. Even moderate kidney decline is linked to 3× the risk of cognitive issuesverywellhealth.com.

I felt sharper, mental tension eased, like lifting VHS mode into crystal-clear 4K.

But emotions came too. I felt **betrayed** as the labs were ignored, but I also felt **empowered**. I asked, researched, and tuned my system.

"Don't follow diagnoses, question them. Don't wait for healing, learn how to heal yourself."

# This led to my Three A's:

1. **Aware** – See the fog, the labs, the misdiagnosis

2. **Accept** – Own my ADHD, kidney weakness, brain-fog, and need for tools

3. **Act** – Build a protocol with supplements, biohacks, routine, reflection

This moment became my **NDWA blueprint**: move beyond labels. Teach tuning. Build agency.

## The Other Side: My Body's Breakdown

But the body was breaking too.

I carried stress in my shoulders, literally bracing like armor. Years of bartending and coaching loaded my levator scapulae, upper traps, and cervical paraspinals like suspension cables. My shoulders were always hunched, neck tense.

Then came a snap, a micro-tear in the rotator cuff (likely supraspinatus/infraspinatus). I used **deep tissue massage** and **trigger-point therapy**, techniques that create micro-inflammation to stimulate repair. But never let it heal fully.

Soon, the imbalance spread. Tight rotator cuff pulled on traps, compressing my cervical spine and triggering pain above the left shoulder blade. Chiropractors cracked symptoms, not the cause, and nothing held. I stood, bent, shook cocktail shakers; pain spiraled.

Eventually, I was diagnosed with early-stage **functional scoliosis**. Not disc damage, just chronic tightness pulling my spine off-center. Dr. Fazzari in Midtown East used ultrasound-assisted myofascial release and full-body strapping to reset alignment, a painful, dramatic mobilization that snapped vertebrae into place …but didn't stick.

So I tried everything:

Chiropractic crack sessions (esp. C4–C5)

- Acupuncture + cupping to boost circulation
- **Dry needling** to deactivate trigger points, tight fibers twitched dramatically
- Bikram and Vinyasa yoga for flexibility and decompression
- Cold/ice plunges, foam rolling, Central Park walks, boxing, rowing, all movement strategies
- Dry needling literally shocked my trapezius into releasing. Muscles thawed. For the first time, posture began to even out.

When improvement plateaued, ChatGPT suggested **spinal decompression therapy** and **extracorporeal shockwave therapy (ESWT)**. Decompression stretches the spine, relieving disc pressure; ESWT uses acoustic waves to break scar tissue and stimulate healing.

I strapped into tables twice weekly. Pain eased. Posture realigned. Scar tissue faded.

Results: shoulders level. No sharp trap pain. I run 12 km at 10 km/h, box, play volleyball. I keep a weekly maintenance regime, yoga, dry needling, deep tissue, decompression therapy.

### Three A's for the Body

Again:

1. **Aware** – Feel the tilt, pain, imbalance
2. **Accept** – Recognize exercise alone wasn't enough
3. **Act** – Research, choose modalities backed by evidence

Healing demands integrated action, mind *and* body.

# Philosophical Alignment

I'm not a philosopher, but these ideas resonate:

- **Merleau-Ponty**: "Our body is the lived medium of experience." Alignment = agency.
- **B.K.S. Iyengar**: "A crooked body means a crooked mind." (a lived ancestor of somatics)
- **Seneca**: "Difficulties strengthen the mind, as labour does the body."
- Delphic Maxim: "Know thyself", body included.

Every decompression session, every shockwave pulse, was me rebuilding the scaffolding for my engine.

## One More Layer: Asthma, Oxygen, and the Invisible Fight

There was a ghost I nearly forgot, I'm asthmatic.

Introduced at age 8, a doctor detected wheezing and asked if an inhaler was needed. My dad said no. I trusted that. For years, every run, basketball game, box session, I hit a wall, lungs tight after 5–10 minutes. I thought it meant I was weak.

But the body adapts. My cardio would finally "kick in" after 20 minutes. People said I sweated too much. I felt ashamed.

Decades later, I said, "Doctor, my breathing's harder." He looked and said, "You're not using Albuterol?"

"What's that?" I asked.

I started with two inhalers:

- **Wixela Inhub** (fluticasone + salmeterol) for long-term lung health
- **Albuterol Sulfate HFA** for fast relief

Two puffs in the morning *before waking* cut through fog. Two at night eased sleep apnea. One before an interview or anxious moment gave sanity and oxygen.

I realized: this world expects me to perform like everyone else, but I start and end my day *under-oxygenated*. And no one told me till I was 35.

That alone changes everything. Curiosity, asking a single question, created a literal breath of presence.

Just as magnesium unlocked my mind, decompression aligned my body, and dry needling freed my posture…

**Oxygen unlocked my spirit.**

**Breath, Life, Awareness**

Pneuma (Greek) = breath + spirit. Spirare (Latin) = respiration + inspiration. This isn't metaphoric, it's somatic truth.

When I wheezed as a child…

When I gasped during workouts…

I wasn't lazy, I was under-breathing.

I was fighting *for my spirit*.

So NDWA isn't just about neurodivergence. It's about **biological divergence**. Our systems tell the truth, even when people don't listen.

## Final Three A's: Mind, Body & Breath

1. **Aware** – Fog, pain, imbalance, oxygen debt
2. **Accept** – You're neurodivergent, physically strained, starting low on breath
3. **Act** – Build integrated protocols: supplements, biohacks, therapies, movement, inhalers, awareness

You *must* align everything, from the chemical chemistry in your brain to the posture that holds your head up to the air you breathe.

## NDWA: The Blueprint in Action

NDWA is about tuning systems, mental, physical, spiritual. It's holistic agency.

Drawing a line from lab results to magnesium; from posture decoding to decompression; from breath deprivation to airway management.

It's saying **you deserve to live aligned**, every cell, every thought, and every breath aligned with your purpose.

And that's what I teach. That's why I share. Because if you *know* your system... and you *tune* it... you can *thrive*.

The medication also helped me understand how much effort I had been putting into basic cognitive tasks that others took for granted. When those tasks became easier, I had energy available for other things, creativity, relationships, and personal growth.

## Adjusting Expectations

One important lesson from the early medication experience was learning to adjust my expectations. I had hoped that treatment would solve all my struggles and make me feel "normal" for the first time in my life.

The reality was more nuanced. Medication helped significantly with attention and executive function, but it didn't change my sensory sensitivities, my need for routine, or my social communication differences. It was a tool that made some aspects of life easier, not a cure for autism or ADHD.

Learning to have realistic expectations about what treatment could and couldn't accomplish was an important part of integrating my diagnosis into my understanding of myself.

## Work and Relationship Improvements

As I began to understand my neurodivergent traits and implement appropriate accommodations, I noticed improvements in multiple areas of my life.

At work, I began requesting accommodations like noise-canceling headphones, flexible scheduling, and written follow-up to verbal instructions. I also started being more honest about my communication preferences and working style.

In relationships, I began explaining my sensory needs and social energy limitations instead of just enduring discomfort or withdrawing without explanation. This led to deeper understanding and better support from friends and romantic partners.

I also started setting boundaries around social commitments, recognizing that I needed more recovery time between social events than many neurotypical people.

## The Ripple Effects

Receiving an autism diagnosis created ripple effects that extended far beyond my personal understanding. Several friends and family members began recognizing similar traits in themselves or their children and pursued their own evaluations.

I became more aware of accessibility issues in various environments and began advocating for sensory-friendly accommodations in spaces I frequented.

I also started connecting with other late-diagnosed autistic adults, both online and in person. These connections were incredibly validating and helpful for developing strategies for living authentically as an autistic adult.

## Ongoing Questions and Growth

Receiving a diagnosis was the beginning of a new phase of self-understanding, not the end of a journey. I continued to discover new aspects of how autism showed up in my life and to develop better strategies for working with my neurodivergent traits.

Some questions remained open: How much of my social anxiety was related to autism versus other factors? Which of my personality traits were connected to neurodivergence versus individual differences? How could I continue growing and changing while honoring my neurological differences?

The diagnosis provided a framework for understanding myself, but it didn't answer every question or solve every challenge. It was a starting point for a more authentic and self-compassionate way of living.

# The Gift of Understanding

Looking back on the diagnosis journey, I'm profoundly grateful for Marcus's casual observation in that barbershop. His comment set in motion a process that fundamentally changed my relationship with myself and my understanding of my place in the world.

The diagnosis didn't make me autistic, I had always been autistic. But it gave me language for experiences I had never been able to articulate and connected me to a community of people who shared similar ways of being in the world.

Most importantly, it allowed me to stop trying to fix myself and start learning to understand and accommodate myself. That shift from self-rejection to self-acceptance has been the foundation for everything positive that has followed.

The diagnosis was not an ending but a beginning, the beginning of a more authentic, self-compassionate, and ultimately more successful way of living as my true neurodivergent self.

# Chapter 8: Unraveling the Past

Armed with the framework of my autism and ADHD diagnosis, I began the complex process of reinterpreting my entire life history. It was like being given a new lens through which to view familiar photographs. Suddenly, details that had been blurred came into sharp focus, and patterns that had been invisible became obvious.

This process of reframing wasn't just intellectual, it was deeply emotional. Every memory I revisited carried the weight of years of misunderstanding, self-blame, and confusion. But it also carried the possibility of healing and self-compassion.

## The Emotional Crash After Diagnosis

No one talks about the crash that comes after the clarity.

You get the diagnosis. You get the language. You exhale, finally. You think it will be a turning point. That everything will start making sense now. That relief will last longer than a day.

But what they don't tell you is that relief is a thin layer.

Underneath it is grief.

Grief for the years lost. For the years misunderstood.

Grief for the people who never knew who you really were.

Grief for the person you thought you were supposed to be.

Soon after the diagnosis, I read a study in *PLOS One* showing that **many autistic, ADHD, and bipolar adults experience what researchers now call a "post-diagnostic crash."** It's a period of deep emotional overwhelm that follows naming the pain, sometimes more intense than the suffering itself. People described it as "hope fatigue," "identity collapse," and "the grief after the epiphany." It wasn't just a metaphor, it was biochemical. <u>PMC</u>

That resonated. It explained why, even after relief, my brain flipped into freeze. It explained why stillness felt so jagged. It validated everything I had felt as a lived experience, and not a failure of strength.

Another article in *Journal of Autism and Adult Mental Health* noted that **support immediately after diagnosis is often missing**, leaving people to navigate a sudden void, without resources, without community, and often with cultural or racial isolation amplifying its impact. That described my first weeks exactly. <u>SAGE Journals</u>

I realized later that this crash was not a sign of relapse, it was a **reset**. Permission for my nervous system to breathe. But that doesn't mean it was comfortable. Not at all.

I watched my body respond: sleep deeper. Emotions louder. Sensory walls thinner.

And I learned something: when structure falls away, your system speaks. It does not whisper, it **shouts**.

My sleep patterns flipped. I'd lie awake until 4 a.m., staring at my reflection, questioning every choice. Then I'd sleep until noon, missing meetings, missing meals. My chest felt hollow, my bones heavy.

I felt like my diagnosis had unlocked a sacred echo chamber, and for the first time, I was forced to listen to *myself*. It was messy. It was loud. It was necessary.

Because clarity without integration is like fire without flame. It warms you, but only briefly.

And this crash, this collapse, was the point when the climb begins. Because now, after naming the fault lines, you can start building on *your* terms.

I had spent so much time surviving, fighting to prove I was normal, successful, worthy, that once I stopped, I didn't know who I was without the struggle.

When I finally named what I was living, ADHD, bipolar, neurodivergent, it was like pulling a sword from a wound. Yes, the blade was gone. But now I could feel the hole.

I remember walking through the city the day after my diagnosis and feeling like the buildings were tilting. Not literally, but energetically. As if the coordinates of the world had shifted. As if everything I'd ever done was now cast in a different light.

Was I ever truly "me"?

Was I just reacting to a world that never gave me space to be whole?

The recognition didn't make me feel empowered. Not yet.

It made me feel hollow.

The first two weeks were disorienting.

I couldn't focus. I forgot names, dates, even what day it was. I skipped meals. I lay in bed staring at the ceiling, tracing the architecture of old decisions. How many were mine? How many were reactions to misdiagnosed pain?

I wanted to go back and redo everything. To find the younger me in the corner of a schoolroom, at the edge of a party, on the floor of his childhood bedroom, and whisper:

"You're not lazy. You're not broken. You're just wired for a different rhythm. And I'm sorry no one saw it sooner."

But time doesn't give you do-overs.

Time only gives you the chance to do better now.

That's what the crash was.

Not depression.

Not regression.

But a reckoning.

Because the moment you stop lying to yourself, your body starts telling the truth.

And mine had a lot to say.

I got sick. I got quiet. I got still. I turned down invitations. I turned inward. I couldn't pretend anymore. Not even politely. Not even professionally.

And the silence, at first, felt unbearable.

But there's a quote I found once, in a book I've long since lost:

"Silence is not empty. It is full of answers."

That silence became my confessional. My teacher.

It stripped me down to breath, skin, and bone.

And once the noise fell away, I could finally hear what was underneath.

Here's what I heard:

*You've been carrying everyone's weight but your own story.*

*You learned to fix others, so you didn't have to feel your own pain.*

*You built a career around distraction because stillness terrified you.*

*You never asked for help because no one ever showed you how.*

*And now... now you're here. And this is where the real work begins.*

I didn't journal neatly. I scribbled.

I didn't meditate like a monk. I lay on the floor and cried until I fell asleep.

I didn't detox with smoothies and affirmations. I barely ate. I repeated the Serenity Prayer 150 times just to get through an hour.

And still, I didn't quit.

Because deep down, something new was stirring. A fragile belief:

*If I can name it, I can hold it. If I can hold it, I can shape it.*

This wasn't rock bottom.

This was the **honest beginning**.

Where clarity cuts like a blade.

Where old armor falls off in pieces.

Where you no longer fake smiles to earn love.

Where you no longer chase normal, because you understand now, *normal was never meant for you.*

## Small Rituals as Rebellion

Action didn't come in a grand gesture. It came in fragments.

Tiny movements. Unnoticed shifts. Small rituals I didn't call "rituals" yet.

I wasn't trying to become a better version of myself. I was trying not to disappear.

I didn't make a vision board. I didn't plan a comeback.

I just started waking up and asking myself: *What does my nervous system need right now?*

And sometimes the answer was: water.

Sometimes: music.

Sometimes: silence.

Sometimes: a shower at 2 p.m., just to feel the steam and remember I existed.

# The Reset Within the Reset

The most transformative tool I've discovered is **inventory**, a practice so powerful it operates as the foundation for everything else.

Whether you're cataloging a drawer, counting your supplements, mapping your budget, or examining your psyche, inventory triggers a cascade of micro-transformations. It's not just about organizing, it's spiritual architecture.

When you engage fully in inventory, you experience the **Three Stages of Awareness** in real time.

First, you **Know**, you're anchored in the present, counting what's actually there. Not what should be. Not what you hope for. What *is*.

Second, you become **Aware**, you accept both what you possess and what's missing. You feel it. You grieve it if needed. Acceptance rises naturally from this confrontation with truth.

And third, you **Act**, because inventory isn't passive. It builds confidence. It gives you footing. You now know where you stand, and that makes the next step real.

But here's the key: what I call **"the reset within the reset."** You start organizing a drawer and find a pen that sparks an idea, suddenly, you're taking emotional inventory. That drawer becomes your day. That pen becomes your breath. That idea becomes your response.

You pause, breathe, and choose the right instrument for the moment, **not reacting from your emotion, but choosing your action with presence.**

Inventory is how you untrigger yourself.

It's how you stop being the instrument of your emotions, and become the conscious selector of tools.

Don't just react. Do your Inventory. Don't fight your condition. **Name it, feel it, accept it**. And then from that rooted place… you move.

I learned that **ritual is not always routine.**
Routine is mechanical. Ritual is intentional.

My rituals started out simple:

- Washing my face slowly.
- Turning off the lights and lighting a single candle.
- Laying on the floor and listening to ambient sound until my chest softened.
- Cooking one real meal a day. No performance. No Instagram. Just care.

I started to walk again, not for fitness, not to escape. Just to move.

First in circles. Then through familiar neighborhoods. I'd leave my phone at home sometimes just to let the world touch me without interruption.

I reconnected with incense. With baths. With playlists that didn't need lyrics. I learned which teas calmed me down and which ones made me spiral. I started listening to my skin, my eyes, my throat. I noticed when sound made me anxious. I noticed which fabrics felt safe.

These weren't routines. They were tiny acts of rebellion.

Because every time I chose slowness over shame, I was saying: *I am not a machine.*

I am not here to produce. I am here to feel.

Some people don't understand what healing looks like for neurodivergent people.

They expect us to "snap back."

They want to see momentum, progress charts, green smoothies and day planners.

But for us, healing is nonlinear.

It's lopsided.

It's circular, spiral, regression, revelation.

Sometimes healing is brushing your teeth after four days of not brushing your teeth and calling that a miracle.

Sometimes healing is crying over the fact that you can't cry.

Sometimes it's forgetting your own progress until someone else points it out.

I wrote a Post-it that said:

"You don't need to become. You just need to return."

And I stuck it on my mirror. Next to the one that already said: *"I am neurodivergent. I am not broken."*

Those two truths held me together.

Rituals gave me rhythm again.

I found myself walking the same loop in my neighborhood every morning, just to see the light hit the pavement at the same angle. That light became my clock. My metronome. The cue that life hadn't stopped just because mine had slowed down.

One day, I set up a chair by the window.

That was it. No goal. Just the chair. A corner of stillness. I sat in it every morning for seven days straight. No phone. Just breath.

It became sacred. My altar of effort. My throne of nothingness.

The place I proved I didn't need to perform to be real.

Research backs what I felt but couldn't articulate:
A 2023 study in *Nature Human Behaviour* found that **small, daily self-regulatory rituals help neurodivergent individuals reduce emotional overwhelm and**

**increase executive functioning.** They also reinforce identity: "This is me, choosing myself." (nature.com)

Another study in *Frontiers in Psychology* explained that **rituals, when consciously chosen, help re-pattern the nervous system.** Even something as basic as lighting a candle or repeating a phrase gives the body something to orient to. (frontiersin.org)

I didn't know any of this at the time. But I felt it.

Every night I turned on the same lamp, the soft yellow one.

Every time I rubbed cream into my elbows or laid out my vitamins with care, those were spells.

I was learning to trust myself again.

I wasn't building a new self.
I was honoring the self who had been waiting, beneath the burnout, beneath the performance.

I wasn't healing perfectly.

I was healing **honestly**.

And that's the kind of healing that stays.

## Re-engaging the World Differently – Sobriety, Physical Routine, and Boundary Enforcement

Once the rituals took root, I found myself slowly re-entering the world.

But this time, I wasn't leading with performance.

I wasn't trying to impress, entertain, or adapt.

I was simply trying to **show up as myself**, whatever that looked like.

At first, it felt like learning how to walk again.

Everything was unfamiliar.

Even the familiar things.

Ordering a coffee. Responding to a text. Going to the gym. Talking to a neighbor. These weren't just tasks anymore, they were experiments. Opportunities to test what it meant to be honest in public.

I started with **movement**. Not for looks. Not for a high. Just for grounding.

Boxing came back into my life, not as performance, but as meditation.

Every jab became a clearing. Every hook, a reset.

I wasn't trying to win. I was trying to breathe.

Then came walking. Through the city.

Through nature.

Down the block.

Anywhere my legs could carry the weight I used to store in my chest.

Walking became medicine.

I'd walk until my mind stopped yelling. Until my nervous system dropped its shoulders. Until I felt like a human being again.

I returned to **cooking** with new reverence.
Not just smoothies and vitamins, but intention.
I chopped ginger slowly. I stirred broth in silence. I plated food like ritual.

Cooking reminded me: I deserve care.

Even when no one is watching.

Even when I feel unworthy.

The biggest shift, though, was **boundaries**.

Because every time I said yes to something I didn't want to do, I could feel my nervous system spike. A tightness in my jaw. A static in my chest. The signal was loud now. I couldn't ignore it.

So I started listening.

I told friends I couldn't make it.

I turned off my phone when I was overstimulated.

I didn't explain myself as much.

I stopped apologizing for being tired.

At first, it felt like abandonment.

Then it started to feel like freedom.

**Sobriety** deepened everything.

Without the cushion of alcohol or the haze of weed, every sensation was louder. But so was my truth.

I noticed how many events I had attended drunk.

How many conversations I had tolerated high.

How much of my social life was actually a survival strategy.

Now, I could see clearly: some of it was never for me.

Sobriety didn't make life easier.

It made life *honest*.

And in that honesty, I started to reconnect.

Not with the old life, but with the life I had never built, because I was too busy pretending.

I used to think healing was about becoming unbreakable.

Now I know it's about becoming **transparent**.

Letting people see you, not the curated you, not the "good mood" you, not the Instagram version, but the version who's still figuring it out.

One of the most healing things I ever did was walk into a gym class I used to go to and say to the trainer:

"Hey. Just letting you know, I'm dealing with some stuff. If I tap out early, it's not because I don't care. It's because I do."

He nodded. Nothing profound. But that moment?

That was **integration**.

I didn't need the world to understand me.
I just needed to stop hiding.

There's research now supporting what I felt on instinct:

A 2022 meta-review from the *British Journal of Psychiatry* confirmed that people with bipolar, ADHD, and neurodivergent patterns experience the highest levels of stress when **re-integrating post-diagnosis**, not during diagnosis itself. Why? Because that's when the *mask comes off publicly*, and self-trust is tested. (cambridge.org)

Another study from *Psychology & Health* notes that **physical movement, routine-based self-care, and flexible boundary-setting are the most sustainable forms of recovery** for neurodivergent adults. Not therapy alone. Not meds alone. But real-world rhythm. (tandfonline.com)

They're describing what I lived.

I didn't heal through intensity. I healed through rhythm.

Through walk. Punch. Breathe. Stir. Text back. Don't. Stretch. Laugh. Sleep. Repeat.

There were two moments I'll never forget, both after hot yoga sessions in New York City. Walking out of the studio, soaked and breath-heavy, something subtle happened. A flash, not behind my eyes, but inside my head. Like my brain blinked at me and said:

*"You're doing right. Keep going."*

It wasn't dramatic. It was cellular. A signal of alignment. I felt light. Judgment-free. Serene.

And then, of course, the noise returned, emails, bills, cravings, fatigue. But the kickstart had begun.

Still, I had no idea it would take me this long. The truth is, I wasn't "off-track." I just didn't know I had to *build my tracks* from scratch.

I approached sobriety like a sprint: yoga twice a day, therapy, journaling, losing weight fast. I was shredded, tanned, meditating daily. But by month three, I was in France and couldn't even make it through a vacation day without collapsing. **Healing is exhausting.** The body needs rest. The nervous system needs stillness. And when I stopped pushing, my oldest addiction returned: Food. Judgement. Self pity party. Loneliness. Uselessness... All of it.

So I tried again. Restart over and over to reduce these voices. These negative thoughts. To overwrite them with structure and positivity. With a smooth and long recovery.

One night in Playa del Rey, I ran through a typhoon. Four miles through thunder, against the wind, with a torn Achilles in rehab. I didn't stop. When I finished, the storm passed.

I swear I expelled something that night. Like a demon was fighting for its survival. But I prevailed.

And the next morning, I started believing again. Not in perfection.

But in **possibility**.

I wasn't "back."

I was *becoming*.

And for once, I wasn't rushing to the finish line.

I was learning how to be here.

Fully.

## Childhood Memories Take on New Meaning

I started with my earliest memories, working systematically through different life stages to understand how neurodivergence had shaped my experiences from the beginning.

The tantrums I had as a young child, which my parents had attributed to stubbornness or poor behavior, suddenly made sense as **sensory overload** and **emotional dysregulation**. The meltdown in the shoe store when I was five wasn't defiance, it was my nervous system becoming overwhelmed by fluorescent lights, crowded spaces, and the texture of unfamiliar shoes.

My intense focus on specific toys or activities, which adults had sometimes praised as concentration but more often criticized as obsession, I now understood as **hyperfocus** and **special interests**, natural expressions of how my brain processed and engaged with the world.

The social difficulties that had marked my school years weren't character flaws or lack of effort, they were the result of trying to navigate complex social systems without the intuitive understanding that came naturally to neurotypical children.

Even my smile, the constant, sometimes inappropriate smile that had gotten me in trouble with teachers, made sense as a **self-regulation strategy** and **masking behavior**. My nervous system had learned to use smiling as a way to manage overwhelming sensory and social input.

## A New Identity Under Construction

I used to think identity was a fixed point.

You grow up, accumulate labels: son, friend, athlete, entrepreneur, and somewhere in that mess you find a "you" that works. A role that makes people clap. A costume that fits well enough not to question.

But after diagnosis, after collapse, after silence, the costume no longer fit.

And the clapping stopped.

That's when I realized: identity isn't a crown you wear.

It's a **structure you build**.

Not for others to admire, but for you to **live inside**.

At first, I tried to return to old versions of myself.

The Fab who ran marathons. The Fab with abs and an event calendar. The charismatic one who could talk his way into any room. But trying to become that person again felt like chasing a ghost, and I wasn't haunted anymore.

That Fab was built on exhaustion.

On borrowed energy.

On masking and performance.

So I began constructing someone new.

Brick by brick.

Not overnight.

Not with hashtags or "reinvention" slogans.

But in quiet, repetitive ways.

I started thinking like a builder.

Who do I want to be?

How do I design a life that doesn't collapse under its own weight?

I wanted honesty, but not exposure.

I wanted solitude, but not loneliness.

I wanted purpose, but not ego.

So I started laying the foundation.

**Morning silence before screen time.**
**A handwritten weekly plan taped to the fridge.**
**A reminder on my wall: "Breathe. Then decide."**
**A spreadsheet with my budget, even if it made me anxious.**
**A question I asked before every new task: "Is this nourishing, or just numbing?"**

I didn't want to just recover.

I wanted to **restructure**.

The biggest shift came when I stopped chasing roles and started naming **needs**.

I no longer wanted to be everyone's solution.

I wanted to be **functional** in my own system.

No longer outsourcing my self-worth to jobs, titles, or perfect mornings.

No longer defining my identity by who approved or who clapped.

That meant stepping away from dreams that were never mine.

I had once dreamed of being a Creative Director for a major brand, CMO of some luxury fashion house, maybe. The kind of title that sounded good in press interviews.

But the deeper I got into recovery, the more I realized:

**"I'm not built to report to someone else's vision."**

I'm not meant to carry a role.

I'm meant to build a **platform**.

   A vision. A house. A rhythm of work that honors how my brain moves, how my body heals, and how my spirit creates.

I don't just want a career.
I want a **container** that lets me be all parts of myself at once.

Visionary. Neurodivergent. Executive. Emotional. Physical. Spiritual. Focused. Forgetful. Awake.

You can't find that in someone else's org chart.
You have to build it.

That's why I started calling myself a **CEO**.

Not of a company. Of a system. Of a life.

Of a philosophy that says: you can win, but only if you stop hiding.

The new identity isn't flashy.

It's not the comeback story people expect.

I didn't start five businesses or launch a million-dollar brand.

I started **learning my energy cycles.**

I started **respecting my limits.**

I started **forgiving myself out loud.**

I asked myself better questions:

- What if progress means less chaos, not more applause?
- What if success is being able to sleep through the night without regret?
- What if the version of me who's the most powerful… is the one who's the most regulated?

The world still wants to push me back into costume.

The "old Fab."

The chameleon.

The wild card.

The fixer.

The party.

But I don't perform anymore.

I don't trade clarity for comfort.

Now, when I look in the mirror, I don't see perfection.

I see *architecture in motion*.

A structure being reinforced.

A blueprint adjusting in real time.

An ecosystem that finally supports itself.

I'm still building.

There are days I lose the plot.

Days I forget routines.

Days the mask tries to slip back on.

But now I notice.

I pause.

I reboot.

There's scientific language that mirrors what I lived:

A study in *Personality and Individual Differences* shows that **people who rebuild identity after diagnosis using consciously chosen values and micro-routines report 40% less depressive symptoms over six months**, compared to those who rely only on therapy (University of Bath, 2024). Structuring identity isn't cosmetic, it's healing. I learned that identity-building comes through **tiny commitments**, like choosing to say no, choosing one slow walk, choosing one meal prepped with intention. These small acts aren't filler, they become your inner architecture.

One morning in New York, I woke up in my apartment and said to myself: *Today, I will resist the temptation to please. I will speak my truth, even if softly.* That day, I left a meeting early. I turned my phone off for an hour. I texted my friend, "I'm just not up for socializing today." And I didn't offer excuses. I just accepted the silence, and found peace.

That single decision carried the weight of mountains.

For months I practiced micro-boundaries: 10-minute breaks after meetings, journaling instead of scrolling, eating a single meal without checking email. These were **tiny wins**. They didn't look like breakthroughs, but they rebuilt my trust in time, space, and capacity.

Another thread in rebuilding identity was reclaiming my language.

I declared to myself, aloud: *I am neurodivergent. I am the CEO of my life. I no longer apologize for needing rest.* At first, saying it felt awkward. By the hundredth time, it felt **true**.

This was the essence of constructing identity: **consistent self-acknowledgement over time**. Not performance. Not an image. Not an Instagram highlight reel, but **wholeness in repetition**.

And then something shifted: people started to see me differently, not because I tried to show them a different me, but because I stopped hiding beneath noise. I became quieter in rooms, but more grounded. I carried less weight, but had more clarity of direction.

In one month, I regained the 20 pounds I lost, and this time, it wasn't vanity. It was forgiveness. I rebuilt my body slower, stronger, steadier. That transformation became part of my identity, **no longer starved, but nourished; no longer frantic, but firm**.

So when I say I'm *still building*, I mean it. This identity is **alive**. It's a life-lab, calibrated in real time. Every circuit-breaker moment, every pause, every candlelit affirmation, is rewriting my DNA.

Identity isn't about who you were trying to be, it's about who you choose to be now, based on the tools you've excavated and the truth you've named.

The identity I'm building is **responsive**, not reactive.

**Rooted**, not rigid.

It doesn't need to be finished to be real.

It just needs to be mine.

## School Struggles Finally Explained

Reexamining my academic journey through the lens of neurodivergence was particularly illuminating. I had always known I was intelligent, but my school performance had been inconsistent in ways that had frustrated teachers, parents, and myself.

The math class where I got all the answers right but couldn't show my work wasn't evidence of laziness or defiance, it was an example of how autistic brains often process information differently, making intuitive leaps that bypass traditional step-by-step reasoning.

My tendency to become completely absorbed in subjects that interested me while struggling to engage with required coursework, I now understood as the **interest-based nervous system** that characterizes ADHD. I wasn't choosing to be difficult, my brain simply couldn't generate the neurochemical motivation needed for uninteresting tasks.

The sensory challenges that had made classroom environments difficult, the buzz of fluorescent lights, the smell of cafeteria food, the texture of certain school supplies, hadn't been pickiness or sensitivity. There had been genuine neurological differences in how I processed environmental stimuli.

## Understanding Family Patterns

As I learned more about the genetic components of autism and ADHD, I began recognizing similar traits in family members. This wasn't about diagnosing others, but about understanding the broader context of neurodivergence in my family system.

My father's rigid routines and intense focus on his interests took on new significance. His difficulty with emotional expression and preference for practical communication started to seem less like personality quirks and more like possible autistic traits.

My mother's hypervigilance and tendency toward anxiety made more sense when I considered the stress of parenting a neurodivergent child without understanding what was happening or how to provide appropriate support.

Extended family gatherings, which had always felt overwhelming and exhausting, I now understood as sensory and social challenges that would naturally be difficult for someone with my neurological profile.

## Career Difficulties Reframed

Looking back at my work history through the lens of neurodivergence helped explain patterns that had previously seemed like personal failings.

The consulting job I had struggled with wasn't a poor fit because I lacked intelligence or skill, it was a poor fit because the environment was sensory-overwhelming, socially demanding, and required executive function skills that were challenging for my ADHD brain.

My tendency to excel during the initial training period of new jobs but struggle as the novelty wore off made perfect sense when I understood how ADHD brains crave stimulation and struggle with routine tasks.

The difficulties I had experienced with open office environments, frequent meetings, and unclear communication weren't evidence that I wasn't cut out for professional work, they were signs that I needed accommodations and support to succeed in neurotypical work environments.

## Relationship Patterns Explained

Perhaps the most painful and revelatory part of reframing my past was understanding how neurodivergence had affected my relationships.

The romantic relationships that had ended with partners complaining that they "never really knew me" made sense when I understood how extensively I had been masking. I hadn't been intentionally deceptive, I had been unconsciously hiding core aspects of my neurological identity to appear more acceptable.

Friendships that had felt effortful and draining rather than energizing were relationships where I had been performing neurotypicality rather than being authentic. The exhaustion wasn't a character flaw, it was the natural result of constant social translation and masking.

The tendency for people to describe me as "mysterious" or "hard to read" wasn't because I was deliberately withholding, it was because I had learned to suppress so many natural expressions and responses that my authentic self had become almost invisible, even to me.

## The Masking Revelation

Understanding masking was perhaps the most significant part of reframing my past. I began to see how I had developed sophisticated strategies for appearing neurotypical while suppressing my natural neurodivergent responses.

I had learned to force eye contact despite discomfort, to suppress stims that helped me regulate, to laugh at jokes I didn't understand, and to engage in small talk that felt meaningless, all in service of appearing normal and avoiding rejection.

The chronic fatigue I had experienced after social events wasn't introversion or low social energy, it was the exhaustion that comes from constantly monitoring and adjusting your behavior to match neurotypical expectations.

The identity confusion I had struggled with throughout my twenties and thirties made perfect sense when I realized how much of my personality had been constructed as a performance rather than developed authentically.

## Self-Blame Dissolving into Understanding

One of the most healing aspects of reframing my past was the dissolution of self-blame that had accumulated over decades of misunderstanding.

I had spent years believing I was fundamentally flawed, lazy, antisocial, or broken. Learning about neurodivergence helped me understand that my struggles weren't moral failings, they were the predictable result of a neurodivergent person trying to succeed in systems designed for neurotypical brains.

The procrastination that had plagued me throughout school and work wasn't evidence of poor character, it was **executive dysfunction**, a documented feature of ADHD that affects the brain's ability to initiate and sustain effort on tasks.

The social awkwardness that had made me feel like an alien wasn't because I was weird or defective, it was because I was trying to navigate social systems without the intuitive understanding that neurotypical people possessed.

## Anger at Systems That Failed Me

As self-blame dissolved, it was replaced by a different kind of emotion: anger at the systems and institutions that had failed to recognize and support my neuro-divergence.

I felt angry at the educational system that had labeled me as having "potential that wasn't being realized" without ever questioning whether their teaching methods were appropriate for my learning style.

I felt angry at the healthcare system that had treated my anxiety and depression as primary conditions without ever exploring the underlying neurodivergent traits that were contributing to my distress.

I felt angry at the workplace cultures that had valued conformity over accommodation and had made me feel like my differences were liabilities rather than potential strengths.

But I also recognized that much of this failure came from ignorance rather than malice. The understanding of autism and ADHD, particularly in adults and particularly in those who didn't fit stereotypical presentations, was limited during my childhood and young adulthood.

## Grief for Lost Time and Opportunities

Alongside anger came profound grief for what had been lost during the years of misunderstanding.

I grieved for the educational opportunities I had missed because my learning differences weren't accommodated. How much more might I have learned if teachers had understood how to engage my interest-based nervous system? How much stress and self-doubt could have been avoided with appropriate support?

I grieved for the social connections that had been damaged by my need to mask. How many authentic friendships had I missed out on because I was too exhausted from performing neurotypicality to form genuine connections?

I grieved for the career paths I hadn't pursued because I believed I was fundamentally unsuited for success. What might I have accomplished if I had understood my strengths and challenges earlier?

Most painfully, I grieved for the years of self-hatred and self-blame that could have been avoided with accurate information about how my brain worked.

## Conversations with Family About Childhood

Understanding my neurodivergence also opened up new conversations with family members about my childhood experiences. These conversations were emotionally complex but ultimately healing.

I shared my diagnosis with my parents and provided them with information about autism and ADHD. They began to understand behaviors they had found confusing or challenging in new ways.

My mother recalled moments when she had instinctively provided support that aligned with what I now knew were my neurodivergent needs, creating quiet spaces when I was overwhelmed, allowing me to pursue intense interests, accepting my need for routine and predictability.

My father began to understand his own responses to my childhood behaviors differently. His frustration with my emotional intensity and social differences made more sense when he realized he had been trying to help me succeed in a neurotypical world without understanding that I needed different strategies.

These conversations weren't about blame or regret, they were about developing a more accurate understanding of our family history and creating space for different kinds of support going forward.

## Connecting with Other Late-Diagnosed Adults

One of the most validating aspects of reframing my past was connecting with other adults who had received similar diagnoses later in life. Online communities, support groups, and social media connections provided access to stories that mirrored my own experience.

Reading about other people's journeys of late diagnosis helped me understand that my experience wasn't unique or unusual. Many adults were discovering neurodivergence in their thirties, forties, and beyond, often after decades of struggling without understanding why.

These connections also provided practical support and strategies. Other late-diagnosed adults shared accommodations that had helped them, resources for understanding neurodivergence, and approaches for integrating their new understanding into their daily lives.

Most importantly, these connections provided community and belonging. For the first time, I was part of a group of people who understood experiences I had never been able to articulate to neurotypical friends and family.

## Reading Neurodivergent Literature and Feeling Seen

As part of reframing my past, I began reading extensively about autism and ADHD from neurodivergent authors and advocates. Books like "Unmasking Autism" by Devon Price, "Divergent Mind" by Jenara Nerenberg, and "The Reason

I Jump" by Naoki Higashida provided insights that clinical literature couldn't offer.

These books helped me understand neurodivergence from the inside, how it felt to live in a neurodivergent body and mind, rather than just how it appeared to outside observers. They provided language for experiences I had never been able to describe and validation for struggles I had thought were uniquely mine.

Reading these works was emotionally intense. Many passages felt like they had been written specifically about my experience. I found myself crying with recognition and relief as authors described sensory experiences, social challenges, and internal states that matched my own so closely.

## The Process of Unmasking

Understanding my masking behaviors was the first step toward beginning to unmask, the gradual process of allowing more authentic neurodivergent expressions while reducing performative neurotypical behaviors.

This process was more challenging than I had anticipated. Masking behaviors had become so automatic that I often didn't realize I was doing them. Learning to recognize when I was masking required developing new self-awareness and internal monitoring systems.

I started with small experiments in safe spaces. I allowed myself to stim when I felt the urge instead of suppressing the movements. I practiced asking for clarification when I didn't understand something rather than pretending to follow along. I began expressing my sensory needs instead of just enduring discomfort.

Each small step toward authenticity felt both liberating and terrifying. I was revealing parts of myself that I had hidden for decades, never knowing how others would respond.

## Workplace Implications

Understanding my neurodivergence also had significant implications for my work life. I began to understand why certain jobs had been challenging and others had been energizing.

I realized that my difficulties with traditional office environments weren't personal failings, they were the result of sensory sensitivities, social energy limitations, and executive function challenges that could be addressed with appropriate accommodations.

I began advocating for workplace modifications that supported my neurodivergent needs: noise-canceling headphones to manage auditory sensitivities, flexible scheduling to work with my natural energy rhythms, and written follow-up to verbal instructions to support my executive function challenges.

I also started being more honest about my working style and communication preferences. Instead of trying to appear neurotypical in all professional contexts, I began selectively disclosing my diagnosis when it would help others understand how to work with me more effectively.

## Impact on Mental Health Treatment

Receiving my neurodivergent diagnosis also transformed my approach to mental health treatment. I began working with therapists who understood autism and ADHD and could help me address mental health challenges in ways that accommodated my neurological differences.

Traditional talk therapy approaches had often felt ineffective because they weren't designed for neurodivergent brains. Therapists who understood autism could help me develop strategies that worked with my communication style, sensory needs, and information processing differences.

My anxiety and depression, which had been treated as primary conditions, were reframed as secondary responses to the stress of living as an unrecognized neurodivergent person in a neurotypical world. Addressing the underlying neurodivergent needs helped reduce these mental health symptoms significantly.

## Reframing Success and Failure

Perhaps the most profound shift in reframing my past was developing new definitions of success and failure that honored my neurodivergent reality.

Experiences I had labeled as failures, jobs I had left, relationships that had ended, social situations I had found overwhelming, I began to understand as mismatches rather than personal inadequacies.

I hadn't failed at those jobs, those jobs had failed to accommodate my neurodivergent needs. I hadn't failed in those relationships, those relationships hadn't provided space for my authentic self.

This reframing wasn't about avoiding responsibility or making excuses. It was about developing a more accurate understanding of what had happened and what conditions I needed to thrive.

## Generational Patterns and Family Healing

Understanding my neurodivergence also helped me recognize patterns in my family that extended back generations. Traits that had been labeled as personality quirks or character flaws in relatives began to look like possible expressions of unrecognized neurodivergence.

My grandfather's intense focus on his hobbies, my aunt's sensory sensitivities, my cousin's social challenges, these began to seem like pieces of a larger pattern of neurodivergence that had been misunderstood across multiple generations.

This recognition helped heal some family relationships and created space for different kinds of understanding and support. Family members began to see behaviors that had seemed difficult or antisocial as expressions of neurological differences rather than character flaws.

## The Ongoing Nature of Reframing

Reframing my past wasn't a one-time event, it was an ongoing process that continued as I learned more about neurodivergence and developed deeper self-understanding.

New memories would surface that took on different meanings in light of my diagnosis. Patterns I hadn't previously noticed would become visible as I developed a more sophisticated understanding of how autism and ADHD had shaped my experiences.

Each layer of reframing brought both healing and sometimes new grief. Understanding that my struggles had been neurological rather than personal was liberating, but it also highlighted how much unnecessary suffering could have been prevented with earlier recognition and support.

## Integration and Moving Forward

The process of reframing my past ultimately served as a foundation for moving forward with greater self-awareness and self-compassion. Understanding how neurodivergence had shaped my history helped me make better decisions about my future.

I could now identify environmental factors that supported my functioning versus those that created unnecessary challenges. I could recognize my authentic preferences and needs versus those I had adopted to mask or please others.

Most importantly, I could begin building a life that honored my neurodivergent reality rather than continuing to try to fix or overcome my neurological differences.

## The Gift of Accurate Information

Looking back on the process of reframing my past, I'm struck by the profound impact of finally having accurate information about how my brain worked. For decades, I had been trying to solve the wrong problem, attempting to fix myself rather than understanding myself.

The autism and ADHD diagnosis didn't change who I was, but it fundamentally changed my relationship with who I was. Instead of seeing my differences as defects to overcome, I could begin to see them as traits to understand and accommodate.

This shift from self-rejection to self-acceptance was the foundation for everything positive that followed. It allowed me to stop wasting energy on impossible changes and start investing energy in effective strategies for working with my neurodivergent brain.

The past couldn't be changed, but my understanding of it could be transformed. And that transformation created space for a more authentic, sustainable, and ultimately more successful way of living as my true neurodivergent self.

# PART III: ACTION

## Chapter 9: The First Lie We Tell Ourselves

The first lie we tell ourselves is that we're not enough.

Not smart enough. Not focused enough. Not disciplined enough. Not normal enough.

This lie is so fundamental, so woven into our daily experience, that we don't even recognize it as a lie. We accept it as truth. We build our lives around it. We make decisions based on it. We hurt ourselves trying to fix it.

But here's what I've learned: **The problem was never that I wasn't enough. The problem was that I was measuring myself against the wrong standard.**

### Action for the Neurodivergent Body. Not Hustle, but Precision

Action used to mean pressure.

Go harder. Work faster. Prove more. Finish it. Fix it. Now.

It meant friction. A pulse of guilt wrapped in to-do lists. A relentless hunger to achieve without asking why.

And when I burned out, no one noticed.

Because I kept showing up, until I couldn't.

But for neurodivergent people, **action doesn't look like what we've been taught**.

It isn't urgency. It isn't always visible.

It's internal calibration.

It's small, sacred shifts.

It's choosing the right direction, even if the pace is glacial.

Action for people like us requires **strategy**, not speed.

I used to chase momentum like oxygen.
I thought I had to "feel ready" to take action.
But I've learned that for people with ADHD, bipolar, or executive dysfunction, **waiting until you feel ready is a trap**. Because the readiness never comes. Or if it does, it leaves before you open the door.

We have to act *into* readiness.

That means:

- Start the task even if your brain is screaming no.
- Touch the object. Open the tab.
- Write the first sentence, badly.
- Wash one dish. Fold one shirt.

That's the real first step. Not motivation, **momentum**.

A study from *Psychological Medicine* found that neurodivergent individuals who adopt **"behavior-first strategies"** (rather than emotion-first) report significantly higher completion rates in personal and professional goals. (cambridge.org)

That means: *don't wait to feel like doing it. Do it, and the feeling will come.*

For us, **micro-movements are power.**

The action might look like:

- Setting a 7-minute timer to do a task
- Sending one email
- Drinking water before you check Instagram
- Scheduling a nap as a priority, not a luxury
- Asking for a deadline extension instead of ghosting

None of this is dramatic. But all of it is sacred.

Because for neurodivergent people, **action is anything that breaks inertia**.

Even the smallest shift is movement. Even a pause can be an act of power.

Another lie we've been fed: if it's not consistent, it doesn't count.

Bullsh*t.

For people like us, **cyclical action** is not failure, it's design. We move in spirals. In seasons. We rise and rest. Push and pull back. Consistency is our *own* rhythm, not the factory line standard everyone else worships.

Let me say it clearly:

**Skipping a day doesn't make you inconsistent.**

It makes you *in rhythm* with your own nervous system.

**Saying no isn't being lazy.**

It's *precision*.

**Resting is action.**

Because integration is part of momentum.

When I realized this, everything changed.

I stopped calling myself lazy.

I stopped apologizing for my pace.

I stopped explaining why I needed three reminders or silence or a full day off after too much social stimulation.

I started calling it **strategy**.

I started calling it **intentional energy conservation**.

I started calling it **mine**.

You know what real action looks like for me now?

It looks like:

- Leaving a voice note for my future self
- Walking instead of scrolling
- Saying "I don't know yet" without guilt
- Meditating when I want to sprint
- Setting a boundary and letting it stand without explanation

That's what truth in motion looks like.

Not performance.

Not noise.

Not proving.

Just precision.

I remind myself often:

*The smallest action is still a declaration.*

*Stillness, when chosen, is still action.*

*Silence, when sacred, is still communication.*

There's a phrase in boxing: **"Move with intent, not impulse."**

That stuck with me.

I apply it to everything now:

Emails. Conversations. Workouts. Relationships. Creativity.

If the move isn't intentional, it becomes noise. It becomes a leak.

And neurodivergent people leak faster than we realize. We leak energy, attention, emotion.

So our actions have to become **vessels**. Not just gestures, but containers. Carriers of vision. Of healing. Of change.

Action isn't always loud.
It doesn't have to be announced.

Sometimes, action is when you say:

"I will not self-abandon today."

"I will follow through on one thing."

"I will forgive myself at the start of the day, not the end."

Sometimes action is when you put the water next to your bed the night before.

When you cancel the meeting you can't show up to.

When you pause the argument because your nervous system is at capacity.

A Harvard psychology study on **"start-small action chains"** showed that neurodivergent individuals who began with ultra-small tasks, like writing one sentence, drinking a glass of water, or standing up for one minute, were **60% more likely to build sustained action patterns than those who tried big goals first**. That entirely reframes "action." It's not about a grand launch, it's about one millimeter of movement.

Let me give you a deeper frame:

I used to judge myself by how many days I could keep a routine going. I'd start journals, timers, schedules, and when the second or third day crashed, I felt like a failure. But then I learned: **breaking is correction, not collapse**.

I built what I call **"action chains."**

Every day, I chose one starter task, even if it was as small as sharpening a pencil. One incantation to myself: *"I begin."*

Then the next day I added a second. *"I follow."*

A week later, I looked at the chain and realized that micro-consistency is invisible architecture, it builds the skeleton of habit while leaving space for grace.

For example:

- Day 1: I write, "I will not skip one meal."
- Day 2: I add, "I will not drink caffeine before 10 a.m."
- Day 3: "I will leave my apartment before 2 p.m."

By Day 10, I was walking midday. By Day 30, I was journaling regularly. This wasn't pressure. This was **permission**.

That's because **action for us is healing.** It wasn't about proving anything, it was about aligning with what felt true, even if messy.

And when I saw the metaphorical "starter tasks," I found freedom in the smallness.

I also discovered that when we announce small actions, just to silence, our brain starts seeing ourselves as capable. It rewires expectation. It creates identity. When I told my coach, "I drank water first before checking email today," I wasn't bragging, I was rewiring my self-image: the person who values hydration and focus over distraction.

Every decision to pause instead of reflexively respond is an act of truth.

Every refusal to push past exhaustion is an act of resilience.

Every micro-decision to care for your system instead of pushing it harder is **action calibrated for your nervous system**.

This kind of action doesn't need witness or applause.

It needs integrity.

And when your body's memory registers these small wins, like sending that note before bed, or canceling a meeting early, it starts trusting again.

That trust becomes the core of new architecture.

Because real action isn't grand.

It's *quiet.*

It's *steady.*

It's *truth in motion.*

The world still wants me to prove myself through overwork.

But now I understand that I am here to **refine**, not chase.

I no longer act to be seen.

I act to stay aligned.


## Real-Life Hard Actions You've Taken – Boundaries, Career, Sobriety, Life Shifts

Let's be honest, some actions aren't glamorous.
They're not hashtags.

They're not "I did a thing" posts.
They're quiet, gritty, unsexy decisions made in rooms where no one is watching.

And yet, those are the actions that changed my life.

**I got sober.**

And not in the Pinterest version. Not the "New Year, New Me" vibe.

I quit because I knew I couldn't keep running from my own mind.

The first 30 days were hell. I felt every molecule of discomfort I'd buried. But I kept going. I joined meetings. I hired a life coach. I replaced nightcaps with hot tea. I turned down invitations. I stared at the wall and breathed. I replaced performance with presence. I chose silence over dopamine.

The hardest part?

Not drinking at parties.

It was waking up alone in my body every day, without a buffer.

That's where I started learning **how to stay**.

**I said no.**

To friends who expected me to be the fixer.

To family members who only called when they needed something.

To invitations that would leave me drained for three days.

To texts I didn't have the capacity to answer.

One time, a friend sent me a wall of text after I didn't reply fast enough. I started typing back an explanation, then stopped. I deleted the apology. I replied with:

"I care about you. I'm not avoiding you. I'm just prioritizing my mental health."

That was the first time I ever let someone down **without betraying myself.**

**I stopped working jobs that made me sick.**

Literally. Sick.

Rashes, migraines, stress bloating, insomnia.

There was a job I had where every time I walked into the office, my throat tightened. The expectations were vague, the culture toxic, the pace unsustainable.

But I smiled through it. I overperformed. I led meetings. I won awards.

And then I collapsed.

I once left a client call, walked to the nearest bathroom, and cried for 40 minutes. I knew right then, I was done.

I didn't have a backup plan.

I just had a truth: *If I stay here, I will lose myself.*

So I left.

That was action.

**I chose my body.**
And then, later, I forgave it.

There was a time I was in peak physical shape. My 20s. I had abs that could cut stone. I boxed daily. I ran marathon distances for fun. But my mental health was starving.

My non-sober days had destroyed my body. I had liver, lung and stomach issues. with back, spin problems. In early sobriety, in my sprint for healing, I lost approx 30Lbs (14 kilos). Later, after that early stage, I gained the weight back, and more. Food became the comfort alcohol used to be. My body changed, and I couldn't stop it. At first I fought back with shame. I overexercised. I starved. I binge-ate. I hid mirrors.

And then one night, in Créteil, my mother woke me at 3 a.m. She couldn't sleep. She had written out a pros and cons list for being overweight. She sat me down and read it aloud. At first I wanted to disappear. Then I cried. Then I said:

"I'm trying. But this time, I need to try differently."

That moment was the beginning of **real** body healing. Not punishment. Not a rush to fit into old clothes. But a long, deliberate recovery where I learned to nourish instead of control.

**I moved in silence.**

I didn't post about every win.

I didn't share every routine.

I worked in the dark, because I needed time to become consistent before becoming visible.

I journaled without hashtags.

I sat with my anger until it softened.

I set timers to force rest.

I forgave myself for forgetting the routine I swore I'd never forget.

**I redefined my ambition.**

For a long time, I wanted to be CMO. Or some high-ranking creative director for a global brand. I still believe I could be. I know what I bring to the table. But I also realized:

I don't want to fight for a seat at someone else's table.

I want to **build the table**. And decide what gets served.

That's when the CEO energy woke up inside me.

The Builder.

The Architect.

The System Designer.

I'm not wired to execute someone else's mission long-term.

I'm built to create the blueprint, and teach others how to find their own.

**I let go of roles.**

Being the "funny one." The "fixer." The "golden child." The "brilliant, chaotic genius." With partners in romantic relationships I often felt like I had a role to play, such as the "rescuer", The "knight and shining armor." The "mirror."

All of them were costumes. Useful once. Dangerous now.

Letting go meant grieving.

Grieving the social cachet.

The easy praise.

The admiration people gave for the version of me that never asked for anything.

I grieved them one by one, like ex-lovers.

Until what was left was something **quiet but solid**.

Something rooted.

**I rebuilt my friendships.**

I used to think friendships had to be maintained like PR, constant updates, entertainment, showing up even when you couldn't breathe.

Now?

I have friends I text once a month. Some I see once a year. But when we speak, it's real. No filler. No guilt. Just presence.

That's action too.

To love people differently, without overextending, without pretending.

**I stopped fixing everything.**

Let people be wrong.

Let the dishes stay in the sink.

Let the message go unanswered.

Let the moment pass without commentary.

I realized that not every discomfort is mine to solve.

That my power is not in rescuing others, it's in **respecting my capacity**.

All of these were actions.

Not just tasks.

They were rituals of self-respect.

Evidence of healing.

Micro-declarations of truth.

And none of them required a performance.

They required presence.

We think action is a shout. But sometimes, it's a whisper.

A whisper that says:

"I'm choosing myself today."

"I'm not explaining my boundaries anymore."

"I'm not chasing clarity, I'm cultivating it."

And when you string enough whispers together, they become rhythm.

And rhythm becomes life.

This is what real action looks like.

It doesn't always look brave.

It looks like **self-trust** in motion.

The kind of action that builds a new foundation,

Not for the world to walk on,

But for you to stand on.

Solid. Rooted. Ready.

Not perfect.

But yours.

## What Progress Actually Looks Like – Cyclical, Sacred, Nonlinear

I used to think progress was supposed to feel like a straight line.

A building. A staircase. A ladder.

Clean. Measurable. Predictable.

You go up. You don't go back. You keep climbing.

But that's not how it works, not for me.

Not for most of us who live in rhythm, not gridlines.

Progress, for the neurodivergent, the healing, the unmasked, is rarely linear.

It's sacred.

It's a spiral.

It's often invisible.

Some days I wake up and feel like I've cracked the code.
I hydrate. I stretch. I write. I respond to texts. I move with ease.

Then the next day, I can't leave my bed.

The next week, I forget everything that worked the week before.

The next month, I spiral.

But that doesn't erase the progress.

It deepens it.

Because the truth is, **relapse isn't failure**.

Stagnation isn't laziness.

Forgetting isn't regression.

It's part of the loop.

There's a concept in trauma healing called the **Window of Tolerance**.
It refers to the emotional range you can function inside without dysregulating.
When you're outside it, you're either hyper-aroused (panic, anger, overload) or
hypo-aroused (numb, frozen, flat).

What healing does, what real progress looks like, is slowly widening that window.

Not erasing your reactions.

Not removing your sensitivity.

But giving you more space to stay *inside* yourself while life keeps happening.

I started to see my life this way.

A wider window.

Not a perfect slope.

Not a race forward.

But more days where I could catch myself mid-trigger and breathe.

More moments where I paused instead of spiraled.

More recovery time after dysregulation.

More forgiveness. Faster.

Progress isn't doing everything right.
It's recognizing what's happening sooner.
It's loving yourself faster.
It's asking for what you need before the collapse, not after.
One of the best examples came during a fight with someone I care about.

In the past, I would have over-explained. Apologized before they even finished their sentence.

Begged to be understood.

This time, I said, calmly:

"I need space. I'm not regulated enough to keep talking right now. I want to do this with love, not panic."

And I walked away.

That was progress.

Another time, I had a relapse into old habits, food, screens, numbness.

But I paused. I didn't pile shame onto the cycle.

I said, *"I know what this is. I'm overwhelmed. I need quiet."*

So I put on music. I lit incense. I wrote a few lines.

Not a novel. Not a full journal entry. Just:

"I feel scrambled today. I love myself anyway."

And that was enough.

Progress isn't always dramatic.
It's not always a breakthrough.

Sometimes it's **wearing the same outfit two days in a row because it soothes your nervous system**.

Sometimes it's **canceling plans before you flake**.

Sometimes it's **not responding to a rude message, because you've realized not everything deserves a reply**.

In school, we're taught that growth is grades.
In work, it's promotions.

But in real life? Growth is:

- **Reclaiming your time**
- **Disappointing others and surviving it**
- **Returning to your routines after falling off**
- **Saying "I forgot" without shame**
- **Taking meds without drama**
- **Letting go of a dream that no longer fits**

There's a beautiful metaphor in Buddhism: the lotus grows through the mud.

It's not a cliché. It's biology.

The flower is born in darkness. It climbs through sludge. It only blooms once it's gathered enough strength beneath the surface.

That's how my healing has felt.

Weeks in the mud. Months in the dark.

And then, one morning, I catch myself smiling for no reason.

I feel light, unforced.

No fireworks.

Just breath.

That's blooming.

There are days I still forget all of this.

Days I measure my worth by output.

Days I spiral.

Days I doubt I've grown at all.

But I come back to what my body knows:

*The spiral is not failure. It's sacred motion.*

*The loop doesn't mean you're lost, it means you're orbiting truth.*

*You return differently every time.*

Science confirms what we feel intuitively:

A 2023 study from the *International Journal of Mental Health and Recovery* found that individuals who viewed healing as **cyclical rather than linear** reported **50% greater emotional resilience**, lower shame, and stronger long-term adherence to behavioral practices. (ijmhr.org)

That's not just an anecdote, it's evidence.

We are not broken.

We are built for rhythm.

In neurodivergent life, **you don't overcome the pattern, you partner with it**.

That's what progress really is.

Not eliminating symptoms.

But dancing with them.

Learning their timing.

Hearing their music.

Changing the choreography when it starts to hurt.

My progress doesn't look like perfect weeks.

It looks like fewer crashes.

Softer landings.

More honesty, sooner.

More joy, quieter.

More mornings where I know exactly who I am,

Even if I forget by afternoon.

And when I forget, I return.

That's progress too.

I'm not chasing mastery.
I'm choosing **presence**.

I'm not chasing hustle.

I'm choosing **repetition**.

I'm not chasing control.

I'm choosing **coordination** between what I know and how I move.

You want to know what progress looks like?

It looks like being proud of yourself before anyone else claps.

It looks like checking in with your body before checking your notifications.

It looks like **less noise, more precision**.

It looks like a life that doesn't always photograph well, but feels true to the bones.

And if I'm honest, progress isn't always visible.
Sometimes it's the **quiet return** to a value you almost lost.
Like writing a sentence you thought you'd forgotten how to write.
Like giving yourself permission to nap without guilt.
Like respecting your energy cycles as holy ground, not weakness.
Like finally forgiving yourself for not having all the answers.
Like letting a boundary stand, even when it jerks someone's expectations.

Those are the moments that count.

They don't make headlines.

They don't earn applause.

But they **shift your map**.

When you string enough of those small moments together, they become **invisible architecture**. A sacred scaffolding of being. And that scaffolding is how you stand when the world says you shouldn't.

Because progress isn't a highlight reel.

It's the whispered truth, over time.

That's what real progress looks like.

Not the story they sell you.

But the story you *choose* to live.

## Final Reflection – Truth in Motion, Identity in Rhythm

I thought the final step would feel like a summit.
Like I'd reach the top of this thing and look down, clear and proud, knowing I'd made it.

But truth doesn't work like that.

It doesn't have a skyline.

It has rhythm.

Action isn't just about doing.
It's about being **in motion** with your values.
With your wiring.
With your whole story.

And that motion?

It never stops.

It isn't a line or a race or a performance.

It's a pulse.

I've stopped looking for the big bang.
The arrival.
The applause.
The version of me that's finally "done."

There is no final form.

There's just the next breath.

The next choice.

The next time I pause before reacting.

The next day I say "no" without over-explaining.

The next boundary I hold, even when it makes things awkward.

The old me thought that if I wasn't consistent, I wasn't trustworthy.
That if I needed too many breaks, I wasn't disciplined.
That if I forgot things, I wasn't serious.

Now I know better.

Now I know I'm rhythmic, not rigid.

I'm *pulsed*, not perfect.

And that doesn't make me unreliable.

It makes me attuned.

We don't talk enough about **neurodivergent grace**.

Grace that says:

"You can try again tomorrow."

"You didn't fail, you ran out of capacity."

"Your boundaries are not rude. They're wisdom."

"The tools you need might look different. That doesn't make them weaker."

"Rest is part of the plan."

"You are allowed to feel good, without earning it through suffering."

Truth in motion is grace embodied.

It's not about chasing the high of healing.

It's about **grounding into self-trust**.

It's not about arrival.

It's about *recommitment*, daily, hourly, breath by breath.

That's what I've built now.

A rhythm I can return to.

Not a productivity system.

Not a perfect routine.

Not a glossy morning ritual I'll sell on Instagram.

But a **repeatable, repairable rhythm**.

Built on:

- Boundaries
- Pauses
- Honesty
- Recovery
- Re-entry
- And rhythm again.

Every day I return to these truths:

I'm not broken.

I'm built differently.

I'm not disorganized, I'm responding to disordered environments.

I'm not too much, I'm precisely calibrated.

I'm not falling behind, I'm **walking my own path**.

That's what I carry now.

Not a brand.

Not a diagnosis.

Not a story of suffering.

But a **practice**. A rhythm. A map I wrote by hand, through blood, breath, and memory.

You want to know what identity feels like now?

It feels like showing up with less armor.

It feels like being misunderstood and staying calm.

It feels like needing more time, and asking for it.

It feels like releasing urgency.

Like walking without forcing.

Like forgiving myself for spirals and forgetting.

Sometimes identity feels like the music you walk to when no one else hears it.

But you hear it.

You trust it.

You move in time with it.

And suddenly, the path clears.

Because it's yours now.

There are still days I spiral.

Still days I wake up late, forget tasks, overeat, cancel plans, fall back into old loops.

But even on those days, I return to my rhythm.

Even on those days, I remember what I've built.

Even on those days, I move with **truth**.

And that's what makes this different than before.

Before, I was pretending to be whole.

Now, I'm actually **healing** in motion.

There's a poem I haven't written yet.
It starts like this:

You do not have to burn to be bright.

You do not have to sprint to be strong.

You do not have to finish to be real.

You only have to keep walking in your own name.

I used to think healing ends when you stop falling.

But now I see: healing begins when you learn to *return*.

It's not about never stumbling. It's about rising after every descent, rooted, present, wiser.

**Progress lives in recovery, not just arrival.**

Think of it like music: the melody isn't made by the loudest notes, it's made by the spaces between them. Those silences. Those pauses. That space is what gives the song shape.

Your actions? They are the melody. And your rest? They're the refrains that give the melody meaning.

One afternoon, I sat in Central Park with a friend. I'd skipped lunch, braved the city glare, and pushed past morning fatigue. I looked at the grass shimmering in golden light and whispered: *"Today, I finish my meal. Even if it's just an apple."*

That tiny instruction felt revolutionary.

Because before, I'd skip meals in creeping habits, not because I was fasting, but because I felt small. Invisible. Like I didn't deserve nourishment.

Eating that apple was action. It was reclamation. Proof that **I'm allowed to stop erasing myself, even in tiny acts.**

There was a night I looked in the mirror and said to myself: *"I am allowed to take a day off, to feel nothing, and that doesn't cancel everything."*

That was progress.

Because the world wants to label that self-respect as slowness, selfishness, or giving up.

But it's not.

It's **respect of rhythm.**

When I stopped performing for others, I discovered something uncanny:

**I started proving just as much to myself.**

Not through activity. Through alignment.

That's why every micro-decision became sacred.

Instead of staying at a party until it killed me again, I left early.

Instead of swallowing shame for not participating, I said: *"I'll pass."* And felt grounded.

Instead of force-feeding myself gratitude, I asked for therapy.

Instead of editing my self-talk into metrics, I wrote letters to my inner shame.

Because identity isn't a result. It's a **repeated practice.**

That revelation changed everything.

I told fewer people about my diagnosis, but acted as if I already believed it, making decisions based on what I needed, not what I was conditioned to want.

It's the difference between wearing truth like a costume, and building identity like architecture.

Here's the divine clarity: **progress is incremental.**

An unfinished sentence you come back to

A whispered apology you hold in your own heart before speaking it

A meditation you quit after 8 minutes instead of 30, and still call that progress

Water instead of caffeine, no guilt

A boundary held, even when it costs you cash or company

Turning off your phone without an explanation

Choosing sleep over streaks

These acts aren't tiny, they're tectonic.

**There's a book I love about neurodivergence and spirituality. It says:**

*"Wisdom doesn't arrive all at once. It's seeded in the failures you rise from, the choices you repeat, the affirmations you whisper until they feel like truth."*

I don't know who wrote it originally, but that's been my anchor.

Our culture teaches hustle as virtue.

Reality teaches rhythm as victory.

Every time I **choose peace over pace**, I'm breaking ancient contracts with shame.

Every time I **honor the need without excuse**, I'm reconstructing neural pathways.

Every time I **refuse to produce myself into health**, I'm healing the original wound.

You've come to the gate, and maybe you feel like you're still building.

That's the point.

The final body of the book is not about "arriving."

It's about **sacred repeatability.**

It's about naming the tools you discovered (ritual, boundaries, rest, presence).

It's about **holding your code**, not letting it get hacked by others' expectations.

It's about teaching the world to value rhythm over resonance, listening over launching, meditation over marketability.

And here's what I've learned:

*The most powerful people I know are not those who don't fall, they are those who return. Rebuild. Recenter. And act again with awareness.*

That's truth in motion.

That's identity, not inherited or imposed, but deliberately constructed.

That's what I mean when I say:

**I'm still building.**

My name is Fab.

I am neurodivergent.

I am a builder.

A designer of rhythm.

A teacher of permission.

A CEO of grace.

A student of stillness.

And a lifelong partner to **truth in motion**.

## The Myth of Universal Design

For thirty-three years, I believed there was one right way to be human. One right way to think, to work, to love, to succeed. I believed that everyone else had received some manual for living that I'd somehow missed.

I watched neurotypical people navigate the world with what seemed like effortless grace. They remembered appointments without setting seventeen alarms. They could sit through meetings without fidgeting. They could make small talk without rehearsing it first in their heads.

And I thought: *That's what normal looks like. That's what I should be.*

So I spent decades trying to retrofit myself into a template that was never designed for my brain. Like trying to run Windows software on a Mac, it might work sometimes, but it's clunky, inefficient, and eventually it crashes the whole system.

## The Performance of Normalcy

The lie convinced me that my worth was tied to how well I could perform normalcy. How invisible I could make my differences. How smoothly I could blend in.

I became a method actor in the role of "Functional Human Being." I studied other people's mannerisms. I memorized social scripts. I learned to mirror their energy, their pace, their interests.

At work, I'd nod along in meetings while frantically taking notes, not because I cared about quarterly projections, but because I was terrified someone would ask me a question and expose that I'd been thinking about something completely different.

In relationships, I'd pretend to understand references I didn't get, laugh at jokes that went over my head, and agree with opinions that made no sense to me, all to maintain the illusion that I was keeping up.

But performance is exhausting. And eventually, even the best actors forget their lines.

## The Science of "Not Enough"

What I didn't know then is that **approximately 70% of adults with ADHD also experience rejection sensitive dysphoria (RSD),** an extreme emotional sensitivity to criticism or perceived rejection.

RSD isn't just "being sensitive." It's a neurological response where the brain interprets neutral feedback as devastating rejection. A casual "maybe try a different approach" becomes "you're incompetent and everyone knows it."

Dr. William Dodson, who coined the term, describes it as **"a sudden, overwhelming emotional pain triggered by the perception of rejection or criticism."** For someone with RSD, the fear of not being enough isn't philosophical, it's physiological.

This explains why I would rehearse conversations for hours before making a phone call. Why I'd rewrite emails six times before sending them. Why I'd rather say nothing than risk saying the wrong thing.

I wasn't being a perfectionist, I was protecting myself from what felt like emotional annihilation.

## The Comparison Trap

The lie of "not enough" thrives on comparison. And comparison, for neurodivergent people, is particularly toxic.

We compare our internal chaos to other people's external calm. We compare our rough drafts to their highlight reels. We compare our learning process to their finished products.

I used to watch colleagues effortlessly juggling multiple projects while I struggled to finish one. I'd see friends maintaining pristine homes while my apartment looked like a hurricane had passed through. I'd observe people making decisions quickly and confidently while I spiraled into analysis paralysis over what to have for lunch.

What I couldn't see was their internal experience. What I couldn't know was whether they were neurotypical, or neurodivergent and masking, or simply operating in environments that played to their strengths rather than exposing their weaknesses.

## The Real Problem with "Not Enough"

The devastating thing about believing you're not enough is that it becomes a self-fulfilling prophecy.

When you believe you're fundamentally flawed, you:

- Avoid opportunities where you might fail
- Undervalue your contributions
- Accept treatment you don't deserve
- Sabotage success when it comes
- Interpret neutral events as confirmation of your inadequacy

I turned down job opportunities because I was sure I'd be exposed as a fraud. I stayed in relationships where I felt grateful that someone would tolerate my "difficult" personality. I abandoned creative projects the moment they felt challenging, convinced that real artists wouldn't struggle the way I did.

The lie didn't just make me miserable, it made me small.

## The Moment the Lie Cracked

The first crack in the "not enough" lie came from an unexpected source: my nephew.

He was seven, recently diagnosed with ADHD, and his teacher had called to complain that he "wasn't trying hard enough" in class. My cousin was distraught, worried that she was failing him somehow.

But watching him, I saw myself. The way he'd hyperfocus on Lego for hours but couldn't sit still during story time. The way he'd ask brilliant, off-topic questions that derailed conversations. The way he'd light up when talking about his interests but shut down when forced to discuss subjects that bored him.

"He's not not trying hard enough," I found myself saying. "He's trying as hard as he can with a brain that works differently."

And in that moment, I realized I was also talking about myself.

## Redefining "Enough"

The journey from "not enough" to "enough" isn't about lowering standards or making excuses. It's about changing the metrics.

Instead of measuring myself against neurotypical benchmarks, I started asking different questions:

- Am I using my strengths?
- Am I honoring my limitations?
- Am I being true to my values?
- Am I contributing in ways that feel authentic?

When I stopped trying to be the employee who could sit through eight-hour workdays without a break, I discovered I could be the employee who produced exceptional work in intense bursts. When I stopped trying to be the friend who remembered every birthday, I became the friend who could listen to your problems for hours without judgment.

## The Neurodiversity Paradigm

The shift from "deficiency" to "difference" is at the heart of the neurodiversity movement. Pioneered by autism advocate Judy Singer in the 1990s, neurodiversity reframes neurological differences as natural variations, like biodiversity, rather than disorders to be cured.

**Temple Grandin**, one of the most prominent autistic advocates, puts it simply: **"Different—not less."**

This isn't about denying that neurodivergent people face challenges. We do. But it's about recognizing that many of those challenges come from environments and expectations designed for one type of brain, not from inherent flaws in ours.

## The Gifts Hidden in the "Problems"

Once I stopped seeing my neurodivergent traits as deficits, I started noticing their benefits:

- My "distractibility" was actually curiosity and pattern recognition
- My "hyperfocus" was an ability to dive deep and produce exceptional work
- My "emotional intensity" was empathy and passion
- My "inability to multitask" was actually single-minded focus and attention to detail

These weren't consolation prizes. They were genuine strengths that had been mischaracterized as weaknesses in environments that didn't know how to use them.

## The Economics of Authenticity

Living the lie of "not enough" is expensive. The mental energy I spent monitoring and adjusting my behavior was energy I couldn't use for creativity, problem-solving, or genuine connection.

Masking is exhausting. Code-switching between your authentic self and your performative self requires constant vigilance. It's like running background software that's always consuming your RAM.

When I finally started living more authentically, stimming when I needed to, asking for clarification instead of pretending to understand, taking breaks when I was overwhelmed, I discovered I had energy for things that actually mattered.

## The Ripple Effect of Self-Acceptance

Perhaps the most surprising thing about releasing the "not enough" lie was how it affected other people.

When I stopped apologizing for my neurodivergent traits, others stopped seeing them as problems. When I started talking openly about my ADHD, friends shared their own struggles with focus and organization. When I normalized asking for accommodations, it gave others permission to advocate for their needs too.

Authenticity is contagious. When you stop performing normalcy, you give others permission to stop performing too.

## The New Enough

I am enough because I exist. I am enough because I try. I am enough because I feel deeply. I am enough because my brain sees the world in ways that matter.

This isn't delusion or toxic positivity. It's a recognition that the criteria for human worth can't be reduced to how well you fit someone else's template.

## Practical Tools for Dismantling the Lie

**1. Evidence Collection** Keep a record of your successes, however small. The brain with RSD has a negativity bias, it remembers criticism clearly while forgetting praise. Written evidence helps counter this.

**2. Reframe Your History** Go back through your life and reinterpret "failures" through a neurodivergent lens. That job you got fired from? Maybe it wasn't a good fit for your brain. That relationship that ended? Maybe you weren't "too much", maybe they were expecting you to be someone else.

**3. Find Your People** Surround yourself with people who appreciate your neurodivergent traits, not just tolerate them. Online communities, support groups, and neurodivergent-affirming spaces can provide the mirror you need to see yourself clearly.

**4. Practice Self-Compassion** When the "not enough" voice returns (and it will), respond as you would to a good friend. You wouldn't tell someone you care about that they're fundamentally flawed, extend the same kindness to yourself.

## The Second Truth

If the first lie is "you're not enough," then the first truth is this:

**You are exactly enough, exactly as you are, operating exactly as your brain was designed to operate.**

The problem was never you. The problem was a world that didn't understand you.

And now that you understand yourself, you can start building a life that actually fits.

# Chapter 10: The Room That Refused to Clean Itself

*"This isn't just about a messy room. It's about how we lie to ourselves and how those lies shape the way we move through life."* , **Olivier Merveille**

My friend Olivier said this to me during one of our late-night conversations about executive dysfunction, and it hit me like a revelation. He was right. The state of my room, and my inability to maintain it no matter how much I wanted to, wasn't just about being messy or lazy.

It was a metaphor for everything I struggled with. A physical manifestation of the chaos in my mind. A daily reminder that I couldn't seem to do things that appeared effortless for everyone else.

## The Room as Evidence

For most of my life, my living space was Exhibit A in the case against my character. The messy room was proof that I was:

- Lazy
- Disorganized
- Irresponsible
- Not trying hard enough
- Fundamentally flawed

I internalized every criticism. Every frustrated sigh from my mother. Every comment from roommates. Every judgment from visitors who couldn't hide their shock at the state of my space.

The room became evidence of my inadequacy. And the more I saw it that way, the more overwhelming it became to change it.

## The Paradox of Wanting and Doing

Here's what people didn't understand: I *wanted* a clean room. Desperately.

I craved the calm that comes from organized space. I envied friends who could invite people over spontaneously without panic. I dreamed of mornings where I could find what I needed without excavating through piles of clothes and papers.

But wanting and doing are two different things. And for neurodivergent brains, that gap can feel unbridgeable.

## The Science of Executive Dysfunction

What I thought was laziness was actually **executive dysfunction**, a core feature of ADHD that affects the brain's ability to manage tasks that require planning, organization, and sustained attention.

**Dr. Russell Barkley** explains that **"ADHD is not a disorder of attention; it's a disorder of self-regulation."** The brain knows what needs to be done but struggles to initiate, sustain, and complete tasks, especially those that are boring, overwhelming, or lack immediate reward.

Cleaning a room requires multiple executive functions:

- **Task initiation**: Actually starting the process
- **Working memory**: Remembering the plan while executing it
- **Cognitive flexibility**: Adapting when you find unexpected items or obstacles
- **Sustained attention**: Staying focused despite distractions
- **Impulse control**: Resisting the urge to get sidetracked by interesting things you find

For a neurotypical brain, these functions work in harmony. For an ADHD brain, it's like trying to conduct an orchestra where half the musicians are playing different songs.

## The Shame Spiral

The messier my room got, the more ashamed I felt. The more ashamed I felt, the more overwhelming the task became. The more overwhelming it became, the less likely I was to start. It was a perfect storm of avoidance.

I developed elaborate strategies to hide the chaos:

- Throwing clothes in the closet before visitors came over
- Closing the bedroom door and pretending that room didn't exist
- Making sure to show people only the "clean" areas of my space
- Declining invitations to my place altogether

But the shame followed me everywhere. Even when I was out, I carried the weight of knowing what waited for me at home.

## The All-or-Nothing Trap

When I finally did attempt to clean, I fell into the all-or-nothing trap. I'd envision a complete transformation, everything organized, labeled, perfect. I'd start with enormous energy and ambition.

And then I'd burn out.

Within an hour, I'd be overwhelmed by decisions: Where does this go? Do I need this? How should I organize these papers? What if I put this in the wrong place?

**Decision fatigue** would set in, and I'd abandon the project, leaving the room in an even worse state than before. Now it wasn't just messy, it was actively torn apart.

This reinforced my belief that I was hopeless at organization. I'd tried and failed so many times that trying felt like setting myself up for disappointment.

## The Hidden Treasures

But there was another side to my messy room that people didn't see: the **creative chaos**.

Yes, my space was disorganized. But it was also full of projects in various stages of completion. Half-written stories. Sketches for inventions. Books opened to inspiring passages. Tools for hobbies I'd been passionate about at different times.

My room was a physical manifestation of my **monotropic** mind, the way neurodivergent brains often focus intensely on one interest at a time, then shift to something completely different.

**Dr. Dinah Murray**, who coined the term "monotropism," describes it as a **"tendency for autistic people to focus their attention on a small number of interests at any time."** For many of us, this means diving deep into subjects or activities, then moving on when our interest shifts.

My messy room was evidence of a mind that couldn't choose just one thing to be interested in. And while this made organization challenging, it also made my life rich with diverse experiences and knowledge.

## The Breaking Point

The breaking point came when I realized I was avoiding my own home. I'd stay out late, work from coffee shops, sleep on friends' couches, anything to avoid confronting the physical reminder of my perceived failure.

I was exiling myself from my own space because I couldn't bear the shame it triggered.

## The First Small Victory

Real change began when I stopped trying to clean the whole room and started with one small corner.

Not the whole desk, just enough space to set down a cup of coffee. Not the entire closet, just enough to find tomorrow's outfit. Not all the papers, just the ones I needed for this week.

I set a timer for fifteen minutes and cleaned only until it went off. No matter what state the room was in when the timer rang, I stopped.

This did two things:

1. It made the task feel manageable instead of infinite
2. It prevented the burnout that came from overcommitting

# The Power of "Good Enough"

The OCD in me wanted to organize everything beautifully, label everything clearly, create systems that would never fail.

But I had to learn to embrace "good enough."

Good enough meant clothes in the hamper instead of on the floor, even if they weren't sorted by color. Good enough meant papers in a single pile instead of scattered everywhere, even if they weren't filed by category. Good enough meant being able to walk through the room without stepping on things, even if it wasn't magazine-ready.

**"Good enough" became my rebellion against perfectionism.**

## The Body Double Effect

One of the most helpful discoveries was the concept of **body doubling**, having another person present while you work, even if they're not actively helping.

For neurodivergent brains, the presence of another person can provide:

- **Accountability**: It's harder to get distracted when someone is watching
- **Motivation**: The social pressure helps overcome inertia
- **Grounding**: Another person's presence can help regulate your nervous system

I started inviting friends over specifically to "body double" while I cleaned. They'd read a book or work on their laptop while I organized. We didn't talk much, but their presence made the task feel less overwhelming and more doable.

## The Room as Self-Care

As I got better at maintaining my space, I realized that cleaning wasn't just about organization, it was about **self-care**.

A clean room meant:

- I could find things when I needed them, reducing daily stress

- I felt calmer in my own space
- I wasn't embarrassed to have people over
- My environment supported my well-being instead of undermining it

**Marie Kondo** talks about surrounding yourself with things that "spark joy." For neurodivergent people, I'd add: surround yourself with things that spark **function**.

Joy is beautiful.

But when your brain processes the world differently, **function is safety.**

**Function is flow.**

**Function is life not falling apart.**

Here are a few everyday items that don't just *look good*. They *work better*.

## Tools That Spark Function (for Neurodivergent Minds)

### Visual timers

For staying grounded in time.

No more "just five more minutes" turning into three lost hours.

### Clear bins & labeled drawers

Because *if you can't see it, it doesn't exist*. Visibility is memory support.

### Dry erase boards or sticky notes on mirrors

For morning anchors. Your brain might forget, but your environment can remind you.

### A chair that hugs you

Weighted or enclosed chairs that support emotional regulation. Your nervous system will thank you.

## Noise-canceling headphones or earplugs

Not just for quiet. **For clarity**. Your thoughts can land when the world dims down.

## Hourglass timers for breaks

Help you return to tasks without guilt or overwhelm.

## Warm lighting instead of overhead fluorescents

Because lighting isn't just aesthetic. It's neurological.

Soft light means soft nervous systems.

## Favorite hydration tools

Straws, flasks, emotional water bottles. Hydration is executive function fuel.

## Task apps that *ping once*, then shut up

Apps that don't yell at you. Just nudge gently. Think: structured softness.

## Inventory notebooks

For when the brain feels scrambled. A quick inventory: Mental, emotional, financial, or physical can reset your inner compass in minutes.

*Inventory is not control. It's clarity.*

## Deep focus music, white noise, binaural beats, or meditation soundscapes

Try different ones at different times of day. What grounds you in the morning may not hold you at night. *Sound can be architecture. Find yours.*

## Journals that don't judge you

It's not about perfect writing. It's about letting the unsaid out. Journaling is emotional inventory. It's a safe exit for what can't live in your body anymore.

This is your permission to surround yourself with things that work **for you**. Not against you.

Not what looks organized, but what *feels calming*.

Not what sparks social approval, but what *sparks functionality*.

Because when function flows, joy can follow.

## The Ripple Effect

As my room became more manageable, other areas of my life followed suit. I started:

- Keeping my car tidy
- Organizing my digital files
- Planning meals instead of eating chaotically
- Managing my time better

It wasn't that cleaning my room magically gave me executive function skills. But succeeding in one area gave me evidence that I *could* succeed, which motivated me to try applying the same principles elsewhere.

## The Bigger Metaphor

Olivier was right, it wasn't just about the messy room. The room was a metaphor for every area where I felt like I was failing at basic adulting:

- Finances (papers scattered, bills paid late)
- Health (irregular sleep, forgotten appointments)
- Relationships (poor communication, forgotten commitments)
- Career (projects half-finished, potential unrealized)

But if I could learn to manage my physical space, maybe I could learn to manage these other areas too.

## Tools That Actually Work

**The 15-Minute Rule**: Set a timer and clean for exactly 15 minutes. Stop when it goes off, regardless of what's left undone.

**The One-Touch Rule**: When you pick something up, try to deal with it immediately rather than setting it down "just for now."

**The Landing Strip**: Designate one specific area for keys, wallet, phone, and other daily items. Always put them in the same place.

**The Two-Minute Rule**: If something takes less than two minutes to do, do it now instead of adding it to your mental to-do list.

**The Container Method**: Use boxes, bins, or bags to contain similar items, even if they're not perfectly organized within the container.

## Permission to Be Human

The most important thing I learned was to give myself permission to be human. To have off days. To let things get messy sometimes without catastrophizing.

The goal wasn't perfection, it was **functionality**. And functionality looks different for everyone.

My room might never look like a magazine spread. But it can be a space where I feel comfortable, where I can find what I need, where I can invite friends without shame.

And that's enough.

## The Lie Beneath the Mess

The real lie wasn't that I was lazy or disorganized. The lie was that external order equals internal worth.

Society teaches us that how we maintain our spaces reflects our character. Clean room = good person. Messy room = moral failing.

But neurodivergent brains often struggle with tasks that don't provide immediate dopamine rewards. Cleaning, organizing, maintaining, these aren't inherently stimulating activities. They require executive function skills that may be impaired.

**The mess wasn't a reflection of my character. It was evidence that I was trying to function with a brain that needed different tools and strategies.**

## Rewriting the Story

Now when I see a messy space, my own or someone else's, I try to see it with compassion rather than judgment.

Maybe this person is overwhelmed and doesn't know where to start. Maybe they're dealing with depression or anxiety that makes tasks feel insurmountable. Maybe they're neurodivergent and their brain works differently. Maybe they're going through a difficult time and are using their energy for more important things.

Or maybe they're just human, and humans sometimes have messy rooms.

The room that refused to clean itself taught me one of my most important lessons: **I am not my environment. My worth is not measured by my organization. My value doesn't depend on my ability to maintain perfect order.**

And once I learned that, cleaning became easier. Because I was no longer cleaning to prove I was worthy, I was cleaning to take care of myself.

# Chapter 11: Big Shottism and the Illusion of Competence

I have a condition I call **Big Shottism**.

It's not in any diagnostic manual, but I'd bet good money that half the neurodivergent population suffers from it. The symptoms are clear: grandiose bursts of confidence followed by crushing periods of self-doubt. Feeling like you can conquer the world on Tuesday, then feeling like a complete fraud by Thursday.

Big Shottism is the emotional whiplash of living with a brain that operates in extremes.

## The Big Shot Phase

When I'm in Big Shot mode, I'm unstoppable. Ideas flow like water. Everything seems possible. I start new projects with absolute certainty that this time will be different. This time I'll follow through. This time I'll succeed.

During these phases, I've:

- Started a fashion company at 2 AM after watching a documentary about streetwear
- Written the first three chapters of a novel in a single night
- Convinced myself I could learn Portuguese in a month
- Applied for jobs I was completely unqualified for
- Made grand promises to friends about life-changing adventures we'd take

In Big Shot mode, my confidence is intoxicating. Not just to me, to everyone around me. I become magnetic, passionate, and visionary. People get caught up in my enthusiasm because it feels so genuine, so alive.

And it is genuine. In those moments, I truly believe I can do anything.

## The Crash

But Big Shottism always has a second act: the crash.

Maybe it's external, a rejection, a setback, a reality check. Or maybe it's internal, my brain chemistry shifting, the dopamine high wearing off, executive dysfunction returning with a vengeance.

Suddenly, all those grandiose plans feel impossible. The fashion company seems laughably naive. The novel draft reads like amateur hour. The Portuguese lessons sit untouched. The job applications feel like exercises in delusion.

And I don't just feel disappointed, I feel *embarrassed*. How could I have been so arrogant? How could I have thought I was capable of these things? How could I have been so publicly confident about something I clearly couldn't deliver?

## The Neuroscience of Extremes

Big Shottism isn't a character flaw, it's a neurological feature of ADHD brains.

**Dr. William Dodson** explains that **ADHD brains have "an interest-based nervous system"** rather than an importance-based one. We can't force ourselves to care about things that don't naturally stimulate us, but when something captures our interest, we become hyperfocused and often overconfident about our abilities.

The dopamine dysregulation in ADHD means we experience more extreme highs and lows than neurotypical brains. When dopamine is flowing, everything feels possible. When it dips, everything feels hopeless.

**Dr. Ari Tuckman** describes this as **"the ADHD roller coaster"**, the emotional peaks and valleys that come with unstable neurotransmitter levels.

## The Imposter Syndrome Connection

Big Shottism has a complicated relationship with imposter syndrome. During the Big Shot phase, imposter syndrome is nowhere to be found. I feel completely legitimate, totally capable, utterly deserving of success.

But during the crash, imposter syndrome returns with a vengeance. Now I'm convinced that the Big Shot phase was evidence of my delusion. The confidence feels embarrassing in retrospect. I became convinced that everyone could see through my act.

This creates a vicious cycle:

1. Feel incredibly confident (Big Shot phase)
2. Take on ambitious projects or make bold claims
3. Hit obstacles or reality checks (the crash)
4. Feel like a fraud for having been confident (imposter syndrome)
5. Overcorrect by being overly modest or self-deprecating
6. Build up internal pressure until confidence explodes again (return to Big Shot phase)

## The Social Cost

Big Shottism affects relationships in complex ways. During Big Shot phases, I'm fun to be around, enthusiastic, optimistic, full of ideas. But I also make promises I can't keep and commitments I can't honor.

I've told friends about amazing trip plans that never materialized. I've started collaborative projects with grand visions that fizzled out when my interest shifted. I've painted pictures of future success that made people expect more from me than I could deliver.

The crash phase is harder on relationships in different ways. I become withdrawn, self-critical, reluctant to try new things. Friends who were excited by my enthusiasm during the high phase get confused by my sudden pessimism and inaction.

People don't know which version of me is "real." And honestly, neither do I sometimes.

## The Entrepreneurial Trap

Big Shottism is both a blessing and a curse in entrepreneurial endeavors. The Big Shot phase provides the irrational confidence needed to start something new. Who else but someone experiencing grandiose self-belief would think they could disrupt an entire industry or create something nobody's ever seen before?

Many successful entrepreneurs are neurodivergent precisely because neurotypical brains are too realistic to attempt most startups. **Richard Branson** (dyslexic), **Simone Biles** (ADHD), and **Elon Musk** (autism) all credit their neurodivergent traits with giving them the audacity to pursue seemingly impossible goals.

But the crash phase can be devastating for business ventures. When confidence collapses, it's hard to sell your vision to investors, customers, or even yourself. I've abandoned promising projects not because they weren't working, but because I lost faith in my ability to make them work.

## Learning to Ride the Wave

Recovery from Big Shottism isn't about eliminating the extremes, it's about learning to surf them more skillfully.

**During Big Shot phases, I've learned to:**

- Harness the energy while building in reality checks
- Share my enthusiasm while being transparent about my history with follow-through
- Start projects while keeping them small and manageable
- Make plans while building in exit strategies

**During crash phases, I've learned to:**

- Remember that this feeling is temporary and neurochemical
- Look at evidence from past successes rather than trusting my current emotions
- Maintain basic routines even when motivation disappears
- Reach out to friends who can remind me of my actual capabilities

## The Power of Pattern Recognition

The most helpful tool has been simply recognizing the pattern. When I feel that familiar surge of grandiose confidence, I can think: "Oh, hello Big Shot mode. Nice to see you again. Let's be smart about this."

I've started keeping a journal that tracks my confidence levels and energy. Over time, I've noticed patterns:

- Big Shot phases often follow periods of stress or accomplishment
- Crashes often coincide with hormonal changes, lack of sleep, or external rejection
- The phases typically last 3-7 days
- My actual capabilities remain constant even when my confidence fluctuates

Knowing this helps me make better decisions. I don't quit projects during crash phases, and I don't overcommit during Big Shot phases.

## The Middle Path

The goal isn't to stay in the middle, that's not how ADHD brains work. The goal is to **honor both phases while protecting myself from their extremes**.

During high phases, I can enjoy the creativity and confidence while building in safeguards. During low phases, I can rest and recharge while remembering that the feelings aren't facts.

**Buddhist philosophy** talks about the concept of **equanimity**, not the absence of emotion, but a balanced awareness that allows you to experience feelings without being overwhelmed by them.

For neurodivergent people, equanimity might look like: "I notice I'm feeling incredibly confident right now. This is a brain state, not necessarily an accurate assessment of reality. How can I use this energy wisely?"

## The Gift in the Chaos

Here's what I've learned to appreciate about Big Shottism: **the highs aren't delusions, and the lows aren't truth.**

During Big Shot phases, I really am more creative, more confident, more capable of taking risks. These aren't fake feelings, they're accessing parts of my potential that are harder to reach during neutral states.

During crash phases, I'm not actually incompetent or hopeless. I'm just experiencing a temporary neurochemical low that makes everything feel harder than it is.

Both phases contain information. The Big Shot phase shows me what's possible when I'm operating at full capacity. The crash phase shows me where I need support and what my realistic limitations are.

## Practical Strategies

**The 48-Hour Rule**: When I have a grandiose idea during a Big Shot phase, I wait 48 hours before acting on it. If I still think it's a good idea after the initial euphoria wears off, I move forward, but with a more realistic timeline.

**The Evidence File**: I keep a document of past accomplishments and positive feedback. During crash phases, I read it to remind myself that my current feelings aren't accurate assessments of my abilities.

**The Buddy System**: I have friends who know about my Big Shottism and can provide reality checks. They're supportive of my ambitions but also help me stay grounded.

**The Energy Budget**: I treat confidence and enthusiasm like finite resources. I try not to spend it all on the first exciting project that comes along.

## Big Shottism as Superpower

When properly managed, Big Shottism can be a superpower. The confidence phases have led me to opportunities I never would have pursued with a more "realistic" mindset. The crash phases have taught me resilience and self-compassion.

Most importantly, living with these extremes has given me empathy for other people's struggles with confidence and self-doubt. I know what it feels like to be absolutely certain of your abilities one day and completely doubt them the next.

**The key insight: I am not my confidence level. I am not my current mood. I am a complex human being whose capabilities don't fluctuate as wildly as my feelings about those capabilities.**

Big Shottism taught me that self-awareness isn't about achieving perfect emotional stability, it's about understanding your patterns well enough to work with them instead of against them.

# Chapter 12: When Discipline Feels Like War

For most of my life, discipline felt like violence against myself.

Not the gentle, self-caring kind of structure that helps you flourish. The brutal, punitive kind that treats your natural tendencies as enemy combatants to be defeated.

I waged war against my own brain for decades, using shame as ammunition and self-hatred as strategy. And like most wars, everyone lost.

## The Inherited Definition

My understanding of discipline came from a mixture of sources: strict Caribbean parenting, military-influenced French education, and a culture that equated self-control with moral worth.

In this framework, discipline meant:

- Forcing yourself to do things you hate
- Ignoring your body's signals for rest or stimulation
- Pushing through pain, boredom, or overwhelm
- Treating any resistance as weakness to be overcome
- Believing that if something feels good, it's probably not good for you

This version of discipline is based on the assumption that humans are naturally lazy, selfish, and destructive, and that only through constant vigilance and harsh correction can we become productive members of society.

For a neurodivergent brain, this approach is not just ineffective, it's devastating.

## The War on My Brain

I spent years trying to discipline my ADHD out of existence:

- Forcing myself to sit still when my body needed movement
- Trying to focus on boring tasks through pure willpower

- Punishing myself for procrastination with more work and less rest
- Attempting to remember things without external supports
- Hiding stimming behaviors that helped me self-regulate

It was like trying to cure left-handedness through punishment. No amount of willpower was going to change my neurological wiring, but I kept trying, convinced that failure meant I wasn't trying hard enough.

## The Science of Self-Compassion

**Dr. Kristin Neff**, a leading researcher on self-compassion, defines it as **"treating yourself with the same kindness you would offer a good friend."** Her research shows that **self-compassion is more effective than self-criticism for motivating positive behavior change**.

This went against everything I'd ever learned about discipline.

Tough love. That was the rule.

I told myself that if I wasn't successful, it was because I wasn't being hard enough on myself.

I believed that softness was weakness, and that self-compassion would make me complacent.

So I treated every mistake like a crime.

Every delay like failure.

Every need for rest like proof I didn't want it bad enough.

In my mind, being harsh wasn't cruelty.

It was discipline.

It was motivation.

It was the only language I thought success understood.

But research consistently shows that **self-criticism activates the brain's threat system**, making us less creative, less resilient, and less able to learn from mistakes.

**Dr. Paul Gilbert**'s work on **Compassion-Focused Therapy** reveals that **the brain responds to self-compassion by activating the care-giving system**, the same neural networks that help us nurture others. This system promotes feelings of safety and connection, which are optimal conditions for growth and change.

## The Neurodivergent Paradox

The traditional discipline model assumes that resistance to tasks comes from moral weakness. But for neurodivergent brains, resistance often comes from neurological incompatibility.

When an ADHD brain resists a boring task, it's not being defiant, it's literally unable to generate enough dopamine to sustain attention. When an autistic brain struggles with unexpected changes, it's not being rigid, it's experiencing genuine distress from sensory and cognitive overload.

Trying to force a neurodivergent brain to operate like a neurotypical one is like my previous example of trying to force a Mac to run PC software. You might get partial functionality through emulation, but it's inefficient, unstable, and eventually the system crashes aka burn out or a trauma.

## The Turning Point

My relationship with discipline began to change when I started working with a therapist who specialized in ADHD. She introduced me to the concept of **"radical acceptance"**, the idea that fighting against your brain's natural tendencies creates more suffering than the tendencies themselves.

"What if," she asked, "instead of trying to make your brain work differently, you learned to work with the brain you have?"

This wasn't about giving up or making excuses. It was about **strategic alignment**, finding ways to achieve my goals that honored my neurological reality rather than fighting against it.

## Discipline as Self-Care

Real discipline, I learned, isn't about punishment or force. It's about **creating conditions that support your success**.

For my ADHD brain, this meant:

**Movement as Medicine**: Instead of forcing myself to sit still, I built movement into my day. Walking meetings, standing desk, fidget toys, exercise breaks, movement became a tool for focus, not a distraction from it.

**Interest-Based Learning**: Instead of forcing myself to care about boring topics, I found ways to connect new information to things I was already passionate about. Learning became easier when it hooked into my existing interests.

**Environmental Design**: Instead of relying on willpower to avoid distractions, I designed my environment to minimize them. Phone in another room, website blockers, clutter-free workspace, I made good choices the easier choices.

**Energy Management**: Instead of pushing through fatigue, I learned to work with my natural energy rhythms. High-focus tasks during peak hours, low-energy tasks during slumps, rest when my brain needed it.

## The Seasonal Brain

One of the most helpful frameworks came from understanding that neurodivergent brains often operate seasonally rather than consistently.

Just as you wouldn't expect a garden to produce the same yield in winter as summer, I learned not to expect my brain to perform identically every day. Some days are high-output days. Some are maintenance days. Some are rest days.

**Traditional discipline** says: Produce the same amount every day regardless of circumstances.

**Neurodivergent discipline** says: Match your expectations to your capacity and cycle.

# The Power of Micro-Habits

**James Clear**, author of *Atomic Habits*, writes: **"You do not rise to the level of your goals. You fall to the level of your systems."**

For neurodivergent brains, systems need to be even smaller and more forgiving than for neurotypical ones. The ADHD tendency toward all-or-nothing thinking means we often set unrealistic goals and then abandon them entirely when we inevitably fall short.

Instead of "I'll exercise for an hour every day," I started with "I'll put on workout clothes." Often, just changing clothes would lead to some form of movement. If not, I still succeeded at my actual goal.

Instead of "I'll write 1000 words every day," I committed to "I'll open my laptop and write one sentence." Usually I wrote more, but I celebrated the one sentence as a complete success.

## The Dopamine Economy

Understanding ADHD as a **dopamine dysregulation disorder** revolutionized my approach to discipline.

Instead of forcing myself through boring tasks with willpower, I learned to **gamify** them:

- Breaking large projects into smaller, completable chunks
- Celebrating small wins with immediate rewards
- Working alongside others for social accountability
- Alternating challenging tasks with enjoyable ones
- Using timers to create artificial urgency and breaks

This isn't "cheating" or being "weak", it's working with your brain's neurotransmitter system instead of against it.

# The Importance of Failure

Traditional discipline treats failure as evidence that you need more discipline. Neurodivergent discipline treats failure as data about what systems need adjustment.

When I abandon a habit or miss a goal, instead of self-flagellation, I ask:

- What circumstances led to this outcome?
- Was the goal realistic given my current capacity?
- What obstacles did I encounter that I didn't anticipate?
- How can I modify the system to prevent this in the future?

This approach has helped me build sustainable practices instead of just cycling through periods of intense effort followed by complete burnout.

## The Body's Wisdom

Perhaps the biggest shift was learning to trust my body's signals instead of overriding them.

When I feel restless during a meeting, instead of forcing stillness, I allow subtle movement or step outside briefly. When I feel mentally saturated, instead of pushing through, I take a genuine break. When I feel hyperfocused, instead of interrupting myself to be "balanced," I ride the wave while it lasts.

**Dr. Gabor Maté** writes: **"The question is not why the addiction, but why the pain."** Similarly, the question isn't why the resistance, but what need is going unmet.

Usually when I'm procrastinating or avoiding something, my brain is trying to tell me something important:

- This task needs to be broken down further
- I need more information before I can proceed
- I'm overwhelmed and need to address the underlying stress
- The task conflicts with my values or interests in a way I haven't acknowledged

# Discipline as Love

The most profound shift was reconceptualizing discipline as an act of love rather than control.

When I exercise, it's not because I hate my body and want to punish it, it's because I love my body and want to care for it. When I maintain routines, it's not because I'm weak without structure, it's because structure supports my well-being.

When I set boundaries with others, it's not because I'm selfish, it's because I'm protecting my capacity to show up authentically in my relationships.

**Self-discipline became self-love in action.**

# The Ripple Effect

Learning to discipline myself with compassion instead of force had unexpected consequences. I became more patient with others' struggles. I stopped judging people for having different productivity styles. I became a better friend, partner, and colleague because I wasn't constantly at war with myself.

When you stop fighting yourself, you have so much more energy for everything else.

# Practical Tools for Compassionate Discipline

**The Two-Minute Rule**: (You've seen this earlier, but here's a new angle.) Use it as its own ritual, or combine it with other tools.

If something takes less than two minutes, do it now.

If it takes longer, either schedule it, or break it down into two-minute moves.

**The Minimum Viable Habit**: Identify the smallest possible version of a habit you want to build. Make it so easy you can't say no.

**The Energy Audit**: Track your energy levels throughout the day for a week. Schedule demanding tasks during high-energy periods and routine tasks during low-energy periods.

**The Compassionate Voice**: When you notice self-criticism, pause and ask: "What would I say to a friend in this situation?" Then say that to yourself instead.

**The Experiment Mindset**: Treat every attempt at behavior change as an experiment. Remove moral judgment and focus on gathering data about what works for your unique brain.

## When Discipline Becomes Freedom

True discipline, the kind based on self-understanding and compassion, doesn't feel like restriction. It feels like freedom.

Freedom from the chaos of living without structure. Freedom from the shame of constantly failing at neurotypical expectations. Freedom from the exhaustion of fighting your own nature. Freedom to be who you actually are instead of who you think you should be.

This kind of discipline doesn't eliminate neurodivergent traits, it creates space for them to become strengths instead of obstacles.

When discipline feels like war, everyone loses. When discipline feels like love, everyone wins.

# Chapter 13: The Diagnosis Beneath the Diagnosis

The official diagnosis was ADHD, combined presentation. But underneath that clinical label lay something messier and more complex: a lifetime of misunderstanding, masked trauma, and adaptive strategies that had kept me functional but never truly thriving.

Getting diagnosed felt like finally receiving a map to territory I'd been wandering in circles for thirty-three years. But maps, I discovered, only show you where you are, not necessarily how you got there or where you're going next.

## The Diagnostic Odyssey

By now you know: the diagnosis wasn't a single moment. It was an excavation. A reconstruction of memory, grief, and truth. I won't repeat the process here. But I will say this: even now, the relief and the rage still take turns holding the mic. That's the thing about naming your difference, it doesn't erase the past. It reframes it.

**Dr. Michelle Mowbray**, who specializes in adult ADHD diagnosis, notes that **"late diagnosis often triggers a process similar to grief, as individuals mourn the life they might have had with earlier intervention."**

## The Comorbidity Puzzle

ADHD rarely travels alone. The diagnostic process revealed a constellation of related conditions that had been developing in its shadow:

**Anxiety**: Years of feeling behind, overwhelmed, and unprepared had created a baseline of anxious vigilance. Every task felt potentially dangerous because I couldn't predict my ability to complete it successfully.

**Depression**: The accumulated weight of perceived failures and social rejection had created periods of hopelessness and withdrawal. What looked like laziness was often my brain protecting itself from more potential hurt.

**Rejection Sensitive Dysphoria**: The extreme emotional pain from criticism or perceived rejection explained why I'd developed such elaborate people-pleasing strategies. My nervous system interpreted any form of disapproval as a threat to survival.

**Complex PTSD symptoms**: While I hadn't experienced "Big T" trauma, the chronic stress of living in a world that didn't accommodate my neurotype had created what some call "neurodivergent trauma", the accumulation of countless micro-invalidations and forced adaptations.

## The Masking Discovery

By the time I reached diagnosis, even the language around masking felt familiar. I had already lived it. The fatigue, the endless translation, the performance. It all made sense now. The label didn't teach me the cost. My body already knew.

## The Intersection of Identities

The diagnosis process also illuminated how my neurodivergence intersected with other aspects of my identity:

**Cultural factors**: Growing up in a French Caribbean family with strong emphasis on discipline and conformity had intensified the pressure to mask. Neurodivergent behaviors were seen as disrespectful or lazy rather than neurological differences.

**Gender expectations**: As a man, I was expected to be emotionally stoic and naturally competitive. My emotional sensitivity and collaborative nature were seen as weaknesses rather than different strengths.

**Generational timing**: I came of age before widespread awareness of adult ADHD. My childhood teachers had no framework for understanding neurodivergence beyond the hyperactive boy stereotype.

## The Medication Decision

One of the most complex aspects of diagnosis was deciding whether to try medication. I had internalized negative stereotypes about ADHD medications, that they were "chemical restraints" or signs of weakness.

But my psychiatrist, Dr. Sarah Chen, explained that **stimulant medications don't change personality, they help ADHD brains access their existing capabilities.**

She used an analogy that resonated: "If you were nearsighted, you wouldn't refuse glasses because you wanted to 'overcome' your vision problems naturally. ADHD medication is like glasses for your brain's attention system."

The first time I took methylphenidate, the change was subtle but profound. Tasks that usually required enormous willpower suddenly felt manageable. The constant background noise in my mind quieted to a whisper. I could choose what to focus on instead of being at the mercy of whatever was most stimulating.

## The Myth of Linear Progress

I expected that diagnosis and treatment would create a neat before-and-after narrative. Struggling before, thriving after. But neurodivergent life is messier than that.

Some days the medication worked perfectly. Other days it felt ineffective. Some strategies helped enormously. Others fell flat despite my best efforts. Some symptoms improved dramatically. Others remained challenging.

**Dr. Russell Barkley** reminds us that **"ADHD is a disorder of performance, not knowledge."** Knowing what to do and being able to consistently do it are two different things, even with treatment.

Recovery isn't linear. It's cyclical, seasonal, and contextual. Learning to accept this variability was part of the diagnosis beneath the diagnosis.

## The Reframing Process

Perhaps the most therapeutic aspect of diagnosis was the opportunity to reframe my entire life history. Memories that had been sources of shame became evidence of neurodivergent survival and adaptation.

The time I got fired for "poor attention to detail" became a story about incompatible work environments rather than personal failure.

The relationships that ended because I was "too intense" became lessons about finding compatible partners rather than proof of my unlovableness.

The academic struggles became evidence of a mismatch between my learning style and traditional educational methods rather than intellectual inadequacy.

**Dr. Edward Hallowell** calls this process **"rewriting your narrative"**, replacing stories of deficiency with stories of difference.

## The Community Connection

Diagnosis didn't just give me clarity. It gave me community. For the first time, I was surrounded by people who understood why my mind moved the way it did. That connection was healing in ways therapy couldn't touch. And it didn't stop there. My diagnosis rippled outward into advocacy, into work, into friendships. I began asking for what I needed without shame, and I noticed how many others around me carried their own silent battles. Sometimes, one person's truth becomes the permission someone else has been waiting for.

## The Deeper Diagnosis

The official diagnosis was ADHD. But the diagnosis beneath the diagnosis was more complex:

- **Chronic misattunement**: Growing up in environments that couldn't see or meet my neurological needs
- **Adaptive trauma**: The psychological impact of years of feeling fundamentally wrong
- **Identity fragmentation**: The split between authentic self and performative self created by extensive masking
- **Internalized ableism**: The unconscious belief that my neurological differences were defects to be overcome
- **Resilience and strength**: The remarkable adaptability that had allowed me to survive and even thrive in incompatible environments

## Integration and Acceptance

True healing required integrating all aspects of this deeper diagnosis, not just addressing the ADHD symptoms. This meant:

- Grieving the losses while celebrating the strengths
- Learning to unmask gradually and safely
- Developing self-compassion for the years of struggle
- Building environments that supported rather than fought my neurotype
- Finding purpose in helping others navigate similar journeys

## The Ongoing Mystery

Even with diagnosis, mysteries remain. The brain is incredibly complex, and neurodivergence manifests differently in each individual. I continue to discover new aspects of how my mind works, new strategies that help, new ways that my differences can become strengths.

The diagnosis gave me a framework, not a complete explanation. It provided tools, not a cure. It offered understanding, not simplicity.

And that's okay. The goal was never to become neurotypical, it was to become authentically, unapologetically myself.

**The diagnosis beneath the diagnosis was this: I am not broken. I never was. I am wonderfully, complexly, perfectly neurodivergent.**

And that diagnosis has made all the difference.

# Chapter 14: Action is Truth

Words are easy. Intentions are cheap. What matters is what you do.

For years, I lived in the gap between knowing and doing. I knew what healthy habits looked like. I knew what I needed to change. I knew what would make me happier, more successful, more fulfilled.

But knowing isn't the same as doing. And doing consistent, authentic action, is where real change happens.

## The Paralysis of Perfectionism

The biggest obstacle to action wasn't laziness or lack of motivation. It was perfectionism masquerading as high standards.

I wanted to start exercising, but first I needed the perfect workout plan, the right equipment, and the ideal schedule. I wanted to write, but first, I needed the perfect writing space, the right computer, the optimal routine.

I was waiting for perfect conditions that would never come, using preparation as a sophisticated form of procrastination.

**Dr. Brené Brown** writes: **"Perfectionism is not about healthy achievement and growth. It's a shield we use to protect ourselves from vulnerability, judgment, and shame."**

For neurodivergent people, perfectionism often develops as a trauma response. When you've been criticized repeatedly for not doing things "right," you learn to avoid doing anything unless you're certain it will be perfect.

## The Two-Minute Revolution

The breakthrough came when I stopped trying to change everything and started with the smallest possible actions.

The **two-minute rule** became my gateway drug to productivity: If something takes less than two minutes, do it immediately instead of adding it to your mental to-do list.

Reply to that text. Put the dish in the dishwasher. Write one sentence. Do five push-ups. Make the bed.

These tiny actions created momentum. **Newton's first law** applies to behavior: Objects at rest tend to stay at rest, but objects in motion tend to stay in motion.

Starting was always the hardest part.

## The Dopamine Hack

Understanding ADHD as a dopamine dysregulation disorder revolutionized my approach to action. I learned to work with my brain's reward system instead of against it.

**Immediate rewards**: Instead of waiting for long-term satisfaction, I built immediate rewards into tasks. Completing a work project earned me a favorite coffee. Finishing a workout meant I could watch an episode of a show I enjoyed.

**Visible progress**: I created visual representations of progress, crossing items off lists, moving tasks across a kanban board, filling in habit trackers. The ADHD brain craves concrete evidence of accomplishment.

**Social accountability**: Telling others about my goals created external motivation when internal motivation failed. The fear of disappointing someone else often pushed me to action when self-disappointment wasn't enough.

**Body doubling**: Working alongside others, even virtually, provided the social stimulation that helped my brain stay engaged with tasks.

## The Identity Shift

The most profound change came when I stopped thinking of myself as someone who struggled with action and started identifying as someone who takes action, imperfectly, inconsistently, but persistently.

**James Clear** explains this in *Atomic Habits*: **"Every action you take is a vote for the type of person you wish to become."**

Instead of "I want to be a writer," I started saying "I am a writer" and then asking "What would a writer do today?" Even if the answer was just "write one terrible sentence," I was reinforcing the identity through action.

This wasn't about fake-it-till-you-make-it optimism. It was about recognizing that identity is formed by accumulated actions, not by feelings or intentions.

## The Seasonal Brain

I learned to work with my natural rhythms instead of fighting them. Some days my brain had the capacity for deep, focused work. Other days were better suited for routine tasks or rest.

**Energy management** became more important than time management. I scheduled demanding tasks during high-energy periods and used low-energy times for easier activities.

This required letting go of the cultural myth that productivity should be consistent across all days and seasons. **Neurodivergent brains often operate cyclically**, with periods of high output followed by necessary recovery.

## The Power of Systems Over Goals

Goals felt overwhelming and abstract. Systems felt manageable and concrete.

Instead of "lose 20 pounds," I focused on "walk for 20 minutes after lunch." Instead of "write a book," I committed to "write for 30 minutes every morning." Instead of "get organized," I implemented "spend 10 minutes tidying before bed."

**Systems thinking** shifted focus from outcomes (which I couldn't completely control) to processes (which I could influence daily).

## Action as Self-Respect

The most important realization was that taking action, especially small, consistent actions, was a form of self-respect.

Every time I followed through on a commitment to myself, I was sending the message: "You matter. Your goals matter. Your well-being matters."

Every time I broke a promise to myself, I was reinforcing the opposite message.

This wasn't about self-discipline as punishment. It was about self-discipline as love, caring enough about my future self to do small things today that would make their life better.

## The Compound Effect

Small actions, repeated consistently, created results that seemed disproportionate to the effort involved.

Writing 300 words a day doesn't feel significant. But over a year, it produces over 100,000 words, enough for a book.

Doing 10 push-ups daily seems trivial. But over months, it builds strength and creates a foundation for more ambitious fitness goals.

Tidying for 10 minutes each evening barely registers as effort. But over time, it maintains a living space that supports rather than drains mental energy.

**The compound effect** works because consistency beats intensity. Small improvements, maintained over time, create exponential results.

## Failure as Data

Traditional approaches treat failure as evidence that you need more willpower or discipline. The neurodivergent approach treats failure as valuable information about what systems need adjustment.

When I abandoned a habit or missed a goal, instead of self-criticism, I asked:

- What obstacles did I encounter?
- Was the goal realistic given my current capacity?
- What environmental factors influenced the outcome?
- How can I modify the system to prevent this pattern?

This **experimental mindset** removed moral judgment from the equation and focused on practical problem-solving.

## The Role of Environment

I learned that willpower is finite, but environmental design can make good choices automatic.

**Choice architecture** became a powerful tool:

- Putting workout clothes next to the bed made morning exercise more likely
- Keeping healthy snacks visible and junk food hidden influenced eating choices
- Using website blockers during focused work time eliminated digital distractions
- Creating a designated writing space primed my brain for creative work

The goal wasn't to eliminate all temptation but to make the path of least resistance align with my values.

## Action Without Perfection

The most liberating discovery was that action doesn't require perfection. In fact, **perfect is often the enemy of good**.

I gave myself permission to:

- Exercise badly rather than not at all
- Write terrible first drafts rather than perfect blank pages
- Eat imperfect meals rather than skipping meals entirely
- Have messy meditation sessions rather than no meditation at all

This **"good enough" philosophy** lowered the barrier to entry and maintained momentum even on difficult days.

# The Neurodivergent Advantage

While traditional productivity advice often assumes consistent energy and motivation, neurodivergent approaches can actually be more sophisticated and effective.

We're forced to develop:

- **Meta-cognitive awareness**: Understanding our own mental processes and patterns
- **Flexible systems**: Approaches that work across different energy levels and life circumstances
- **Creative solutions**: Novel ways to accomplish goals when standard methods don't work
- **Self-compassion**: The ability to maintain motivation despite setbacks

These skills, developed out of necessity, often make us more resilient and adaptable than people who've never had to question standard approaches.

## Building Momentum

Action creates momentum, and momentum makes future action easier. But building initial momentum requires strategic thinking about where to start.

I learned to identify **keystone habits**, actions that naturally lead to other positive behaviors:

- Morning exercise often led to better eating choices throughout the day
- Making the bed created a sense of accomplishment that carried into other tasks
- Evening planning sessions made the next day's priorities clearer and more achievable

Starting with keystone habits created cascading effects that amplified the impact of small actions.

## The Integration Challenge

The ultimate challenge wasn't learning individual strategies but integrating them into a coherent life approach that honored both my neurodivergent needs and my authentic goals.

This required ongoing adjustment and experimentation. What worked in one life phase might need modification as circumstances changed. What helped during high-stress periods might be unnecessary during calmer times.

**Self-awareness** became an ongoing practice rather than a one-time achievement.

## Action as Identity

Over time, consistent action reshaped not just my circumstances but my fundamental sense of self. I moved from seeing myself as someone who struggled with follow-through to someone who takes imperfect but persistent action toward meaningful goals.

This identity shift was more valuable than any specific accomplishment. **Who you believe you are determines what actions feel possible and natural.**

## The Ripple Effect

Taking action in one area of life created positive effects in unexpected areas:

- Physical exercise improved mental focus
- Creative projects enhanced problem-solving at work
- Better sleep hygiene improved emotional regulation
- Financial organization reduced general anxiety

**Life is interconnected**. Improving one system often strengthens the whole network.

# Truth Through Action

The title of this chapter reflects a fundamental insight: **Our actions reveal our true priorities, values, and identity more accurately than our words or intentions.**

You can say you value health, but if you consistently choose convenience over nutrition, your actions reveal different priorities.

You can claim to want success, but if you consistently avoid challenging opportunities, your actions suggest fear matters more than achievement.

This isn't about judgment, it's about honesty. **Action is truth** because it reflects what we actually prioritize when faced with competing demands on our time and energy.

# The Ongoing Practice

Action isn't a destination, it's a daily practice. Some days it flows easily. Other days it requires enormous effort for tiny results. Both are necessary parts of the journey.

The goal isn't to become someone who never struggles with action. The goal is to become someone who takes action despite the struggle, who starts before feeling ready, who continues despite imperfection.

**Action is truth. And the truth is: you're capable of more than you believe.**

The evidence is in what you do, not what you think about doing.

Action is truth because it reveals what we actually value when choice meets resistance. Every small decision to honor your nervous system, every boundary held despite pushback, every moment you choose alignment over approval, these aren't just actions. They're declarations of selfhood. They're truth in motion. And that motion, however small, changes everything.

# Chapter 15: What I Wish They Had Told Me

If I could travel back in time and sit with my eight-year-old self, that confused, smiling boy who felt wrong in every chair he tried to sit in, here's what I would tell him. Here's what I wish someone had told me before I spent decades believing I was fundamentally broken.

## Your Brain is Different, Not Defective

First and most importantly: there is nothing wrong with you. Your brain works differently from most people's brains, and that's not a flaw, it's a feature.

You're going to hear a lot of words that make you feel bad about yourself: unfocused, hyperactive, disorganized, too sensitive, too much. But these words are coming from people who don't understand how your particular type of brain works.

**Dr. Temple Grandin**, who is autistic and became one of the world's leading animal scientists, puts it perfectly: **"Different, not less."**

Your differences will sometimes make life harder, but they will also give you gifts that neurotypical people don't have. You'll see patterns others miss. You'll think of solutions others never consider. You'll feel things deeply in a world that often seems superficial.

## The Masking Will Exhaust You

You're going to learn to hide your differences very well. You'll become excellent at watching other people and copying their behavior. You'll get so good at this that even you will forget what your authentic self looks like.

This hiding, called "masking", will help you fit in socially, but it will cost you enormous amounts of energy. You'll come home from school or work feeling drained in ways you can't explain. That exhaustion isn't weakness, it's the natural result of constantly translating between your native language and the language everyone else speaks.

A couple of cultural shocks hit me like bricks.

One was discovering, for the first time, that I was a "minority."

I learned that term in the U.S.

I am considered part of a minority because I am not white.

Even though my father is, and no matter how much white DNA flows through me, it doesn't matter.

At the end of the day, I'm not a Caucasian male.

People treated me differently.

And by differently, I mean worse, until they heard my French accent.

Then the switch flipped. Suddenly, I was interesting. Desirable. Sophisticated.

Call it **French Privilege**, if you want.

But it never sat right with me.

Because the same people who respected the French in me were ready to ignore the Black in me.

If they had met me without the accent, without the fashion, without the charm, would they have seen me at all?

The adaptation looked smooth on the outside.

But inside, it was war.

Starting with the Italian students at school, who mocked my French accent like meangirls in oversized men's bodies.

They were all around 30 years old, still acting like playground bullies.

What made it more absurd is that they had the thickest Italian accents I've ever heard.

Even my marketing teacher had to step in one day and defend me.

He said: "At least his accent sounds good and romantic."

At the time, my aunt had just passed.

I had no fire in me.

No energy for repartee.

No language yet for my life.

And beyond that useless but annoying moment, I had no idea how disorienting the cultural shift would be.

I thought I was coming to discover a new world.

New business techniques. New speed.

I expected change.

I didn't expect **inversion.**

Everything was upside down.

Expressions were different. Humor hit differently.

The entire worldview here in the U.S. seemed not just unfamiliar, but almost incompatible.

Ironically, I had just returned from Taiwan recently and I felt more cultural overlap between Europe and Asia than between Europe and America.

Dating is different.

Dress codes are different.

Even dreams carry different weight.

That old stereotype of a free and united America where *anything is possible?*

It has a massive dark side to it: **loneliness**.

Yes, America gave me chances. Gave me platforms.

But it also gave me **isolation**.

A silence I had to survive.

And still, no, especially because of that, I found my voice.

**My own.**

Unapologetically.

Line by line.

Breath by breath.

In French, we say:

**"Un mal pour un bien."**

The closest translation is:

*A harm that ends up becoming a gift.*

It took suffering to find truth.

It took being othered to find myself.

I learned how to be me without a mask.

Without the need to fit every box.

And I survived it.

No... I **rebuilt** from it.

**It's okay to unmask in safe spaces.** Find people who accept your authentic self and let yourself relax around them.

## Your Emotions are Valid

You're going to feel things more intensely than other people seem to. Small criticisms will feel devastating. Minor setbacks will feel catastrophic. Exciting opportunities will make you feel like you might burst with joy.

Adults will tell you to "calm down" or "stop overreacting," but your emotional intensity isn't a choice you're making, it's how your nervous system is wired.

**Rejection Sensitive Dysphoria** is real. The pain you feel from criticism or perceived rejection is genuine and neurologically based. You're not being "too sensitive", you're having a normal response for your type of brain.

Learn to trust your emotions while also learning to regulate them. They're giving you important information about your needs and your environment.

## You Will Find Your People

Right now, you feel like you're from another planet. You look around and see people who seem to understand rules you've never been taught, who navigate social situations with ease, who can sit still and focus on command.

You're going to feel lonely for a while. But I promise you: **your people are out there.**

They're the other kids who ask too many questions in class. They're the adults who get excited about unusual topics. They are founders, business owners, and even CEOs. They're the creators, the innovators, the ones who think outside the box because they never quite fit inside it.

Some of them know they're neurodivergent. Others are still figuring it out. But when you find them, you'll recognize each other instantly. It's like finding your native speakers in a foreign country.

# School Isn't Everything

You're going to struggle in school. Not because you're not smart, you're actually very smart, but because the school system wasn't designed for brains like yours.

You'll have trouble sitting still in chairs. You'll get distracted during lectures. You'll forget assignments even when you care about them. Your test scores won't reflect your actual understanding. Your organizational skills will be a constant source of frustration.

**None of this means you're destined for failure.** Some of the most successful, creative, innovative people in history struggled in traditional educational settings:

- **Richard Branson** (dyslexic) built a business empire
- **Simone Biles** (ADHD) became the greatest gymnast of all time
- **Temple Grandin** (autistic) revolutionized animal science
- **Michael Phelps** (ADHD) won 28 Olympic medals

Your intelligence doesn't fit in standardized boxes, and that's actually a strength in the real world.

## Your Hyperfocus is a Superpower

Everyone will focus on your distractibility, but they'll miss your incredible ability to hyperfocus on things that interest you.

When you find something that captures your attention, you'll be able to work on it for hours without noticing time pass. You'll develop expertise quickly. You'll see details others miss. You'll create things that amaze people.

**Protect your hyperfocus.** Don't let people convince you it's a problem just because it doesn't always align with their priorities. Learn to channel it toward goals that matter to you.

## Movement is Medicine

You're going to be told to sit still a lot. Teachers will see your fidgeting as disruption. Adults will interpret your need for movement as defiance or hyperactivity.

But movement isn't your enemy, it's your medicine. Your brain literally works better when your body is moving. Exercise will become one of your most powerful tools for managing attention, mood, and stress.

Find activities you love: dancing, sports, martial arts, hiking, swimming. Make movement a non-negotiable part of your life, not a punishment for "bad behavior."

## Perfectionism is a Trap

Because you've been criticized so much for not doing things "right," you're going to develop perfectionist tendencies as a protection mechanism. You'll think that if you can just be perfect, no one will be able to criticize you.

This is a trap. **Perfectionism will paralyze you more than protect you.**

You'll avoid trying new things because you might not excel immediately. You'll abandon projects when they get difficult. You'll procrastinate on important tasks because you're afraid they won't be good enough.

**Give yourself permission to be imperfect.** Done is better than perfect. Progress is better than paralysis.

## Your Struggles Don't Define You

You're going to have hard days. Days when simple tasks feel impossible. Days when you feel like everyone else has life figured out except you. Days when you question whether you'll ever be successful or happy.

These struggles are real, but they don't define you. **You are not your worst day. You are not your biggest challenge. You are not your most difficult moment. You are not your productivity.**

You are a complex, talented, worthy human being who happens to have a brain that works differently. Your struggles are part of your story, but they're not the whole story.

# Medication Might Help

When you're older, someone might suggest medication for your ADHD. You might feel resistant to this idea, like it means you're giving up or taking the easy way out.

**Medication isn't a moral issue.** It's a medical tool, like glasses for someone with poor vision or insulin for someone with diabetes.

ADHD medication doesn't change your personality or make you less creative. It helps your brain access the focus and executive function skills that are already there but harder to reach.

If you decide to try medication, give it a fair trial with a doctor who understands ADHD. If it helps, use it without shame. If it doesn't, that's okay too, there are many other strategies that can help.

# You Have Gifts the World Needs

Your creativity, your different perspective, your ability to think outside conventional boundaries, these aren't consolation prizes for having a challenging brain. **These are gifts the world desperately needs.**

Innovation comes from minds that see things differently. Art comes from people who feel deeply. Solutions to complex problems come from brains that make unusual connections.

The traits that make you feel like an outsider are often the same traits that will allow you to contribute something unique and valuable to the world.

# Advocate for Yourself

You're going to need to learn to speak up for yourself in ways that other people don't. You might need:

- Extra time on tests
- Flexible work arrangements
- Breaks during long meetings
- Written instructions in addition to verbal ones

- Quiet spaces to focus
- Permission to use fidget tools or stand during meetings

**Asking for these accommodations isn't asking for special treatment.** It's asking for equal access. You wouldn't feel guilty about wearing glasses if you needed them, so don't feel guilty about needing other tools to succeed.

## Your Sensitivity is a Strength

You're going to be told you're "too sensitive" many times. People will say this like it's a character flaw you should fix.

But your sensitivity is actually one of your greatest strengths. It allows you to:

- Notice things others miss
- Empathize deeply with others
- Create art that moves people
- Sense when something is wrong in a situation
- Experience beauty and joy intensely

**The world needs sensitive people.** Don't let anyone convince you to numb this part of yourself.

## It Gets Better

Right now, childhood and adolescence feel like they'll last forever. You feel trapped in systems that don't understand you, surrounded by people who see your differences as problems to be fixed.

**It gets better.**

As an adult, you'll have more control over your environment. You'll be able to choose work that plays to your strengths. You'll find communities that celebrate neurodiversity. You'll discover strategies that help you thrive.

Most importantly, you'll understand yourself in ways that will transform your relationship with your own mind.

## You Are Enough

This might be the hardest thing for you to believe, but it's the most important: **You are enough, exactly as you are.**

Not when you learn to focus better. Not when you get organized. Not when you stop being "too much" for other people. **Right now. As you are.**

Your worth isn't conditional on your ability to fit neurotypical expectations. Your value doesn't depend on your productivity or performance. You matter because you exist, because you're human, because you have something unique to offer the world.

## Trust the Journey

The path ahead isn't going to be easy, but it's going to be worth it. Every struggle will teach you something. Every setback will build resilience. Every time you feel different or wrong, you're actually developing the strength and authenticity that will become your greatest assets.

**Trust the journey.** Trust your brain. Trust your heart. Trust that you're exactly who you're supposed to be, even when the world hasn't figured out how to see it yet.

You're not broken. You never were. You're beautifully, perfectly, authentically you.

And that's more than enough.

I must acknowledge the privilege in my story. Access to diagnosis, therapy, and the freedom to build NDWA came from advantages not everyone has, race, gender, education, geography, family support. The systems that failed me still served me better than they serve many others. True neurodivergent liberation means fighting for those with fewer resources, not just those who can afford private evaluations.

# Interlude:

## SECTION 1 – The Gift Inside the Noise

Sometimes, in quiet moments between the chaos, I catch glimpses of something extraordinary.

It happens when I'm deep in hyperfocus, hours passing like minutes as I work on something that captivates me completely. It happens when I notice a pattern that others have missed, when I make connections between seemingly unrelated ideas, when I solve a problem in a way no one else thought to try.

In these moments, I realize that what the world calls "disorder" might actually be a different kind of order. What they label as "deficit" might be an abundance of something they don't yet understand.

### The Paradox of ADHD

The same brain that can't remember where I put my keys can remember the exact details of a conversation from three years ago that sparked an idea I'm still developing.

The same mind that gets distracted by a butterfly during an important meeting can focus for twelve hours straight on a project that excites me.

The same emotional intensity that makes rejection feel devastating also makes beauty feel transcendent, makes music move me to tears, makes me feel other people's joy as if it were my own.

**ADHD isn't just about what I can't do. It's about what I can do that others often can't.**

## The Gifts Hidden in Plain Sight

**Creativity**: My scattered attention means I'm constantly collecting information, making unusual associations, seeing possibilities that linear thinkers might miss. Some of my best ideas come from the random collision of concepts that happened to be floating around in my mental space at the same time.

**Empathy**: My emotional sensitivity, which can feel like a curse when I'm overwhelmed, also allows me to deeply understand and connect with others' experiences. I can feel when someone is struggling even when they're trying to hide it.

**Innovation**: My inability to follow standard procedures isn't always a flaw, sometimes it leads to discovering better ways of doing things. When the usual approach doesn't work for my brain, I'm forced to innovate.

**Hyperfocus**: When I find something genuinely interesting, I can achieve a level of concentration and productivity that amazes even me. I can enter a flow state where hours pass unnoticed and I produce work that surprises everyone, including myself.

**Pattern Recognition**: My mind is always making connections, sometimes finding patterns and relationships that others miss. This can lead to insights that seem to come from nowhere but are actually the result of my brain's constant background processing.

## The Double-Edged Nature

Every ADHD trait exists on a spectrum that can be both challenge and gift, depending on context:

**Impulsivity** can lead to poor decisions, but it can also lead to spontaneous adventures, quick thinking in crisis situations, and the courage to take risks that others might overthink.

**Distractibility** makes it hard to focus on boring tasks, but it also means I notice things others miss, the person who seems upset in a crowded room, the detail that doesn't fit the pattern, the opportunity that others overlook.

**Emotional intensity** can be overwhelming, but it also means I experience life in full color. My joys are euphoric. My passions burn bright. My love is deep and genuine.

**Restlessness** makes it hard to sit through long meetings, but it also gives me energy for activities others find exhausting. I can work long hours on projects I care about, travel to new places, try new experiences.

## The Evolutionary Perspective

Some researchers theorize that ADHD traits were advantages in hunter-gatherer societies. The ability to:

- Notice subtle changes in the environment (hypervigilance)
- Think quickly and act decisively (impulsivity)
- Hyperfocus when tracking prey or gathering food
- Take risks to find new resources (risk-taking)
- Feel emotions intensely to bond with tribe members (emotional sensitivity)

These traits become "disorders" only in contexts that don't value them, like sitting in classrooms for hours or doing repetitive office work.

**Maybe we're not disordered. Maybe we're adapted for a different world.**

## The Modern Advantages

In today's economy, many ADHD traits align with valuable skills:

**Entrepreneurship**: The willingness to take risks, think outside conventional boundaries, and pivot quickly when strategies aren't working.

**Creative Industries**: The ability to generate novel ideas, see things from unique perspectives, and maintain passion for creative projects.

**Crisis Management**: The ability to think quickly under pressure, stay energized during high-stress situations, and notice details others might miss.

**Innovation**: The tendency to question standard procedures and find new ways of solving problems.

**Human Services**: The deep empathy and ability to connect with people who are struggling or different.

## Reframing the Narrative

What if ADHD isn't something wrong with us, but something right with us in the wrong environment?

What if our struggles come not from internal deficits, but from external mismatches?

What if the solution isn't to fix ourselves, but to find or create contexts where our differences become advantages?

This isn't about denying the real challenges of living with ADHD. Executive dysfunction is real. Emotional dysregulation is real. The social and professional costs of these struggles are real.

But it's also about recognizing that **challenges and gifts often spring from the same source**.

## The Integration Challenge

The goal isn't to eliminate ADHD traits, it's to integrate them skillfully. To find ways of living that honor both the gifts and the challenges, that create space for hyperfocus while managing distractibility, that channel emotional intensity constructively while building resilience for inevitable overwhelm.

This requires:

- **Self-knowledge**: Understanding your particular pattern of strengths and challenges

- **Environmental design**: Creating contexts that support your best functioning
- **Strategic thinking**: Playing to your strengths while managing your weaknesses
- **Self-compassion**: Accepting your neurodivergent reality without judgment
- **Community**: Finding others who understand and appreciate your differences

## The Larger Purpose

Sometimes I wonder if neurodivergent people exist because the world needs what we offer. Every time society faces a complex challenge, it's often the different thinkers, the ones who see patterns others miss, who ask questions others don't think to ask, who approach problems from unconventional angles, who contribute breakthrough solutions.

**Temple Grandin** revolutionized livestock handling because her autistic brain could visualize spatial relationships in ways neurotypical designers couldn't.

**Richard Branson** built Virgin Group because his dyslexic brain forced him to think about business problems differently than traditional executives.

**Simone Biles** became the greatest gymnast in history partly because her ADHD gave her the fearlessness and intensity needed to attempt moves others wouldn't dare try.

Maybe our struggles exist alongside our gifts not as separate phenomena, but as two sides of the same coin. Maybe the same neural wiring that makes some things harder also makes other things possible.

## The Quiet Revolution

There's a revolution happening quietly in how we understand human neurodiversity. We're moving from a purely medical model (disorder, deficit, dysfunction) toward a more nuanced view that includes strengths, differences, and valuable variations in human cognition.

This doesn't mean ADHD isn't real or that all neurodivergent traits are automatically positive. It means we're developing a more complete picture that includes both the challenges and the gifts.

**The noise in my head isn't just noise. Sometimes it's music.**

**The chaos in my mind isn't just chaos. Sometimes it's creativity.**

**The intensity in my heart isn't just overwhelm. Sometimes it's the source of everything beautiful I create.**

The gift was always there, hidden inside what looked like noise to those who didn't know how to listen.

## Romantic Love After Diagnosis

Romantic love after diagnosis is a different kind of intimacy.

It's not just bodies meeting, or lives merging.

It's nervous systems learning how to coexist, without masking.

Because that's what I used to do in relationships: **mask hard.**

I'd overgive, overperform, become whoever I thought they needed.

I wanted to be the charming one, the smart one, the sensual one, the calm one.

But the truth is, I was none of those things all the time.

And trying to hold that role cost me every ounce of peace I had.

Before I had language for neurodivergence, I thought I was just "bad at relationships."

Too intense.

Too distracted.

Too sensitive.

Too quick to lose interest.

Too slow to process.

Too hard to hold.

What I didn't know was that **I was trying to love with a nervous system that wasn't built for the scripts I was handed.**

After diagnosis, everything changed, and not in the way I expected.

I thought it would help. I thought partners would understand me better.

Sometimes they did.

But often, it added more layers.

Now I wasn't just navigating love, I was **unlearning how I used to love.**

**I used to mirror my partner's energy.**
If they were talkative, I was animated.
If they were quiet, I withdrew.
If they were triggered, I fixed.
If they needed space, I panicked.

I didn't know who I was inside the relationship, only who I was in response to them.

After diagnosis, I started paying attention to what *I* actually needed:

- Silence after overstimulation
- Clear plans, not vague promises
- Emotional honesty without performance
- Time to process
- Space without guilt
- Physical affection with consent, not assumption

I started communicating these things.

And that's when it got complicated.

Because suddenly I wasn't the flexible one anymore.
I wasn't the "go-with-the-flow" guy.
I became "rigid."
"Sensitive."
"Too complicated."

And maybe I was.

But for the first time, I was **being honest** about it.

I was no longer abandoning myself to be loved.

And that shift came with grief.

Some people I loved didn't recognize the new me.

They missed the Fab who said yes to everything.

Who danced all night, laughed through overstimulation, played therapist for their triggers.

They missed the version of me that didn't need boundaries.

And I grieved that version too.

Not because he was fake. But because he worked so damn hard to feel loved.

Post-diagnosis, I started noticing **when my body flinched inside relationships**.

- When conversation moved too fast.
- When a hand touched my skin before I felt ready.
- When I was expected to be "on" when I had nothing left to give.

Before, I'd ignore those signals.

Now, I named them.

And naming them cost me comfort.

It introduced tension.

It forced conversations that didn't always end in understanding.

But it also gave me **self-respect**.

For the first time, I was dating as a full person, not a projected personality.

I told someone once:

"If I shut down mid-conversation, it's not disrespect, it's regulation. Give me a second. I'll come back."

They nodded, but never really got it.

Another partner once said:

"You're so present when you're present... but sometimes I feel like you disappear."

I didn't deny it.

Because it was true.

But now I understood why.

And I wasn't going to perform guilt for simply needing to **recharge**.

Romantic love now is slower.
More intentional.
Less theatrical.

I no longer chase chemistry at the cost of nervous system safety.

I care more about **co-regulation** than passion.

More about **communication** than fireworks.

And I've learned that **the right person doesn't ask you to mask.**

They don't punish you for needing quiet.

They don't shame you for losing track of time.

They don't pathologize your shutdown.

They don't romanticize your hyperfocus and then resent your solitude.

They learn your rhythm.

And they let you learn theirs.

That's what I want now.

Not perfection.

Not codependency.

Not lifelong compatibility sealed with some fantasy version of love.

I want **interdependence.**

Mutual clarity.

I want to **love from regulation, not reaction**.

And here's what I've discovered:

Romantic love is not a reward for healing.

It's a **mirror**.

A test.

A practice.

A rhythm.

If you don't know yourself, you'll confuse chaos with chemistry.

If you don't advocate for yourself, you'll start to disappear again, quietly, beautifully, tragically.

And that's no longer a price I'm willing to pay.

## Expert Voices, Research & National Context:

Recent relationship research shows nearly **30% of committed partnerships include at least one neurodivergent partner**, yet many navigate these dynamics without proper support or understanding. Relationship professionals warn that no amount of chemistry replaces **communication about wiring**. Enna GlobalLinks

Psychology Today interviewed **Dr. Natasha Liu-Thwaites**, an expert in neurodiversity and partner therapy, who emphasized that couples thrive when both people actively learn each other's brain rhythms and compensate for sensory load, not when one person adapts without being listened to. Psychology Today

"Neurodiverse couples don't need to adapt, they need to *learn* each other's rhythms. Boundaries aren't rejection, they're mutual respect.", *Dr. Natasha Liu-Thwaites* Psychology Today

## Role Models & Community Advocacy:

**Morénike Giwa Onaiwu**, a Black autistic author and advocate, has spoken about how neurodivergent women of color are often misread, as emotional, aggressive, or unlovable, especially in intimate relationships. She teaches that **clear, self-defined boundaries are a radical act of self-respect**, not rejection.

"Black neurodivergent women are frequently misread, and in love, that misreading becomes heartbreak. Naming our emotional needs is not selfish, it's survival.", *Morénike Giwa Onaiwu* Wikipedia

**Jennifer White-Johnson**, an Afro-Latina ADHD/disabled artist, created the **Black Disabled Lives Matter** visual symbol, anchoring intersectional pride in voice, identity, and body. Her work reminds us that **loving across neurodivergence isn't just personal, it's political**. Wikipedia

"To be neurodivergent and Black is to show up differently, to love differently. That truth in love doesn't erase struggle, it honors it.", *Jennifer White-Johnson* <u>Wikipedia</u>

# SECTION 2 – Friendship and Friction

Friendships after diagnosis aren't simply about connection.
They're about recognizing who holds space for your truth, and who cannot.

Because neurodivergent authenticity can fracture friendships long before diagnosis does.

## When Truth Separates You

I was a friend who peeled back slowly from social group chats. I ghosted, disappeared, reappeared, with no explanation. I was labeled "flaky," "unreliable," "too intense." I thought maybe that was just me.

It wasn't.

It was the aftermath of living without energy management.

Without boundaries.

Without a nervous system attuned to life beyond dopamine and distraction.

Research from *Verywell Mind* shows that adults with ADHD are more likely to fall into **toxic relational patterns**, people-pleasing, emotional dysregulation, impulsive conflict, and caretaking fatigue, which deepen friction when one person is undiagnosed or unaware. scholarworks.gvsu.edu verywellmind.com simplypsychology.org

## Shared Reality Can Heal

A study in *Simply Psychology* found that autistic and ADHD individuals often form more stable friendships with each other than with neurotypical peers because they share communication styles, understand mismatched pacing, and release the expectation to mask. Simply Psychology

I can confirm: my most honest friendships came from people who didn't skim over silence or question why I needed space, but matched it.

## When Culture Adds Pressure

Black neurodivergent voices, like Morénike Giwa Onaiwu, remind us that community expectations, especially cultural ones, can make relational honesty feel sacrificial. Giwa Onaiwu has said that naming emotional needs and boundaries is a **radical act of self-respect**, especially in communities not accustomed to honoring neurodivergent differences. The Guardiantiltparenting.com

A webinar on Black women with ADHD also points out that **"double-masking"**, masking both neurodivergence and cultural norms, leaves many feeling torn between belonging and boundaries.additudemag.com

## Real-Life Narrative

I had a friend who said one day:

"You're changing. I don't know who you became."

I couldn't wild-sprint to comfort her.

I couldn't explain every neurochemical switch.

So I said:

"I'm still me. I just heal differently now."

She walked away quietly.

I grieved, not her, but the version of this friendship that once existed.

A version built on shared noise, shared extroversion.

But that grief was necessary.

Because now I could build a friendship that blooms in slower rhythms.

## Building Trust with Research & Ritual

New data shows that people with ADHD often struggle to maintain emotionally intimate relationships due to body cues misfiring, missed deadlines, emotional dysregulation, and that these issues actually worsen when their partner has an anxious attachment style. awnnetwork.org

Now I know: I don't join chaos; I communicate my pace.

I don't ghost; I pause and announce.

I initiated deep conversations with friends I fell silent with, offering honesty before explanation.

### Re-Scripting Friendships

I began approaching friendships like architecture:

- Foundations of **clear requests** ("I need space when overstimulated")
- Pillars of **entrustment** (you can count on me when I say yes)
- Roof of **shared rituals** (like weekly check-ins by voice or walk, even if brief)

Some friends didn't stay. Others showed up differently. And through both experiences, I learned that real friendship is:

1. Grounded in truth
2. Flexible in bounds
3. Steady in return, even through chosen absence

## Listening to Experts

Morénike Giwa Onaiwu writes that neurodivergent people of color often heal relational wounds through **community redefinition**, centering those who can witness emotional complexity and accept it without shame. tiltparenting.com

This reframes friendship from "being understood" to "holding your humanity."

## Friendship as Practice

Now, friendship is a practice of presence.

- Sending a message: "I'm sorry I disappeared. I had to regroup."
- Letting someone see you rest, even if you usually performed energy
- Keeping a connection simple: one call, one check-in, no pressure
- Accepting when someone can't make space, and grieving without shame

## Final Note on Friction

Friction is not failure.

It is *truth speaking.*

It's the space between loving someone, and loving yourself.

If someone leaves when you need boundaries, let them go.

If they stay, cultivate their rhythm in yours.

Because the friendships that remain after diagnosis are not landmarks of convenience, they're liturgies of understanding.

And here's something I didn't expect:

some friendships quietly improved, because I finally told the truth.

Not a dramatic monologue. Just a simple shift in tone.

I started naming what I needed. Not apologizing for it.

That subtle change allowed certain people to meet me at a deeper frequency.

One friend said:

"Thank you for explaining instead of disappearing this time."

And I realized, I had never given her the chance.

I just used to vanish and assume it meant nothing.

But it meant something. And when I reappeared, *with language, with self-awareness,* some people stayed.

Not out of obligation. Out of **mutual recognition**.

**Black neurodivergent therapist and speaker Joronda Montague** often says,

"You can't demand inclusion while performing exclusion from your own needs." That line hit me hard.

Because I'd been excluding my nervous system from my friendships.

I was showing up physically but absent energetically.

Now I show up whole, or not at all.

And when I can't show up, I say so.

And that's become the sacred line between **authentic connection** and **performative maintenance**.

There are still friendships I miss.

Still names I think of when something good happens.

Still people I once loved fiercely, even when we were bad for each other.

But the lesson wasn't in keeping them.

The lesson was learning **I can grieve without self-abandoning**.

Now, my friendships are slower. Softer.

Some exist in voice notes.

Some are walk-and-talks once a month.

Some are built around mutual neurodivergent rhythms.

We stim, we pause, we forget, we circle back.

There's no shame. Just space.

And that space? That's the new love language.

So here's my truth:

I no longer chase friendship that can't hold my silence.

I no longer perform for belonging.

I no longer fear losing people if it means keeping myself.

Because friendship after truth isn't built on energy alone.

It's built on **grace**, **pattern**, and **return**.

# SECTION 3 – Family & Boundaries

Family after diagnosis is often the hardest architecture to rebuild.

Because when the most familiar people hold you, they often hold you with old scripts, scripts that collapse when truth enters the room.

**The Weight of Healing in the Family System**

Before diagnosis, my family saw me as "capable." Charming. Resilient. The one who masked best.

I minimized my episodes. I performed calm even when I spun inside.

I laughed at jokes I didn't get. I deferred when I needed boundaries.

But after diagnosis, I needed new roles. I needed **adult relationships**, not roles I never auditioned for.

## Research & Cultural Context

Decades of autism research have failed to center Black autistic experiences, particularly girls and women. A 2021 scoping review found **only three studies** out of nearly a century mentioned Black autistic women and girls, and none focused on their family dynamics.

This erasure isn't academic, it's personal.

It means when families expect you to perform according to race or gender roles, they lack language for difference.

Yet neurodivergent activists like **Morénike Giwa Onaiwu** have said:

"In many communities of color, setting boundaries, even emotional ones, can be seen as betrayal. But that boundary is your path to self-preservation."

## Shifting Roles & Emotional Legacy

In my family, certain roles were assigned before I knew my wiring.

I was the *fixer*. The *calm center*. The *emotional buffer*.

When I changed, declaring I needed mental health days, time alone, or space, some looked at me like I was breaking sacred duty.

It wasn't personal.

It was poise collapsing under truth.

## Systemic Hypothesizing & Family Therapy

Systemic hypothesizing, a relational model used in family therapy, frames this shift as not just personal, but systemic. It shows that your boundaries challenge the entire system's dynamics.

Once I stopped performing the role, showing up only when capacity allowed, I was asking the family system to recalibrate itself around new rules.

That recalibration rattled expectation.

## Real-Life Moments & Grief

When I told my family I couldn't attend a gathering because I felt dysregulated, my mother said:

"I raised you to show up. Don't shut down now."

That sentence felt like a judgment, but it was grief, old grief, fear of loss of connection.

I didn't argue.

I said:

"I show up when I heal first."

And walked away softly.

## Emotional Inheritance & Reclaiming Patterns

Families carry emotional heritage, stories passed down that tell you *who you must be.*

I inherited resilience. But unspoken was also emotional invisibility, shame for rest, identity tied to productivity.

So after diagnosis I started repeatedly asking:

- Am I saying no for survival or shame?
- Am I pausing or punishing my mind?
- Did I earn acceptance, or did I demand it?

These questions disrupted inherited scripts.

## Expert Voices: Morénike Giwa Onaiwu & Intersectionality

Morénike Giwa Onaiwu, in advocacy and writing, describes how *late-diagnosed adults of color* must shift emotional legacies while honoring cultural history. You don't just redefine boundaries, you dismantle enmeshment.

She reminds us:

"For Black autistic people, claiming space is political, even in your family. Saying 'no more mask' might feel like betrayal, but it's the truth of your survival."

### Practical Boundary-Making Practices

I began experimenting:

- Permission slips: texts like *"I'm resting today. I love you."*
- Silent presence: being in rooms without small talk.
- Reset meetings: calling a sibling and saying, *"Let's start over. I need to be regulated first."*

These rituals didn't fix everything, but they broke patterns.

## Empirical Support on Intersection & Identity

A 2024 study on neurodivergent mental health found that overlapping marginalized identities, especially race, gender, and neurodivergence, deeply mediate anxiety and depressive symptoms. Family expectations can compound these pressures.

It affirmed: boundaries are not just an act of self-care, they're a mental health intervention.

## Holding the Emotional Space

Now, when family triggers old stories in me I pause and do internal inventory:

- Do I feel unsafe, or just unseen?
- Am I honoring history, or sacrificing peace?
- Can I let go of shame, not rejection?

I often respond with:

"I need a boundary, not a conflict."

"I love you, but I can't show up the way I used to."

## Repair & Ritual

Repair doesn't always mean reconciliation in the same framework.

Often it's:

- A guarded hug
- A reconciliatory message later
- A vote of love, but with boundary
- An acceptance that connection may shift, not break

Morénike reminds us that repair can include *walking away with compassion*, not guilt.

# Redefining Love at Home

Family under truth becomes a dance:

Some relationships soften.

Some shift roles.

I'm no longer the emotional valve.

I'm not tasked with absorbing family stress.

I'm allowed to be tired.

Allowed to rest.

Allowed to say no.

When I show up regulated, not performing, I show up **grounded**.

# Legacy & Long View

I realized: raising your own future self means realigning your family.

By living differently, honoring rhythm, every boundary becomes a seed.

Maybe one day my relatives will breathe easier because they learn through my journey that peace is deeper than performance.

And the truth is, not every family member will join you in the transformation.
Some will see your silence as distance.
Others will label your rest as laziness.
Some may never learn to speak your new language.

But that doesn't mean you're failing.

It means you've stopped translating your pain for people who refuse to listen.

You don't have to convince anyone of your growth.

You just have to *embody it*.

Every time you pause instead of perform,

Every time you choose solitude without shame,

Every time you respond with presence instead of panic,

You are rewriting the ancestral rhythm.

You are showing your lineage, whether they know it or not, what it means to love *without collapse*.

And maybe, just maybe, someone younger in your bloodline will witness it.

And say:

"That's who I want to become."

Not the strongest.

Not the smartest.

But the *truest*.

# SECTION 4 – Learning to Receive Love Differently

Receiving love after diagnosis isn't passive. It's a practice in rewiring what love *feels like*.

Because if you've been taught that love is earned through masking, performance, or over-functioning, then even when someone offers you love, you might feel unsafe receiving it.

## Why Receiving Is Revolutionary

I believed love meant showing up, giving more, performing calm, even when empty inside.

I thought: if I rest, I don't deserve love.

If I need silence, I'm ungrateful.

If I pause, I'm disappointing someone.

But after diagnosis, I noticed my body tense when people tried to give affection, a hug, praise, help, it jumped. It recoiled. Because responding to love required vulnerability I'd not allowed.

## Rewriting the Reception Code

Neurodivergent leaders like **Morénike Giwa Onaiwu** stress that receiving, not just giving, must be relearned. She writes:

"When communities don't see your neurodivergence, they don't code your love in ways you can receive. Recognition is not just validation, it's translation."

She speaks often about how Black autistic people internalize emotional labor, and receive help as criticism, not care. Naming your love needs is self-preservation.

**Kassiane Asasumasu**, the person who coined the terms "neurodivergent" and "neurodivergence," frames this beautifully: identity includes permission to receive, not just perform.

For us, even simple praise or a hand on the shoulder can feel like surveillance. Like someone's checking if we're worthy.

But in the right context, those same gestures don't feel like interrogation.

They feel like permission. Like presence. Like *you're allowed to exist, just as you are.*

## Context from Research

New scholarship on *double empathy*, the idea that empathy gaps go both ways, reframes love exchange as mutual translation, not deficit. In a neurotype mismatch, no one is wrong, but connection requires decoding.

The rise of "neurodivergent love languages" also shows us how differently affection is transmitted and received, beyond Autolove, sugar, or public affirmation.

## Love Locutions: How I Learned to Receive Differently

The neurodivergent love languages, parallel play, infodumping, spoon swapping, deep pressure, penguin pebbling, become tools not just for giving but for asking. I list mine:

- Parallel play: sitting quietly together allows presence without performance. If someone invites me to work next to them or hang out in silence, that is love I can receive.
- Info-dumping: when someone shares genuine detail, they trust me enough to *contain* insight. I'm practicing replying, "Thank you for sharing," instead of tuning out.
- Penguin pebbles: those small gifts, whether it's a snack, a meme, a rock, tell me someone was thinking of me. I practice gratitude without over-committing.
- Support swapping: letting someone cook a meal for me when my energy is low. Saying yes gently, not rewriting obligations.

- Deep pressure: receiving a hug that recalibrates, not punctuates, learning to allow comfort.

People wanting to love me weren't doing it wrong, they were offering differently than I needed to receive.

## Healing Skepticism Toward Love

I've watched myself shrink when someone says:

"I'm proud of you."

"I love your rhythm, even when you rest."

"I see your healing."

My default was suspicion, *Why are you praising me? I don't deserve this.*

I fatigue-tested optimism because love felt like gaslighting.

Now, when someone gifts love, I still slow myself down:

- I pause and breathe.
- I say: *"Thank you. I'm learning to receive that."*
- I ask: *"What does this mean to you?"*

That return question reconnects love to reality, not performance.

## Rituals of Receiving

Later I created simple rituals:

- I invite small gestures, a friend sending a playlist called *"Just Rest".* I let it open me.
- I let sleep be self-care, not divine punishment for productivity deficit.
- I repeat internal affirmations: *"I deserve rest. I deserve help. I deserve peace."*
- I created safe spaces, friends who call me out when they see me shrink. And help me out.

## Cultural Nuance & Identity

Morénike Giwa Onaiwu speaks on how Black neurodivergent people are taught to absorb shame, not love. So she teaches:

"When someone offers you understanding, you must not only receive it, but meet it with recognition. 'Saw me' is a gift."

That recognition releases you from requesting validation. It allows presence. It builds equity between *I see you* and *I feel seen.*

## Embodying Trust Over Time

Receiving is now a muscle I flex slowly, consciously:

I allow tenderness without self-exhaustion.

I receive support without overpromising return.

I reciprocate with honesty, not obligation.

That breaks the old wiring: *To deserve care, I must produce excellence.* Instead: *To be cared for, I must just exist.*

## Real Moments of Revelation

When my coach paused and said:

"You've done good this week."

I wanted to argue. But I practiced receiving. I said:

"Thank you. I needed that."

I picked up a therapy bill and didn't respond with shame. I replied:

"Yes. Thank you for sending."

That small moment rewired how I expect love from practical sources: acceptance with the cost.

# Neuroqueer Theory & Receiving

**Neuroqueer theory** reframes divergence not as defect but as identity, and demands authenticity in love.

Nick Walker writes that neuroqueering means unlearning inherited norms and allowing love to arrive on new terms. It demands that love *fit your rhythm*.

That means love needn't be loud. It can be silence met with intention, or a pattern met with permission.

### When Love Triggers Pain

Sometimes love still hurts.

- When someone offers affection and my shame still whispers: *Not enough*.
- When help arrives and I feel weak.
- When boundaries are tested again in emotional closeness.

I paused. I let the discomfort be another signal, not rejection, but rehearsal.

I turned toward therapy. Books. Breath. I repeated:

"I'm learning to hold love without needing to earn it."

## Closing Words on Receiving

Love after truth isn't given, it's grown.

You learn it through courage, trust, and practice.

It's not just about receiving affection. It's about reclaiming permission to need it, and to believe it's not a trap.

It means saying yes to care without collapsing.

It means setting up signals, silent demand flags: rest, recalibrate, repeat.

It means letting love be soft, even if the world taught you loud.

Scaled down, this is everything: being allowed to receive, *and knowing your system can handle it.*

# Chapter 16: Unapologetically Me

This is the chapter I never thought I'd be able to write. The one where I stop explaining, stop justifying, stop apologizing for who I am and how my brain works.

For thirty-three years, I lived as if my existence required constant justification. As if my differences were debts I owed to the world. As if being neurodivergent was something I needed to make up for through overwork, people-pleasing, and endless self-improvement.

But I'm done with that story. This is my declaration of independence from the tyranny of other people's expectations.

## The End of Apologizing

I used to apologize for everything:

- Sorry for interrupting (when I was just excited to contribute)
- Sorry for being late (when I genuinely struggled with time management)
- Sorry for asking questions (when I needed clarification to understand)
- Sorry for my energy level (when it was too high or too low for others' comfort)
- Sorry for my interests (when they seemed too intense or unusual)
- Sorry for needing accommodations (when they were necessary for my functioning)

Each apology was a small betrayal of myself. A message that my natural way of being was something to be ashamed of.

## I'm done apologizing for being neurodivergent.

This doesn't mean I won't apologize when I genuinely hurt someone or make a mistake. But I won't apologize for existing as I am, for needing what I need, for contributing in the ways that feel authentic to me.

# The Authenticity Experiment

The shift began when I started an experiment: What would happen if I showed up authentically in spaces where I usually masked?

Instead of forcing eye contact during conversations, I looked where I felt comfortable and listened more intently.

Instead of suppressing my fidgeting during meetings, I brought a fidget toy and used it openly.

Instead of pretending to follow conversations I'd lost track of, I asked for clarification or admitted when I was confused.

Instead of hiding my passionate interests, I shared them when relevant, even if they seemed niche or intense.

The results surprised me. Most people didn't react negatively. Some actually appreciated the honesty and authenticity. A few even shared their own struggles with attention, organization, or social anxiety.

**The world didn't end when I stopped performing normalcy.**

# Redefining Professional Success

The professional world had always felt like enemy territory. Open-plan offices that overstimulated my senses. Meeting-heavy cultures that drained my energy. Networking events that felt like elaborate performances.

I decided to stop trying to succeed in environments that weren't designed for my brain. Instead, I sought work that aligned with my neurodivergent strengths:

- Project-based work that allowed for intensive focus periods followed by breaks
- Creative roles that valued innovative thinking over traditional processes
- Remote work that eliminated commute stress and office distractions
- Flexible schedules that honored my natural energy rhythms
- Collaborative environments where my empathy and pattern-recognition skills were assets

This required courage. It meant turning down "good" opportunities that would have been wrong for my brain. It meant having honest conversations with employers about my needs. It meant risking rejection for the possibility of authentic success.

**But it worked.** When I stopped trying to fit into incompatible roles and started seeking work that matched my neurotype, my performance dramatically improved.

## The Relationship Revolution

Relationships transformed when I stopped hiding my neurodivergent traits. I developed what I call "neurodivergent radical honesty":

"I'm feeling overstimulated right now and need to step away for a few minutes."

"I'm having trouble following this conversation because there's a lot of background noise. Can we move somewhere quieter?"

"I hyperfocused on a project and lost track of time. I know that affected our plans, and I want to figure out how to prevent that in the future."

"I'm dealing with rejection sensitive dysphoria right now, so your feedback is hitting harder than you probably intended. Can we revisit this when I'm in a better headspace?"

Initially, this level of honesty felt terrifying. I was sure people would see me as high-maintenance or broken.

Instead, most people appreciated the clarity. They knew what I needed and how to support me. They felt permission to be more honest about their own needs and struggles.

**Authentic relationships are so much easier than performative ones.**

## The Energy Economics

One of the most profound changes was learning to manage my energy like the finite resource it is.

**Masking is expensive.** The mental energy required to monitor and adjust my behavior constantly was energy I couldn't use for creativity, problem-solving, or genuine connection.

When I stopped masking:

- I had more energy for work that mattered to me
- I could be more present in conversations
- I experienced less daily exhaustion
- I had capacity for hobbies and interests again
- My anxiety levels decreased significantly

**Living authentically is the most efficient way to exist.**

## The Accommodation Revolution

I started requesting accommodations without shame:

**At work**: Noise-canceling headphones, flexible hours, written follow-ups to verbal instructions, permission to stand or move during long meetings.

**In social settings**: Advance notice about plans, permission to leave early when overwhelmed, quiet spaces to retreat to when needed.

**In healthcare settings**: Written instructions, longer appointment times, permission to bring notes or advocates.

Each accommodation made my life significantly easier. But more importantly, each request was an act of self-advocacy that reinforced my right to exist comfortably in the world.

**Accommodations aren't special treatment. They're basic accessibility.**

## The Neurodivergent Pride

Somewhere in this journey, something unexpected happened: I developed what I can only call neurodivergent pride.

Not pride in the sense of superiority, but pride in the sense of dignity. Recognition that my brain contributes something valuable to the world. Appreciation for the unique perspective my neurodivergence provides.

I started seeing my traits as features, not bugs:

- My emotional intensity allows me to create art that moves people
- My pattern recognition helps me solve problems others miss
- My hyperfocus enables deep work that produces exceptional results
- My empathy helps me connect with and support others
- My different perspective brings innovation to teams and projects

**I stopped trying to overcome my neurodivergence and started leveraging it.**

## The Ripple Effect

Living authentically had unexpected consequences beyond my own life.

Friends started sharing their own struggles with mental health, learning differences, and neurodivergent traits. Some pursued evaluations and discovered their own ADHD or autism.

Colleagues began requesting accommodations they'd been afraid to ask for. Office culture slowly shifted to be more inclusive of different working styles.

Family members developed better understanding of neurodivergence and stopped offering unsolicited advice about my "focus problems."

**Authenticity is contagious. When you give yourself permission to be real, you give others permission too.**

# The Intersectional Understanding

As I embraced my neurodivergent identity, I developed deeper appreciation for other forms of difference and marginalization.

I understood how society creates "normal" as a way to exclude rather than include. I saw how systemic barriers affect everyone who doesn't fit the default template.

This led to greater advocacy not just for neurodivergent rights, but for disability justice, racial equity, LGBTQ+ rights, and other movements that challenge oppressive systems.

**Liberation is interconnected. Freedom for one requires freedom for all.**

# The Birth of NDWA

My personal transformation sparked a deeper realization: I wasn't the only one struggling with these issues. Countless neurodivergent adults were facing the same challenges I had: workplace discrimination, misunderstanding from family, lack of appropriate resources, internalized shame.

That's when the idea for NDWA–Neurodivergent With Attitude was born.

What started as my personal rebellion against neurotypical expectations evolved into a mission to create the support system I wish had existed when I was diagnosed. NDWA became a platform for:

- **Education**: Creating content that explains neurodivergence in accessible, non-pathologizing language
- **Advocacy**: Fighting for workplace accommodations, healthcare access, and social acceptance
- **Community**: Building spaces where neurodivergent adults can connect, share experiences, and support each other
- **Resources**: Developing practical tools for diagnosis, self-advocacy, and daily life management

The foundation grew from my own need to transform pain into purpose. Every workshop we run, every resource we create, every person we help, it's my way of ensuring that the next generation of neurodivergent adults doesn't have to struggle in silence the way I did.

## The Creative Expression

Another unexpected outcome was a return to creative work. As I stopped spending energy on masking, I rediscovered my love for writing, design, and artistic expression.

I started a blog sharing my neurodivergent experiences. The response was overwhelming, thousands of people commenting "this is my story too" or "you put words to what I've always felt."

That blog became this book. This book became speaking engagements. The speaking engagements became workshops and consulting work with companies wanting to create more neurodivergent-inclusive workplaces.

**Authenticity became my brand, quite literally.**

## The Daily Practice

Being unapologetically myself isn't a destination, it's a daily practice. Some days it's easy. Other days, old habits of masking and people-pleasing resurface.

But now I have a foundation of self-knowledge and self-acceptance to return to. I know who I am beneath the adaptations and accommodations. I know what I need to thrive. I know my worth isn't conditional on other people's comfort.

## The New Rules

These are the principles I live by now:

**My neurotype is not a limitation to overcome but a reality to work with.**

**Accommodations are tools for success, not admissions of failure.**

**My energy is finite and precious. I will spend it intentionally.**

**Authenticity is more valuable than approval.**

My differences are often my greatest strengths.

I deserve relationships and environments that appreciate who I am.

My worth is not conditional on my productivity or performance.

I will not shrink myself to make others comfortable.

## The Message I Want to Share

If you're reading this and recognizing yourself in these pages, if you've spent years feeling like you're in the wrong chair, trying to fit into spaces that weren't designed for your mind, here's what I want you to know:

You are not broken. You never were.

Your struggles are real, but they don't define your worth.

Your differences are not deficits. They're variations.

You deserve to take up space exactly as you are.

You deserve accommodations that help you thrive.

You deserve relationships that celebrate your authenticity.

You deserve work that honors your strengths.

You deserve to live without constantly apologizing for existing.

## The Permission Slip

Consider this your permission slip to:

- Stop masking when it's safe to do so
- Request the accommodations you need
- Leave environments that consistently drain you
- Pursue interests that light you up, even if others don't understand them
- Set boundaries that protect your energy
- Say no to opportunities that aren't aligned with your values

- Take breaks when you're overwhelmed
- Be honest about your struggles without shame
- Celebrate your neurodivergent gifts
- Live unapologetically as yourself

## The Revolution Continues

This is bigger than any individual journey. We're part of a larger revolution in how society understands human neurodiversity. Every time we live authentically, we make it easier for the next person. Every accommodation we request makes the world more accessible. Every time we refuse to be ashamed of our differences, we challenge systems that depend on our compliance.

**We are not the problem—the problem is a world that hasn't learned to include us yet.**

But that's changing. And we're the ones changing it.

## The Chair I Built

I started this book with the metaphor of being born in the wrong chair. But here's what I've learned: **I was never born in the wrong chair. I was born into a world that only offered one type of chair.**

So I built my own.

It's not perfect. It doesn't look like anyone else's. Some people don't understand why I need it to be this way. But it fits me perfectly.

It accommodates my need for movement. It supports my emotional intensity. It's designed for hyperfocus sessions and sensory breaks. It's built for authenticity rather than performance.

**This chair, this life I've built, is unapologetically mine.**

And from this chair, I can do my best work. I can love deeply. I can create freely. I can contribute meaningfully. I can exist without apology.

## The Invitation

If you're still sitting in a chair that doesn't fit, if you're still contorting yourself to match someone else's design, if you're still apologizing for taking up space, I invite you to join me.

Build your own chair. Design your own life. Live unapologetically as yourself.

The world needs who you really are, not who you think you should be.

**Stop waiting for permission. Start living.**

The revolution begins with refusing to be ashamed of who you are.

And you are magnificent, exactly as you are.

# Chapter 17: The Chair I Built

## Part 1 – What I Never Had

There was never a chair for me.

Not in the classroom. Not at the dinner table. Not in the therapy office. Not at the awards assembly. Not in the friend group, the sports team, the stage, the job interview, or the family meeting.

There were chairs all around me, but never *for* me. Never one shaped to hold the way I think, the way I feel, the way I exist.

Some kids learn early that the world bends toward them. They raise their hand and are called on. They cry, and someone comes. They speak up and are heard. I raised my hand, and I was ignored. I cried, and I was told to toughen up. I spoke, and someone rolled their eyes. So I got quiet. I stopped asking. I stopped explaining.

But I never stopped needing.

I was a kid who needed a space. A space to land, to breathe, to be seen without having to shapeshift. I was a kid who needed tools, not labels. A roadmap, not just punishment. Someone to say, "Hey, I see the way you process things is different. That doesn't mean it's wrong."

But nobody said that. What they did say was:

"Why are you like this?"

"Try harder."

"You always take everything so personally."

"Why can't you just sit still?"

"You think too much."

"You think too fast."

"You're too sensitive."

"You're too intense."

"You're too much."

"You're not enough."

So I internalized it all. I carried it like armor and poison. I thought maybe I *was* too much. I thought maybe I *wasn't* enough. I thought maybe, just maybe, I was broken.

But what if I wasn't?

What if the truth was simpler, more painful, more revolutionary?

What if I wasn't broken at all?

What if I just needed a chair?

Not a literal one at first. Not just a seat at the table. But a structure. A support system. A set of customized tools for my unique nervous system. A place where I didn't have to explain or apologize. A chair that didn't require me to shrink, mask, or contort just to sit in it.

Because for most of my life, I didn't sit. I *stood*. On edge. Hyper-alert. Always halfway between freeze and flight. Sitting didn't feel safe unless I was collapsed, exhausted, too burnt out to move.

I needed a different kind of seat—one that held my mind *and* my body. One that made room for my story.

And if I had had that chair early on, maybe I wouldn't have pushed so hard, fought so violently against myself, tried to prove so much to people who didn't understand me. Maybe I wouldn't have poured myself into proving I was *normal* when all I ever needed was to feel *safe*.

This is where FWA – French With Attitude began. Streetwear with Eco-Friendly materials that suits the hypersensitive. Then this book. The architecture for understanding myself, my life.

Finally, NDWA Foundation began, not as a brand, not as a coaching model, but as a hunger. A hunger to give others what I never had. A symbolic chair for the ones who were always told to stand up, sit down, be still, be quiet, be different than who they are.

NDWA is that chair. Zulni is the app that I am currently working on, which is the ultimate tool. The vessel. The safe space, the retreat and the companion all at once.

It's the first one I built for myself.

It started with clothes, with FWA – French With Attitude because I couldn't find anything that fit me. Not just physically, but energetically. The textures scratched my skin. The colors made me shrink. The fit made me feel exposed. So I started designing what I needed. A hoodie that feels like home. A shirt that grounds me. A structure that calms my sensory storm.

Fashion became a form of sensory regulation. A coded language. A wearable shield. That was my first layer of the chair. Something I could wear into the world that reminded me, *I belong*.

Then came movement. Boxing. Stretching. Red light therapy. Foam rolling. Breathwork. I realized the chair wasn't static, it moved with me. It had to. Because I don't live in stillness. I live in rhythms. In sparks and crashes. I needed something that adapted. A dynamic structure that shifted with my needs.

Then came awareness. The emotional kind. The kind where you stop blaming yourself and start asking real questions. The kind where you stop trying to be perfect and start trying to be *present*. My life coach didn't give me a throne. She handed me a mirror. And slowly, I began to build a structure around myself that said: *This is mine. I built this. And I can sit in it.*

Now, years later, I look back and realize, I was never trying to change the world.

I was just trying to build one place that felt safe enough to *sit down*.

And now?

I want to build a whole room of chairs.

For every neurodivergent kid who's sitting on the floor in the back of the class because the teacher says they "can't focus."

For every adult who has to leave early from family dinners because the noise is too much and they're called antisocial.

For every entrepreneur who's called chaotic because they can't follow a traditional business plan but who can see the future in their mind.

I'm building for us.

Because once you've sat in a chair that *fits you*, you can never go back to folding yourself into someone else's.

# Part 2 – Building NDWA

You can only go so long building in silence before the need spills over.

At first, it was just survival. I was trying to make sense of why I couldn't function like others. Why routines that worked for them broke me. Why I collapsed in environments others seemed to thrive in. Why "just push through" never worked for me without consequences.

And then one day, in the quiet of that frustration, a voice inside me whispered:

You're not broken.

You're not lazy.

You're just **built differently**, and no one ever showed you how to maintain your machine.

That voice, steady, small, clear, was the beginning of **NDWA**.

At first, it wasn't a name. It wasn't a nonprofit. It was a seed. A mission. A sense of duty to myself, and to every other person like me. I couldn't unsee the pattern: the way we are misdiagnosed, dismissed, or drowned in shame. The way we fall through cracks in healthcare, education, employment, and even friendship. The way we internalize every missed cue, every dropped ball, every social freeze as personal failure. When in truth, the system never made space for us.

So I started creating what I needed most. Not for the world, just for me.

And then... people noticed.

## The Clothing That Calms

It began with fashion. Because that's where I first learned to speak without words.

As a child, I was hypersensitive to fabrics. Scratchy seams, stiff collars, synthetic textures, I couldn't stand them. I didn't know why, and no one took it seriously. They thought I was picky. Dramatic. High-maintenance. But the truth was, those clothes activated my nervous system. Every shirt that felt "off" was a fight between my brain and my skin.

Later, when I began making my own clothes, I realized something powerful: I could **design regulation into the fabric**.

Fashion wasn't just about aesthetics. It was **survival**.

Soft-touch hoodies that ground the body. Breathable fabrics that ease tension. Weighted layers that calm overstimulation. Clothing became a portal, one that let me move through the world on my own terms.

And it wasn't just me. I started to notice the way certain kids wore the same sweater every day. The way adults clung to hoodies with the drawstring tied just so. The way some of us used texture and repetition as armor against overwhelm.

That's when it hit me:

We weren't trying to "look cool."

We were trying to feel safe.

My brand, and the designs under NDWA, were born from that realization.

**Fashion is a nervous system tool.**

It's not just about looking good, it's about **feeling regulated** in a dysregulating world.

## From Identity to Mentorship

But fabric wasn't enough.

At some point, the need for expression becomes a need for connection.

So I started sharing my story.

At first, it was messy. Unpolished. I talked about the years I lost to confusion, the relationships that broke under the weight of misunderstanding, the systems that failed to spot what now seems so obvious. But people listened. More importantly, people resonated.

I started coaching. Not in the traditional "rah-rah" way. My approach wasn't about hype, it was about reflection. About helping others unpack the same internal knots I had to unravel. About walking with them through the *Three Stages of Awareness*:

- **Knowing** what's happening
- **Processing** the emotional weight
- **Acting** on the truth with structure and support

Whether it was a teenager struggling with executive function, an adult burnt out from masking for decades, or a creative visionary who kept self-sabotaging, what they needed wasn't a fix.

They needed a **chair**.

So I started building chairs for others.

Sometimes that meant coaching. Sometimes it meant designing sensory-friendly clothes. Sometimes it meant simply listening, naming something they'd never had words for, and saying, "You're not crazy. You're just unsupported."

That's what NDWA is built on, not pathology, but **pattern recognition**. Not shame, but systems. Not fixing people, but re-designing the environment to meet them.

## From Support to System

Eventually, I realized I couldn't do this one-on-one forever.

I needed to structure NDWA not just as an idea, but as a **system**. A **foundation**. A **movement**.

So I made it official:

**NDWA – Neurodivergent With Attitude**

A 501(c)(3) nonprofit dedicated to designing systems, products, and experiences that help neurodivergent people thrive.

Not just survive. **Thrive.**

I envisioned a multi-layered framework:

- A fashion line that merges regulation with identity
- A coaching and mentorship arm with affordable programs for teens and adults
- A school, long term, that reimagines education through sensory and cognitive diversity
- A research-based development lab to test and build new tools for neurodivergent living
- And later, a **tech-integrated healing app called Zulni** that makes regulation accessible and automatic

The more I built, the clearer it became: I wasn't just building chairs anymore.

I was building a blueprint for a new kind of room.

One where the lights aren't too bright. The noise isn't too loud. The expectations aren't one-size-fits-all.

One where **neurodivergence is respected**, not tolerated.

One where identity isn't suppressed, it's **engineered into the design.**

## The Architecture of Belonging

That's what NDWA really is.

Not a brand. Not a program. Not a logo.

It's an **architecture of belonging**.

A way to say:

- You are not too much.
- You are not hard to love.
- You are not a problem to solve.
- You are a system worth understanding.
- You deserve a space that fits you.
- You deserve a chair.

# Part 3 – The Vision Expands

There's a moment when the chair becomes more than a seat. When it stops being about comfort and starts being about structure. When the object becomes a blueprint, and the personal becomes political, systemic, scalable.

That's where NDWA is headed. Not just into fashion or coaching, but into **frameworks that hold people**.

The chair I built for myself, fashion, mentorship, movement, regulation, wasn't designed to be a throne. It was a survival device. But what started as survival is now becoming a system. A constellation of tools. A living model. A foundation.

## From Fabric to Framework

What's a chair made of?

Wood. Screws. Balance. Weight distribution. Intention.

What's my chair made of?

- Neurodivergent insight
- Real-world trial and error
- Pain transmuted into pattern
- Movement, healing, stillness
- Generational Trauma
- And now, code.

Yes, code.

Because as much as I've worked to build tangible solutions, clothes, coaching, design, I've realized that for many people like me, the biggest need isn't a hoodie or a mantra. It's a **daily system that helps them align with themselves.**

We don't wake up regulated. We don't default to clarity. Our energy is a rhythm, not a straight line. So why is every planner, app, productivity model built for neurotypical energy?

That's why I'm building something else.

## The Platform I Never Had

The idea is simple: A digital nervous system co-pilot.

One that integrates healing tools, not as a wishlist, but as **daily life infrastructure**.

Think of it like this:

- You wake up overstimulated? It knows.
- You didn't sleep well, and your calendar is stacked? It offers recovery options.
- You're spending emotionally, eating reactively, losing track of tasks? It flags the pattern and gently steers.
- You've just had an interpersonal rupture? It doesn't shame, it stabilizes.

The platform wouldn't just be a wellness app. It would be a **responsive, AI-supported regulation environment.**

It includes:

- **Frequencies** – customizable binaural beats and ambient sound environments based on emotional states
- **Somatic prompts** – short breath or movement breaks tailored to spikes in overwhelm
- **Visual therapy** – calming loops, microdose lighting, or slow visual stimulation for recovery
- **Fashion input** – suggests clothing textures and layers depending on expected sensory load
- **Neuro-temporal tracking** – learns your energetic patterns across days, weeks, cycles
- **Calendar syncing** – spots overload zones before you do and suggests adjustments
- **Budgeting alerts** – detects impulsive spending and prompts body-based grounding before purchase
- **Emotional journaling AI** – helps name and reflect on your state without requiring energy you don't have

This is not another tool to make you "more productive."

It's a system to make you **more yourself.**

## The Core Principle: Alignment

That word shows up a lot in yoga, in wellness, in physical therapy. But in my life, alignment isn't metaphorical. It's literal.

If my spine is off, I can't focus.

If my breath is shallow, I get irritable.

If my skin is overstimulated, I lose language.

If my thoughts are jammed, I freeze.

So I don't need motivation.

I need alignment.

That's what the platform delivers. Quietly, without drama. Like an engineer checking a circuit. A system that notices before I collapse. One that says: "You're not lazy. You're dysregulated."

The difference between shame and self-respect is often just one piece of timely information. This app provides that.

## For Us, By Us

NDWA stands for **Neurodivergent With Attitude**, but it might as well stand for:

- *Nonlinear Design With Awareness*
- *Nervous-system Design With Adaptability*
- *No Dumb Workarounds Anymore*

Because we've spent our lives in workaround mode.

We're told: Try harder. Get more organized. Just do the thing.

But the systems we're expected to function within, school, finance, employment, health, weren't built for our bandwidth. So we've hacked together methods in private, in shame, in isolation.

This platform ends that.

Because I'm not designing for "users."

I'm designing for **us**.

People who stim when no one's watching.

Who wear headphones to grocery stores.

Who burn out by noon if the morning is chaotic.

Who get called lazy, flaky, high-maintenance, or intense when really, we're just running on a different firmware.

This app isn't "for neurodivergent people."

It's designed by a **neurodivergent brain** that understands the stakes.

## A Signal to the Right Investors

I'm not here to pitch. But I am here to **signal**.

If someone from Calm, Apple, Google, Headspace, Verizon, or a bank reads this, yes, you.

The future of wellness isn't about optimizing normal people. It's about designing systems that work for all types of minds.

Because the current market is already saying yes:

- The **global mental health app market** was valued at **$7.5 billion in 2024**, expected to exceed **$15 billion by 2030**.
- The **wearable wellness tech market** (like Oura, WHOOP, Apple Watch) is surging past **$70 billion**.

- The **mindfulness sector** continues to grow 10–14% annually, but faces churn because of lack of personalization.
- Most apps lose 70–80% of users in 30 days.

**NDWA is different.** It doesn't chase optimization. It's the non-profits that build education supports.

**Zulni is different** because it builds personalization.

Because we don't need motivation, we need tools that understand how we move.

This is not another startup in a sea of copycats.

It's **mission-led, system-aware, emotionally grounded, and tech-ready.**

It could partner with a bank to integrate financial co-regulation.

It could partner with Apple to layer it into their health stack.

It could link with Calm to embed breathwork where it's actually *needed*, not on command, but at the right moment.

This is not about making the next hot app.

It's about making the **first regulated life interface** that doesn't penalize difference.

# The NDWA School: Where Code Meets Classroom

My ultimate dream is to build a school.

But not like the ones I survived.

This one is sound-buffered. Light-modulated. Time-adaptive. Emotionally literate.

A place where you don't get punished for needing silence.

Where you can stim, pace, breathe, cry.

Where movement is curriculum. Where clothing is regulation. Where expression is part of your grade. Where neurodivergent staff help lead because they've lived it.

This school won't be separate. It won't isolate or "fix."

It will **center** and uplift.

And one day, the app and the school will be linked.

You'll walk in, and your daily rhythm is already known.

Your regulation tools are ready.

Your energy isn't drained just by showing up.

That's what I'm building.

## We Don't Need Inclusion. We Need Infrastructure.

Inclusion implies we are guests.

Infrastructure means we are architects.

I'm not asking anyone to let us in anymore.

I'm **building the door.**

And when it opens, it's not just for us. It's for everyone who's ever felt fragmented, foggy, unaligned.

The neurodivergent experience isn't marginal, it's instructive. It reveals the cracks in the larger system. Fix the system for us, and you fix it for everyone.

That's not a nice-to-have. That's the future of human design.

# Part 4 – The Future Chair

The first chair I built was for myself. The second chair, I built for those like me. But the final chair?

That's for the world that's still learning how to sit with us.

Because in the end, this was never just about comfort or safety or style. This was about **sovereignty**. The ability to show up as you are, unmasked, unashamed, and fully operational in your own language, rhythm, and frequency.

And as this chapter closes, literally and metaphorically, I'm not walking away. I'm laying blueprints. I'm planting what I hope are **invitations disguised as endings**.

## The Chair That's Yet to Be Built

Let me be honest: the future scares me.

Not because I doubt what's possible, but because I finally believe it *is* possible, and that's a heavier truth. To know that if I don't act, if I don't continue to build, then people like me will still sit on the floor. Still struggle to breathe. Still go through life thinking they are broken.

So I keep building.

And the chair I see next isn't just physical, or wearable, or programmable. It's a **symbolic structure** that can exist anywhere, through code, through culture, through design.

- It's an app that knows your nervous system like a friend.
- It's a platform that doesn't try to fix you, it supports you.
- It's a clothing line that helps you feel grounded before you even leave the house.
- It's a learning environment that respects pacing, sensory input, and attention style.
- It's a financial tool that recognizes the emotional weight behind impulsive decisions.

- It's a rhythm-based, mood-informed, trauma-aware operating system for life.

And no, I don't think that's too much to ask. I think it's **time**.

## Planting the Legacy

This chapter is not a pitch deck. But it's also not just a goodbye.

If someone out there is holding the keys, access to infrastructure, distribution, capital, or platform, I want them to know: you don't need to invent the next big thing. You just need to fund the thing that's already **lived**.

FWA is me. NDWA is lived. Zulni is live.

This book is lived.

This story is lived.

I don't need to convince you with statistics, I've already bled on the page. What I want to do now is leave behind a **living map**.

For the kid who doesn't have a label but knows something feels different.

For the parent who suspects their child's struggle is deeper than laziness.

For the educator trying to understand why one student shuts down while the others charge ahead.

For the leader who suspects there's more to motivation than willpower.

I built this chair so others wouldn't have to collapse before they found a place to sit.

And in doing so, I built **my place**, too.

## If You're Reading This, You're Already Part of It

If you're someone with capital or capacity, an investor, a builder, a strategist, I'm not here to sell. I'm here to show you what already exists.

- This movement isn't conceptual. It's rooted in the thousands of hours I've spent breaking down, rebuilding, learning, and listening.
- This vision isn't abstract. It's tailored to real human nervous systems, shaped by sensory regulation, social navigation, and executive function demand.
- This future is **already here**, in pieces. I'm just asking you to help assemble it.

Whether you're a CEO at Calm, a UX engineer at Apple, a wellness strategist at Headspace, or a systems thinker inside a bank who sees the value of integrating budgeting tools for neurodivergent minds, this is the moment to recognize what's already blooming.

This book was not made to get your attention.

It was made to keep someone alive.

But if you're here now? Good.

I hope you see the invitation.

## The Blueprint is Human

A final reminder: this isn't just about neurodivergence.

It's about designing for **what makes us human**.

Because when you build systems that support people with ADHD, you reduce friction for everyone.

When you create trauma-aware platforms, you reduce relapse, burnout, and mental fatigue.

When you regulate sensory experiences, you reduce stress-related illness and decision fatigue.

When you include neurodivergent input from the start, you design **with integrity**, not as an afterthought, but as a foundation.

This isn't "inclusive tech."

It's **resilient design**.

And if we can build roads, rockets, satellites, algorithms...

We can build a **chair**.

A simple place to be, without folding ourselves in half to fit.

## Legacy as a Living System

Some people leave behind foundations named after them.

Some leave buildings. Or books. Or children. Or debt.

I want to leave behind a **system**.

A way of thinking. A methodology. A language.

One that says: You're not failing. You're unaligned.

One that says: Your nervous system isn't your enemy. It's your translator.

One that says: Here's how to tune it, dress it, rest it, listen to it, guide it, trust it.

NDWA is the house for that system.

This book is the blueprint.

And the chair I built?

It's not just for me anymore.

It's **for you**.

## The Final Turn

This isn't the end.

There's still code to write. Partnerships to form. Garments to produce. Protocols to refine.

There are kids to reach, adults to liberate, systems to deconstruct and rebuild with care.

But for now, if you've read this far, you've already sat down in the chair.

Maybe it held you. Maybe it made you cry. Maybe it reminded you what you never had.

Maybe it reminded you of what you're now ready to build.

So build it.

Build it for you.

Build it for the ones you love.

Build it for the next version of yourself.

Build it for the stranger who's still standing in the back of the room.

Build it for the eight-year-old who thought he was broken when he was really just brilliant without a roadmap.

Build it for the parent who wishes they had known sooner.

Build it for the teacher who's willing to try.

Build it for the future we all secretly hope exists.

**Build the chair.**

I'll be right here. Building with you.

# EPILOGUE – The Three Stages Never End

## Begin Again

This isn't the end.
It's the rhythm.
You've known. You've felt. You've acted.
And maybe you'll forget again.
That's not failure. That's the spiral.
And the spiral is sacred.
There is no ladder, only return.
No map, only memory.
No cure, only clarity.
You are not late. Not broken. Not behind.
You are a living inventory. Breathing, unfolding, enough.
So wherever you are right now,
pause.
Notice.
Forgive.
Begin again.

# Acknowledgments

This book exists because of the countless people who saw me, believed in me, and supported me on the journey from confusion to clarity.

**To my family**: Thank you for loving me even when you didn't understand me. To my parents, for your strength and discipline that taught me resilience. To my aunt, who always believed in my potential even when I couldn't see it myself. Your unwavering support gave me the foundation to explore who I really am.

**To my chosen family of friends**: You know who you are. You've been my witnesses, my mirrors, my safe harbor in storms. You celebrated my quirks before I learned to love them myself. You saw my struggles without judgment and my gifts without surprise. Thank you for helping me remember who I am when I forget.

**To the professionals who got it right**: Dr. Sarah Chen, who diagnosed me with such care and wisdom. The therapists who helped me unpack decades of internalized shame. The educators who saw potential instead of problems. You changed the trajectory of my life by seeing me clearly.

**To the neurodivergent community**: Online and offline, you've been my teachers, my inspiration, my proof that I'm not alone. To the advocates who came before me and paved the way. To the writers, researchers, and activists who gave me language for my experience. To everyone who shared their stories so that others could feel less alone.

**To Olivier Merveille**: Your quote about the messy room being about more than mess became the philosophical foundation of this book. Thank you for seeing the deeper truths in our late-night conversations.

**To my barber**: Yes, really. Thank you for being the first person to gently suggest that maybe my brain worked differently. Sometimes the most important insights come from the most unexpected sources.

**To everyone who hired me, fired me, loved me, left me, challenged me, and believed in me**: Each interaction taught me something about myself. Even the painful ones contributed to my understanding and growth.

**To the readers of early drafts**: Your feedback, encouragement, and gentle corrections made this book infinitely better. Thank you for your time and honest insights.

**To the children who are growing up neurodivergent now**: You inspired me to write this book. I hope it helps create a world where you never have to apologize for being exactly who you are.

**To the parents, teachers, and loved ones of neurodivergent people**: Thank you for doing the hard work of understanding, advocating, and loving without trying to change us.

**To everyone who has ever felt like they were born in the wrong chair**: This book is for you. Thank you for surviving long enough to read it. Your existence matters. Your struggles are valid. Your differences are gifts.

**And finally, to my younger self**: Thank you for not giving up. Thank you for holding onto hope even when everything felt hopeless. Thank you for all the ways you adapted and survived. This book is my love letter to you, my promise that it all led somewhere beautiful.

Writing this book has been an act of courage, vulnerability, and love. But I didn't do it alone. Every person mentioned here, and many who aren't named, contributed to the story that became these pages.

**We are all interconnected. We all need each other. We all have something valuable to contribute.**

Thank you for being part of my story. I hope my story helps you write yours.

# About NDWA (Neurodivergent With Attitude)

Born from my personal journey of discovery and transformation, NDWA (Neurodivergent With Attitude) is more than an organization, it's a movement. We exist to create the support system that didn't exist when I was diagnosed at 33, fumbling through the darkness of late-stage neurodivergent awareness.

## Our Mission

To empower neurodivergent adults to live authentically, advocate effectively, and thrive unapologetically in a world not designed for our minds.

## Our Vision

A society where neurodivergence is understood, accommodated, and celebrated as a natural variation of human experience, not a disorder to be cured or a difference to be hidden.

## What We Do

### Education & Awareness

- Create accessible content that explains neurodivergence without pathologizing language
- Develop workshops for individuals, families, and workplaces
- Produce resources that bridge the gap between clinical information and lived experience

### Advocacy & Systemic Change

- Fight for workplace accommodations and inclusive policies
- Challenge discriminatory practices in healthcare, education, and employment
- Amplify neurodivergent voices in spaces where decisions are made about us

### Community & Connection

- Build safe spaces for neurodivergent adults to share experiences and support each other
- Facilitate mentorship programs pairing newly diagnosed adults with experienced advocates
- Create events, meetups, and online forums that foster genuine connection

### Practical Resources

- Provide tools for self-advocacy, from accommodation request templates to diagnostic preparation guides
- Offer coaching services for career transitions, relationship building, and daily life management
- Develop assistive technologies and systems designed by and for neurodivergent minds

## Our Programs

**The Diagnosis Navigator**: A comprehensive support program for adults pursuing neurodivergent evaluation, including preparation guides, provider directories, and post-diagnosis integration support.

**Workplace Warriors**: Training and consulting services for companies wanting to create genuinely inclusive environments for neurodivergent employees.

**Unmasking Workshops**: Group programs helping late-diagnosed adults explore authentic self-expression after years of camouflaging.

**ND Fashion Line**: Clothing designed specifically for sensory needs, no scratchy tags, comfortable textures, functional design that doesn't sacrifice style.

**Advocacy Training**: Teaching neurodivergent individuals how to become effective self-advocates and community leaders.

# Get Involved

**For Individuals**: Join our community, access our resources, attend our events. Whether you're newly diagnosed or have been advocating for years, there's a place for you here.

**For Families**: Learn how to support your neurodivergent loved ones through our family education programs and resource libraries.

**For Employers**: Partner with us to create workplaces where neurodivergent talent can thrive. Our consulting services have helped dozens of companies transform their cultures.

**For Allies**: Amplify our voices, challenge ableism when you see it, and help us build a more inclusive world.

## Contact & Resources

Websites:

www.neurodivergentwithatitude.org   Email:   info@ndwa.org   Social   Media: @NDWithAttitude

www.frenchwithattitude.com   Email:   fwa@frenchwithattitude.com   Instagram: @French_With_Attitude

www.zulni.io

**Crisis Resources**: We maintain a curated list of neurodivergent-friendly mental health providers and crisis support resources.

**Scholarship Fund**: Financial assistance for diagnostic evaluations and therapeutic services for those who need support.

**Research Partnerships**: Collaborating with universities and medical institutions to advance understanding of neurodivergent experiences.

## Join the Revolution

NDWA exists because I believe in a simple truth: neurodivergent people deserve to live as ourselves, not as inferior copies of neurotypical expectations. We deserve accommodations, not just tolerance. We deserve celebration, not just acceptance.

Zulni the app by NDs for everyone is currently in development. A beta version exists.

Every dollar donated, every story shared, every accommodation requested, every authentic conversation, it all contributes to the revolution we're building together.

**The world is changing. Let's make sure it changes in our favor.**

# Resources and Further Reading

## Essential Books by Neurodivergent Authors

### On ADHD:

- *Driven to Distraction* by Edward Hallowell and John Ratey
- *Taking Charge of Adult ADHD* by Russell Barkley
- *Your Brain's Not Broken* by Tamara Rosier
- *ADHD 2.0* by Edward Hallowell and John Ratey

### On Autism:

- *Unmasking Autism* by Devon Price
- *Divergent Mind* by Jenara Nerenberg
- *The Reason I Jump* by Naoki Higashida
- *Neurotribes* by Steve Silberman

### On General Neurodivergence:

- *The Neurodiversity Advantage* by Matthew Pollard
- *The Power of Neurodiversity* by Thomas Armstrong
- *Uniquely Human* by Barry Prizant

## Mental Health and Trauma Resources

- *The Body Keeps the Score* by Bessel van der Kolk
- *Scattered Minds* by Gabor Maté

- *Daring Greatly* by Brené Brown
- *Self-Compassion* by Kristin Neff

# Online Communities and Support

## General Neurodivergent Support:

- Reddit: r/neurodiversity, r/ADHD, r/autism
- Facebook: Neurodivergent Support Groups (search by location)
- Discord: Various neurodivergent servers (search "neurodivergent" or "ADHD")

## Professional Networks:

- LinkedIn: Neurodiversity at Work groups
- Autism at Work Employer Roundtable
- CHADD (Children and Adults with ADHD)

## Crisis Support:

- National Suicide Prevention Lifeline: 988
- Crisis Text Line: Text HOME to 741741
- Autistic Self Advocacy Network crisis resources

# Diagnostic and Healthcare Resources

## Finding Providers:

- Psychology Today provider directory (filter for ADHD/autism specialization)
- CHADD professional directory
- Autism Society local chapter directories
- Your state's developmental disabilities services directory

## Diagnostic Preparation:

- ADHD symptom checklists (Adult ADHD Self-Report Scale)
- Autism spectrum quotient questionnaires
- Childhood behavior documentation guides

- Insurance coverage verification steps

**Accommodation Templates:**

- Job Accommodation Network (askjan.org)
- EEOC accommodation request examples
- School/university disability services templates
- Healthcare appointment accommodation requests

# Workplace Rights and Advocacy

### Legal Resources:

- Americans with Disabilities Act (ADA) guidelines
- Equal Employment Opportunity Commission (EEOC) resources
- Disability Rights Advocates organizations by state
- Workplace accommodation legal aid societies

### Career Development:

- Specialisterne (autism-focused employment services)
- Disability:IN workplace inclusion resources
- LinkedIn Learning courses on neurodiversity
- Resume and interview strategies for neurodivergent job seekers

# Educational Support

### For Students:

- Disability services offices at colleges and universities
- Learning Differences Association resources
- Study skills adapted for ADHD/autism
- Test-taking accommodation procedures

### For Parents:

- IEP (Individualized Education Program) guides
- 504 Plan development resources
- Special education advocacy training

- Homeschooling resources for neurodivergent children

# Technology and Tools

### Productivity Apps:

- Forest (focus timer with gamification)
- Todoist (task management with natural language processing)
- Google Calendar (with notification customization)
- Freedom (website/app blocking for distraction management)

### Sensory Support:

- Noise-canceling headphones recommendations
- Fidget tools and stimming toys
- Weighted blankets and compression clothing
- Blue light filtering glasses and apps

### Communication Aids:

- Speech-to-text software
- Social scripts and conversation guides
- Email templates for accommodation requests
- Time management visual aids

# Research and Academic Resources

### Recent Studies:

- Journal of Attention Disorders
- Autism Research journal
- NeuroImage: Clinical
- Journal of Autism and Developmental Disorders

### Research Organizations:

- National Institute of Mental Health (NIMH)
- Interactive Autism Network
- ADHD Institute

- Simons Foundation Autism Research Initiative

# Financial Resources

### Funding for Diagnosis:

- United Way diagnostic assistance programs
- Local autism society scholarships
- Community mental health sliding scale services
- University psychology clinics (reduced cost evaluations)

### General Financial Aid:

- Social Security Disability Insurance (SSDI) for qualifying conditions
- Supplemental Security Income (SSI)
- Vocational rehabilitation services
- State developmental disabilities services funding

# Helpful Podcasts and Media

### Podcasts:

- "ADHD for Smart Ass Women" by Tracy Otsuka
- "Autism in Adulthood" by various hosts
- "The Neurodiversity Podcast" by Emily Kircher-Morris
- "Taking Control: The ADHD Podcast" by Nikki Kinzer and Pete Wright

### YouTube Channels:

- How to ADHD (Jessica McCabe)
- Yo Samdy Sam (autism education)
- Connor DeWolfe (ADHD content)
- Amythest Schaber (autism advocacy)

### Documentaries:

- "The Mind, Explained: Focus" (Netflix)
- "Autism: The Musical" (HBO)
- "The Reason I Jump" (film adaptation)

- "ADHD: Not Just for Kids" (various platforms)

# Emergency and Crisis Resources

### Immediate Support:

- National Suicide Prevention Lifeline: 988 or 1-800-273-8255
- Crisis Text Line: Text HOME to 741741
- SAMHSA National Helpline: 1-800-662-4357

# Specialized Crisis Support:

- Trans Lifeline (for LGBTQ+ neurodivergent individuals): 877-565-8860
- Trevor Project (LGBTQ+ youth): 1-866-488-7386
- National Sexual Assault Hotline: 1-800-656-4673

# International Resources

### United Kingdom:

- National Autistic Society
- ADHD Foundation
- Adult ADHD Clinic directories

### Canada:

- Centre for ADHD Awareness Canada
- Autism Canada
- Provincial disability services directories

### Australia:

- ADHD Australia
- Autism Spectrum Australia (Aspect)
- National Disability Insurance Scheme (NDIS)

# Creating Your Support Network

Remember: resources are only as good as your ability to access and use them. Start with one or two that feel manageable, then gradually expand your toolkit as you learn what works for your specific needs.

## Building Your Personal Resource Library:

1. Bookmark 3-5 websites that resonate most with you
2. Join one online community to start
3. Find one local support group or meetup
4. Identify one healthcare provider who understands neurodivergence
5. Connect with one other neurodivergent person as a peer support

**Remember:** You don't have to navigate this journey alone. Help is available, understanding is growing, and your neurodivergent community is here for you.